BUGS BUNNY

Fifty Years and Only One Grey Hare

BUGS BUNNY

FIFTY YEARS AND ONLY ONE GREY HARE

By Joe Adamson

Prefaces by Friz Freleng and Chuck Jones

A Donald Hutter Book

Henry Holt and Company

New York

Henry Holt books are available at special discounts
for bulk purchases for sales promotions, premiums,
fund-raising, or educational use. Special editions
or book excerpts can also be created to specification.

For details contact:
Special Sales Director
Henry Holt and Company, Inc.
115 West 18th Street
New York, New York 10011

THIS WAY TO RABBIT

First Edition

Produced and prepared by Layla Productions, Inc., and
Sammis Publishing, Inc.

Designed by Allan Mogel
Project Editor: Lori Stein

Printed in the United States of America
Recognizing the importance of preserving
the written word, Henry Holt and Company, Inc.,
by policy, prints all of its first editions
on acid-free paper.

10 9 8 7 6 5 4 3 2 1

Library of Congress Cataloging-in-Publication Data

Adamson, Joe.
    Bugs Bunny : fifty years and only one gray hare / by Joe Adamson :
prefaces by Friz Freleng and Chuck Jones. — 1st ed.
        p.   cm.
    "A Donald Hutter book."
    Includes bibliographical references (p.   ).
    Filmography: p.
    ISBN 0-8050-1190-0 (alk. paper)
    1. Warner Bros. Cartoons—History. 2. Bugs Bunny (Fictitious
character). I. Title.
NC1766.U52W37327   1990
741.5'09794'93—dc20   90-4074
                                                       CIP

For Jan and Joe

THIS WAY TO RABB

Page 1: *The official Warner Bros. logo for Bugs Bunny's 50th anniversary.* Page 2: *Cel from Friz Freleng's* Captain Hareblower, *1954. These pages: Background from Chuck Jones' Duck! Rabbit, Duck!, 1953; layout by Maurice Noble, background painted by Philip DeGuard. Following pages: A collection of publicity and production art from the late '40s to the present; Chapter 4 illustration is a production cel from Chuck Jones'* Haredevil Hare, *1948.*

CONTENTS

Preface

Bugs Bunny?—Yes. *I* know Bugs Bunny.

You have to know Bugs to create a cartoon with Bugs Bunny—you must *think* like Bugs Bunny, *act* like Bugs Bunny, and *be* Bugs Bunny.

Much as any good actor, when he portrays a character is no longer himself; he becomes that character, or he doesn't come across at all.

So it is with the director who is producing and directing a Bugs Bunny cartoon. He is acting through the graphite at the end of his pencil.

To be Bugs you must be young at heart, stimulating, inventive, daring, and imaginative. He *is* fantasy brought into the realm of believability.

When I sit down at my desk to do a Bugs picture, I hear a voice that goes something like this:

"Red Alert! Red Alert! I am confronted by small man with a large red moustache. He is threatening to eliminate all flea-bitten, fur-bearin' critters!"

As the director of this Bugs Bunny cartoon, I am now Bugs Bunny. What do I do?

This book is the story of how we answered that question.

Friz Freleng

Below and opposite*: Cel and animation drawing from Mark Kausler's animation of Bugs in the Odradek Production* A Political Cartoon, *1973.*

8

My admiration for Bugs is immeasurable. When I look in the mirror I see Daffy Duck, but when I look into my heart I see Bugs Bunny. Who in his right mind would not like to find himself a combination of Henry Higgins as played by Rex Harrison, Robin Hood as played by Douglas Fairbanks, and Dorothy Parker as played by Dorothy Parker? Fit them deftly into a sleek and stylish rabbit skin and you have Bugs Bunny. Yes! Daffy Duck is a rueful recognition of my own (and your own) ineptitudes, Bugs Bunny is a glorious personification of our most dapper dreams. We love Daffy because he is us, we love Bugs because he is as wonderful as we would like to be.

CHUCK JONES

The Rabbit

One of our national heroes is a rabbit.

It's tempting to call Bugs Bunny a cartoon character. It doesn't work. It's like calling Woody Allen a comic, Charlie Chaplin a buffoon, the Beatles a band. It's too easy, too pat, a pigeonhole with the door flapping. Bugs Bunny doesn't *behave* like a cartoon character.

Any cartoon character can get his own television show. What kind of character gets his own show in 1960, keeps it for thirty years without a break, is on the air every day in most video markets, and has video cassettes available in virtually any video store?

Any cartoon character can get his image on drinking glasses, his face on beach balls, his mug on mugs. It's your once-in-a-lifetime character who gets his own star on Hollywood Boulevard.

Any cartoon character would get cheers from the Saturday matinee crowd when his face filled the screen to signify the start of one of his adventures. With Bugs Bunny, the reaction tended to blow the roof off the theater.

In the small, suburban, post-World War II theater where I was first acquainted with The Rabbit, just about any one of those cartoon icons flashed on the screen for our approval was received with generous helpings of applause, yells of delight, cheers of joy—but with Bugs, a sort of a "WHOOP!" went up from the crowd, a scream of unalloyed exultation, jubilation, delirium in excelsis, that carried on well into the action of the cartoon, only to be resumed again as he bid us Farewell and That's All Folks. (And this was a *Philadelphia* audience.)

Mickey Mouse clearly wowed 'em in the 1930s—with those solar rays emanating celestially from that sunny countenance, he wasn't just a star, he was the Sun in the dark days of the Depression. But throughout World War II and for the Baby Boomers arriving thereafter, it was that Warner Bros. shield dissolving into Bugs' beam, the Warner concentric circles reduced to a series of orbits around Bugs Bunny, that worked its cartoon magic on the crowd. He was always something you couldn't pinpoint, categorize, or describe—a phenomenon in the form of a "WHOOP!" and then pandemonium.

When his classic cartoons were being made and regularly released to theaters in the 1940s, 1950s, and 1960s, it was his stardom that caromed his studio, Warner Bros. to prominence in the animation field. In a poll conducted by the *Motion Picture Herald* of theater owners (the leading poll indicating the preferences of their customers), his individual series, the "Bugs Bunny Specials," was voted the most popular in the entire short-subject field in the United States and Canada for the year 1945, and then stayed in the Number One spot for the next sixteen years straight.

More recently, Robert Klein drew applause on *Late Night with David Letterman* with the remark, "Creatures like Donald Duck and Mickey give [children] comfort—but they're not *funny* like Bugs and Daffy." In unlikely places such as New York's *Village Voice*, we have this endorsement from writer Charles M. Young: "Bugs, an inhabitant of the Garden who also has smarts, represented the yearning for psychological health, the unity of opposites, the polymorphous perverse, the way out . . . Bugs could do more with the raising of an eyebrow than most comedians can accomplish with an entire monologue."

Bugs has been welcomed in bookstores, record stores, toy stores, video stores, movie theaters, haberdashers, sports arenas, universities, Macy's Thanksgiving Day Parade, the Museum of Modern Art, the Library of Congress, the National Archive, and the Smithsonian Institution. He was voted "Best Puppet or Cartoon Character" in *People* magazine's 1985 national poll. In a nationwide survey conducted in June of 1989 by C.A. Walker and Associates, Bugs was yet again proven to be one of the most popular cartoon and fantasy characters in the country, scoring well with children and adults, even against the classic Disney creations and more recent additions to the tel-

Above: *Bugs playing exactly what he is in* Bugs Bunny: All-American Hero, *Friz Freleng's CBS Special of 1981.*

Preceding pages: *A miscellaneous assortment of Bugs poses from his classic days.*

evision menagerie, like Garfield and the Peanuts gang. When market research in popular reaction to established media figures both real and imaginary was done in 1976, it was found that nobody but Abraham Lincoln tested higher than Bugs Bunny. This is rarefied territory. When you talk about Abraham Lincoln, you're not exactly in the realm of Republican politicians; and when you get around to Bugs Bunny, you're not really talking cartoon character.

Bob Clampett, who directed many of Bugs' pictures in the 1940s, used to give tours of the cartoon studio to the winners of contests in drawing or imitating Bugs;

they could watch the animators at work, watch the characters being painted onto cels, look at the exposure sheets and the model sheets, and still ask, "Yes, but when do we get to meet Bugs Bunny?"

When Bill Scott, later famous as the voice and head writer for Bullwinkle the Moose, went to work for Warner Bros. Cartoons in the mid-1940s, he told his grandmother that he was writing scripts for Bugs Bunny. Her reply to that was "Why? He's funny enough just as he is."

Leonard Maltin, *Entertainment Tonight*'s resident film historian, and no stranger to the mysteries of film production, has himself remarked of Bugs and Daffy,

Above: *The face that launched a thousand WHOOPs when it flashed on the screen in post-World War II America.*

13

"They've always been very real to me — as real as any other movie star!"

Well, how real is that?

People who are surprised at these reactions to Bugs may be laboring under the delusion that people like Groucho Marx, Cary Grant, Marlene Dietrich, Marilyn Monroe, and W.C. Fields were living beings, rather than what they were—farfetched fantasy figures dreamed up by people named Julius Henry Marx, Archie Leach, Josef Sternberg, Norma Jean Mortenson, and William Claude Dukenfield, and sustained by creative teamwork with even less visible folks like Leo McCarey, George Stevens, Gregory LaCava, George S. Kaufman, Morrie Ryskind, and Howard Hawks. The fact that they are dream figures, creatures of the night, doesn't mean they aren't strong enough to overshadow their creators, be confused with them, and sometimes come to possess them. Those are the characters who *live*, and Bugs is one of them.

Friz Freleng, one of the directors of the classic Bugs cartoons, doesn't deny it: "I thought of Bugs myself as a character that existed. I never thought of him as a drawing. I always feel that Bugs Bunny lives somewhere, and I'm just making a drawing *of* him. It's like your own child; you created that child, and the child grows up with you, and you can never lose the love for that child. I believe this character will live on for years to come, because he held true."

Chuck Jones, another of Bugs' directors, feels the same way: "It never occurred to me that these were not living things. I don't think you can make comedy unless you're involved with the characters. When I'd go home and I'd say to [my wife] Dorothy a line which just occurred as I was working, I'd say, 'You know what that guy Bugs did today?' and I'd repeat the line. She never got used to this. She'd say, 'Well, you were *drawing* it, you *did* it.' I'd say, 'That isn't *true*! It developed! That's what he said, it was *natural* for him to say it.' Of course it happens to anybody doing this sort of thing: it comes out of you because it's part of you."

In his cartoon *Duck Amuck*, Jones depicts a cartoon character (Daffy) as slave to his cartoonist (Bugs); in his book *Chuck Amuck*, he makes it sound more like a collaborative process: "When you are engaged in full animation, or in character live action comedy, the character takes over, pushes you aside; you become the interpreter of his actions. You respond to another personality, moving as it *needs* to go—as it *must* go.

Drawing becomes as unconscious a necessity to you as body mechanics are unconscious to the dancer during the performance. You cannot practice mechanics during a performance, because you are now the life force, the moving response. You *are* the interpreter of actions which surprise both you and the character you vitalize; you and he together become the series of surprises that is animation."

If there's one thing Hollywood could always do well, it was create living screen personalities. They called it the Star System, usually in terms of derision; but when it worked right, it produced authentic legends who gave people what one of those legends, Jimmy Stewart, called, "pieces of time."

Bugs got his Hollywood Boulevard plaque on December 21, 1985, declared "Bugs Bunny Day" by Los Angeles' mayor, Tom Bradley. (Mickey Mouse is the only other animated personality to be so honored.) Telegrams were read from Foghorn Leghorn and Pepe LePew. In their own voices. Daffy Duck asked when his time would come to get a star. Bill Walsh, the president of the Hollywood Chamber of Commerce, made his own little speech: "We're really honoring an idea today, but an idea that's become so real to all of us that I think we look upon it as another person in our lives." Ideas are gossamer things, but they've been known to work miracles.

On the night of January 24, 1961, another chrome-cruncher crucified a couple more cars on Sunset Boulevard's treacherous "Deadman's Curve" in Western Los Angeles. One driver emerged with only lacerations on his knee and forehead. The other was crushed inside the wreckage of his Aston Martin, requiring a special police unit with metal-cutting torches to spend half an hour peeling his unconscious body from the debris. Paramedics worked hard to see if there was a flicker of salvageable life, and if anything inside the jacket pocket would yield up legible ID. That's when they found the photograph.

Left: *Bugs' star is a Hollywood landmark at 7007 Hollywood Boulevard.* Above: *Bugs with Friz Freleng at the dedication ceremony, December 21, 1985. Chuck Jones also participated in the ceremony. Clearly, an attempt was being made to convince us that Chuck Jones and Friz Freleng were flesh and blood entities, almost as real in their own way as Bugs Bunny or Daffy Duck.*

Bugs Bunny's Voice Is Hurt Badly in Auto

West Los Angeles, Jan. 25 (UPI).—Comedian Mel Blanc, man of a thousand cartoon voices, including Bugs Bunny's "What's up, doc?" today fought to survive critical injuries received in a head-on collision on Sunset Blvd.

UCLA Medical Center said Blanc, 52, a frequent guest star on the Jack Benny television show, was in critical condition and "has not regained full con-

Above: *Even the press saw Mel Blanc's devastating accident as something that had happened to Bugs Bunny.* Right: *A small bunny, Bugs casts a large shadow. Frame from Chuck Jones'* What's Opera, Doc?, *1957.*

"Holy cow!" one of them exclaimed. "It's Bugs Bunny!"

"Knock off the jokes," said the other. "This guy's in rough shape."

His partner just insisted, "It's Bugs Bunny, I tell you! Look here."

He was close. The man in the Aston Martin who had just broken about every bone in his body was Mel Blanc, Bugs Bunny's voice man, identified by an autographed photo of himself in a rabbit suit, chewing on a carrot. Suffering from compound fractures and a concussion, Blanc was rushed to the UCLA Medical Center, just blocks away, where a team of eight surgeons worked on him throughout the night. The next day, the *Honolulu Herald* carried the grim news: Mel Blanc was dead.

Close again. Blanc's chances for survival were indeed slim, but they weren't invisible. Papers across the country reported the more accurate news that his condition was critical and the odds against his seeing the light of day again were something like a thousand to one. The papers referred to him as the man of a thousand voices, but the one they invariably singled out was the "What's up, Doc?" of Bugs Bunny. Fifteen thousand cards and letters came pouring in from children and adults both, some addressed only to "Bugs Bunny, Hollywood, USA." So many telephone calls wishing for Blanc's recovery flooded the hospital switchboard that extra lines and operators had to be put on. Gifts of pennies, nickels, sticks of gum, and carrots arrived in the mail, with fervent prayers from every religious denomination, messages scrawled in crayon reading, "Please, God, let Bugs Bunny get well."

A human being was in critical condition, and the first thought on the minds of millions of people was that something might happen to Bugs Bunny.

After twenty-one days and nights, and no amount of talking, pleading, whispering, or praying had succeeded in rousing Mel from his coma, his neurosurgeon, Dr. Louis Conway, got an idea. "How are you feeling today, *Bugs Bunny*?" he asked.

"Eh, just fine, Doc. How're you?" came the voice from the bandages.

"Mel was dying," said the doctor years later, "and it seemed as though Bugs Bunny was trying to save his life."

Defying the odds and his doctors, and delighting his family, his friends at Warner Bros. Cartoons, and millions of fans all over the world, Blanc rallied and began a slow but steady recovery to total health. Bugs Bunny was going to be OK.

Michael Maltese, one of Bugs' writers, once said, "After a while, Bugs Bunny was so well loved by the audience that he could do no wrong. We had quite a few lousy Bugs Bunnies. We'd say, 'Well, we haven't got time. Let's do it.' And we'd do it, and the audience would laugh. They loved the rabbit, and what he *stood* for."

If that's true, then what, exactly, did he stand for? If what we're talking about is an idea, then what's the big idea?

16

The Real Bugs Bunny

Bugs Bunny is that irrepressible rabbit who always chews nonchalantly on a carrot and asks that impertinent question, "What's up, Doc?"

The real impertinence, of course, is in a writer's trick like this, the pretense that a great character is reducible to a few words on a page. It actually involves a sort of double-edged literary conceit: that the writer can come up with the right phrase, and that a popular film character is predictable, easily categorized, and harmless. Any character who could be captured so easily is probably not a great character, and so probably not worth capturing. Bugs is a character who's spent fifty years proving he *couldn't* be captured.

"Even the people who write about animation," complains Chuck Jones, "just don't seem to understand that when you have a drawing, you don't have a character. It's like seeing a photograph of an actor and then saying, 'We're choosing this actor.' I don't understand these casting directors: What do you know when you look at him? OK, he looks the part, but until I see him move, I haven't any idea whether he *is* the part or not. If it's anything, it's the bodily style, bodily movement, gestures, mistakes that you make, that identify you, not what you wear, or the facial movements, or even the voice. Even with a talkative character like Bugs Bunny, we wanted to be certain that the action demonstrated what we were talking about—in other words, our characters were actors."

Bob Clampett tried encapsulating the character in the first person to Michael Barrier in 1969: "Some people call me cocky and brash, but actually I'm just self-assured. I'm nonchalant, imperturbable, contemplative. I play it cool, but I can get hot under the collar. And above all I'm a very 'aware' character. I'm well aware that I am appearing in an animated cartoon . . . And I sometimes chomp on my carrot for the same reason that a stand-up comic chomps on his cigar . . . it saves me from rushing from the last joke to the next one too fast. And I sometimes don't act . . . I react. And I always treat the contest with my pursuers purely as 'fun and games.' When momentarily I appear to be cornered or in dire danger and I scream, don't be consoined — it's actually a big put-on. Let's face it, Doc, I've read the script and I already know how it all comes out.

"Of course," he finally admitted, "Bugs Bunny is much too complex a personality for us to fully explore his 'psyche' in these few minutes."

The idea that a "cartoon character" like Bugs Bunny might be "too complex a personality" to describe in a few sentences might seem at first a contradiction in terms. After all, a character like Bugs exists for only seven minutes of screen time at a stretch, as opposed to characters in two-reel comedies, half-hour sitcoms, and full-length features, who must carry twenty, thirty, ninety minutes, or three or four hours. But a great series character has to pull off a neat trick: he has an identity made up of hundreds of sep

Above: *Robert McKimson's wartime drawing of Bugs for a Los Angeles department store's Easter show has since become a standard publicity pose.* Left: *Just a few of the many facets of Bugs Bunny, as illustrated by selected cels from his appearances: a clown in Chuck Jones'* Barbary Coast Bunny, *1956; a genial host on* The Bugs Bunny Show, *1960-62; a dashing sophisticate in Friz Freleng's* Slick Hare, *1947.*

arate episodes (about 175, in Bugs' case) that must each stand alone, but all interconnect strongly enough to establish a consistent personality in the minds of the audience. If he's too schematic, he fades into nonentity; but if he's too vague and ill-defined, he never takes hold. Part of Bugs' great achievement has been to establish a strong personality that can exist for seven minutes at a time, show us a facet of that personality, disappear for weeks, months, maybe years, then reappear and be recognizable, familiar, a buddy, yet still surprise us enough to be entertaining once again. His possibilities are not exhausted by any single episode. ("And thank God," adds Chuck Jones.) A certain amount of complexity, a whole other dimension, is required for that to work. The trick is not to sustain seven minutes, but to live for fifty years.

Take Bugs' ears. "Draw ears to suit mood," says one of his early model sheets. This the artists did. Bugs plays piano with his ears in *Rhapsody Rabbit,* conducts a full orchestra with them in *Baton Bunny,* runs on them in *A Hare Grows in Manhattan*, and in both *The Big Snooze* and *Slick Hare* he dances on them. In *Rabbit of Seville*, he massages Elmer Fudd's scalp with them; in *Rabbit's Feat*, he uses one as a corkscrew to dig into his rabbit hole. In both *The Wabbit Who Came to Supper* and *The Heckling Hare*, Bugs' ears are capable of operating autonomously and even develop a pantomimic rapport with each other; they also operate like periscopes, implying that they are able to *see.*

Bugs uses his ears for additional expression, for gags, for extra appendages, and the way a cat uses his whiskers—the way *we* used to use rabbit ears—as sensing devices tuning him in to his environment. They don't sum him up, but graphically they point in the right direction. Bugs enjoys being a rabbit, but he's flexible. For a considerable stretch of *Rabbit Rampage* he's a horse; for a few seconds in *Knight-Mare Hare* he has to put up with being a pig, and in *Transylvania 6-5000,* a baseball bat.

Bugs is an appealing force for good. He comes on television and sells the kids vitamins that are good for them; he instructs them about fire prevention and earthquake safety. That overwhelming charm, Mel Blanc's ear-nuzzling voice—syrupy smooth without getting sticky sweet—that face carefully input by skilled artists with every time-tested element of eye appeal they can think of, after an evolution that took years—his ability to please, to be lovable and non-threatening—surely it's *that,* in its purest and simplest form, which accounts for his success as a character.

But when British documentarian John Needham interviewed moviegoers in line for *The Bugs Bunny/Roadrunner Movie,* he found that more than one person singled out Bugs' "anarchistic" qualities as the element they most responded to in the character—especially one man who called him "sort of the major character influence in my life, basically being [an] anti-establishment, disrespectful, anti-authoritarian kind of character."

And Tom Shales of the *Washington Post* has explained his inordinate love for The Rabbit in pretty much the same way: "I love Bugs Bunny, because of his attitude toward the Establishment, his absolute refusal to take any . . . *stuff* . . . from anybody." Franklin Rosemont, leading spokesman for the American chapter of the international Surrealist movement, has written, "Bugs Bunny stands as a veritable symbol of irreducible recalcitrance . . . one can scarcely imagine a better model to offer our children than this bold creature who, with his four rabbit's feet, is the good luck charm of total revolt."

This was basically the explanation for Bugs' popularity offered by the motion picture trade periodical *Showmen's Trade Review* in 1943: "The unpredictable antics of this brash hare, his amazing contrast to other animated favorites, proved not a little perplexing to adults and children alike . . . Why, when most spectators are inclined to sympathize with the underdog, should a presumptuous bumpkin like this win their approval? The answer might well lie in the fact that the average person, in life a hardworking introvert striving to get along, found in this character the nerve and bluster, the boldness and self-assurance, he himself would like to possess."

For the people questioned in the C.A. Walker poll, the qualities contributing to the popularity of Bugs and his Warners cohorts were "Adamant and unyielding" and

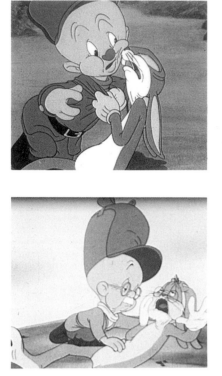

Bugs in not above repeating an old trick, but he generally reworks it each time out. The death scene that fakes Elmer Fudd (top) was animated by Robert McKimson in the first Bugs Bunny cartoon, Tex Avery's A Wild Hare, *1940. The gag is repeated in old age in Bob Clampett's* The Old Grey Hare, *1944 (center), then set to the operatic music of Richard Wagner in Chuck Jones'* What's Opera, Doc? *1957, seen in a detail of a background study by Maurice Noble (bottom).*

"Always persistent in the face of adversity." Chuck Jones agrees that this is a key element of the character, and believes that "What a child wants to be able to see on television is that the individual can survive . . . the whole idea that you're capable, you *personally*. I have known kids who have told me that what they like about Bugs and Daffy and the rest of them are that they are individuals, they solved their own problems."

Bugs has somehow been able to do both things, and superbly well—to be The Rebel to developing adolescents and the "polymorphous perverse" to writers in *The Village Voice*, and yet still be considered an innocuous diversion for children by their parents.

Friz Freleng remarks, "The cocky characters, for some reason, the public seems to like. They don't like those kinds of people in real life." Mel Blanc believed that "Bugs Bunny appeals to the rebel in all of us. Everybody loves a winner, and Bugs Bunny always wins."

When Tex Avery, credited by most people as Bugs' creator, attempted to synopsize his rabbit for the Kool-Aid people, he told them, "You should visualize him like Groucho Marx. If he ever runs from anyone, he has a trick in mind. If you look back at the old Grouchos, he would run, real slow, with that funny lope, but then he'd stop and make some crack. He was always in command; he knew what he was doing."

And Bugs (who appears perfectly natural as Groucho in both *Slick Hare* and *Wideo Wabbit*) is someone we think of as "a winner," as "always in command." But how true is that, really? As a detective in *The Unmentionables*, he gets the handcuffs on the crooks but loses the keys, so he's forced to serve their prison time along with them. His last line in *Captain Hareblower*, after he's gotten himself blown sky-high, is "I could be wrong, ya know." *Mad As a Mars Hare* leaves him transformed, much against his will, into a Neanderthal rabbit. He claims in *The Hare-Brained Hypnotist* that he could never be hypnotized by Elmer Fudd, but he closes the picture by taking off like a B-19 because he thinks he's overdue at the airport. At least three cartoons find him running, screaming, for the hills at their conclusion, and in one of them, *Bugs Bunny and the Three Bears*, his screams are still audible after the picture has irised out.

Again Bugs reconciles the apparent opposites—he can suffer defeats that most characters could never bounce back from and still leave the overriding impression that he is a winner.

There's virtually nothing you can say about Bugs' character without hearing Bugs' voice from *Racketeer Rabbit*: "No no, too obvious . . . No no, won't fit," or from *Rabbit's Feat*: "Nah nah, too complicated . . . Uh-uh, too much detail."

Even to say he's a winner seems to miss the boat. He's not Hulk Hogan with ears, exactly. There's a moment in *A Hare Grows in Manhattan* when Bugs dives into a manhole to escape the bulldog pursuing him, and between the time the dog leaps in the air and the time he reaches the manhole, Bugs has managed to resurface, grab the manhole cover, and pull it into place—turning the dog's face into something resembling a waffle. It's a simple enough gag, but the point is that there is a look of such total *delight* on Bugs' face as he performs the act that he turns the whole business into something else altogether, a conflict of viewpoints rather than a physical conflict between two animals. Bugs is Puck reborn; he *enjoys* the scrapes he gets into because he *knows* he'll win eventually. This goes a long way toward making him the irresistible character he is: he holds out the possibility that the battle is winnable, that we can vanquish the foe and have fun doing it, that every setback can become another challenge, another excuse for high spirits.

Most of the generalizations found in write-ups seem to be based on the viewing of a handful of cartoons. Once you've covered the entire Bugs Bunny canon, it's the *range* that gets impressive, not the formula. Are you talking about the wild, anything-goes Bugs of the '40s cartoons, or the debonair, catch-me-if-you-can Bugs of the '50s? Are you talking about the active, impulsive Bugs of Friz Freleng's cartoons, or the calm, suave Bugs of Chuck Jones' films? Do you mean the noble Bugs of *Ballot Box Bunny* and *Hare Trimmed* who combats Yosemite Sam because he sees it's the right thing to do, or the feisty, anarchistic, even savage animal of *Buckaroo Bugs*, *Fresh Hare*, and *Rebel Rabbit*?

About the only thing Bugs does with any consistency is assume new identities. His transformations, not only into Groucho, but into cops, kids, geriatric cases, women,

seamen, foremen, and apparitions of unknown identity is nothing short of legendary. In the space of a few seconds in *What's Cookin' Doc?* he becomes Katharine Hepburn, Edward G. Robinson, Jerry Colonna and Bing Crosby—then follows that minutes later with Charles Boyer and the Frankenstein monster. This ability probably reaches its peak in *Racketeer Rabbit*, where, in quick succession, he assumes the identities of five separate Damon Runyonesque mobsters and one American Indian chief.

And when Bugs assumes another identity, he's not just donning a new wardrobe or hiding behind a moustache. He enters into a new full-bodied characterization with complete panache. As Steve Schneider points out in his history of the Warner Bros. cartoon, *That's all Folks!*, when Bugs impersonates a detective for the benefit of a gangster he's got locked in a trunk, in *Racketeer Rabbit*, he's careful to put on and take off his detective "disguise" for each new line of this characterization's dialogue, even though he's not visible to the ostensible audience of his charade. When the supposed argument escalates into fisticuffs, he gets in a couple good ones on himself. If he's going to play two people in conflict, there's By George going to be conflict!

This syndrome reaches a kind of schematic high in *Bugs' Bonnets*, where an army helmet is enough to turn Bugs into a tough sergeant, a game warden's cap gives him authority over hunter Elmer Fudd, a feathered headdress makes him an Indian, a white wig turns him into a judge, and a topper makes him the groom at the wedding of a blushing Fudd.

In *Baton Bunny*, he does all this without need of hats: his magic ears alone are sufficient wardrobe to effect these transformations. When they twist to resemble a ten-gallon hat he's a cowboy, when they loop into the form of a headdress he's an Indian again, pursuing himself, and, as the cap of a cavalry officer, they allow him to ride to his own rescue. His ears can do everything hats can do, allowing him to contain multitudes inside himself and become the chameleon of rabbits, without for a second ceasing to be Bugs Bunny.

"No one Warner Brothers character's role is sacred," says animation commentator Roger Bullis. "No humiliation will necessarily be spared for humor's sake. The Looney Tunes cast is immersed in a cartoon repertory system."

Above: Bugs and his magic ears stage an entire Indian attack and rescue unassisted in frames from Chuck Jones' Baton Bunny, *1959.*

Right and opposite: Bugs' characterization varies by the second, as does his gender. Right: Chuck Jones' layout drawing from Bugs' Bonnets, *1956. Far right: animation drawing from Clampett's* Buckaroo Bugs, *1944.*

Clockwise, from above: *Bugs as a flapper in an animation drawing from Friz Freleng's* The Unmentionables, *1963; as Cupid in a cel from his* Hare Splitter, *1948; as Carmen Miranda in an animation drawing from Bob Clampett's* What's Cookin', Doc, *1944; as a mermaid in an animation drawing by Robert McKimson from his* Hare Ribbin', *1943; and as a bride in an animation drawing by Virgil Ross from Freleng's* Hare Trimmed, *1953.*

23

Bugs is an actor: When he masquerades as a Frenchman, he is a Frenchman—but with all the verve and impudence we associate with Bugs Bunny. Animation drawings by Virgil Ross for Friz Freleng's Hare Trimmed, *1953.*

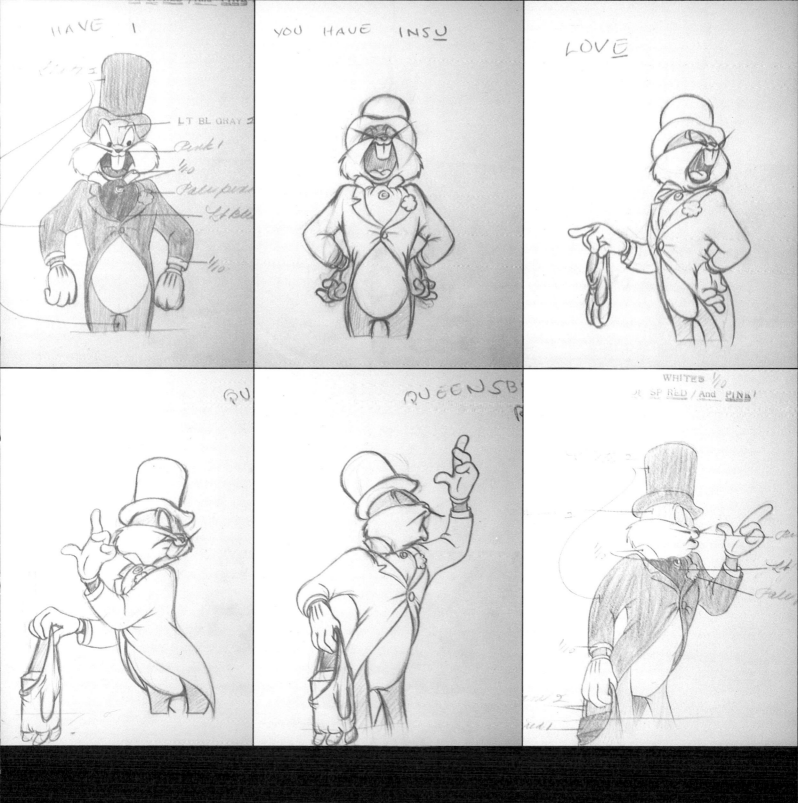

But after working with Bugs for a few years, Jones, Freleng, McKimson, and the writers felt they knew what his demands were. As Bugs himself told a Warners publicist in New York in 1946, "The boys on the Coast try to think of situations in which I get involved through no fault of my own, and then have me turn the tables on the trouble-makers. It's the old story of an underdog getting the best of his oppressors, and do they love it!"

It made sense to start Bugs' adventures in a natural woodland setting—his rabbit hole, if possible, or any other location where a rabbit seemed to belong. Then trouble would come in the form of some outside force, and the more mindlessly vicious the better. Yosemite Sam, the Tasmanian Devil, or some all-purpose brute.

Then, as Jones describes it, "Bugs resists in every way he can imagine, and he is a very imaginative rabbit. Two or three things would happen before he got mad enough—no, he wasn't *mad* enough, just the *logic* would move in, and he'd say, 'All right, so much has happened to me—of course you realize this means war.' Which is not a pugnacious statement, it's a logical statement. Karl von Clausewitz said, 'War is politics carried a step further.' At that point, you say, 'OK, hostilities start *here*.' So Bugs simply says that war has begun, and you couldn't get rid of him then. He is willing to engage danger, but only because he's put upon. This is very important, because there are a lot of characters in animation who simply go out and bedevil people, and to me it's vital that the character have sympathy—particularly an heroic character like Bugs.

"He is that unusual comedian: a comic hero, and they are very few. Bugs is based on many things, but one of them is the idea of how wonderful it would be to be a superrabbit, which is really what he is. Bugs *is* what I would like to be: debonair, quickwitted, very fast on the comeback. I'd like to have that ability to be a sort of male Dorothy Parker, and to have the quip ready every time. I think of beautiful quips, but they're always late. You go home and think, 'I should have said *that*.' You didn't say it at the time, unfortunately. Well, wouldn't it be wonderful to be able to think that fast! And Bugs can, you see."

Below: *Bugs' home: the natural woodland setting most Bugs Bunny adventures take off from. Background painted by Robert Gribbroek from layout by Robert Givens for Robert McKimson's* False Hare, *1964—the last theatrical Bugs cartoon.* Opposite: *There is more of Bugs Bunny's character in these expressive drawings by Friz Freleng, finished by Hawley Pratt, than in any prose poem a writer could conjure up. Made for* Foxy by Proxy, *1952.*

And that is the Union of Opposites that sets off the sirens and red lights. This is possibly the critical factor of what we love about Bugs: that he will not only make us laugh but make us feel victorious and triumphant. There are heroes and there are comedians; rarely the twain meet. This made him difficult for the people who created his cartoons, but it's also what gave him that special spark that makes him the phenomenon that he is. Once you have created that alloy, you have box-office gold and a place in the hearts of millions.

American filmmakers discovered early on that if you could get an audience laughing, they'd come back eagerly for more, and so series like the Keystone and the Our Gang Comedies came into being, and people like Mack Sennett and Hal Roach got rich. Funny is Money: the formula is still in use today.

But when you have a comedian who is in *control*, a character who can satisfy our hunger for laughter as well as our quest for a hero, you have an item with virtually limitless appeal. A character like Bugs has to be stumbled upon, built up by trial and error, kept alive through manic creation, slow caution, freewheeling spontaneity, and hard-as-nails discipline, reconciling opposites all over the place. In this way, comic heroes like Chaplin's Tramp have found their way to the screen, been discovered by their audience, burst through the common-sense border that separates art from commerce, and made assembly-line products into a modern mythology—in Gerald Weale's term, "Canned Goods as Caviar."

From the time he first asked Elmer Fudd "What's up, Doc?" until his Jubilee celebration in 1990, Bugs has been both winner and loser, sophisticated and naive, innocent and guilty, child of nature and street-tough smart guy, foole and hero, cartoonist and character, one of the most rounded and all-around characters in the history of film, a multi-faceted gem who constantly surprises and rarely disappoints, not just a successful character on-screen and off-screen, but Success itself.

Not for nothing that "WHOOP!"

Above: *Bugs as foole in frame from Friz Freleng's Oscar-winning* Knighty-Knight Bugs, *1958*. Below: *Bugs as hero in a publicity pose for Chuck Jones'* Super Rabbit, *1943*. Opposite: *Cel from Jones'* Rabbit Hood, *1949*.

29

2
BIRTH O' DA BUGS

CHUCK JONES

Above: *Bugs with Chuck Jones and Daffy Duck celebrates the second of his two 40th birthdays in 1979.*

The Big Bang

Bugs Bunny, being Success, has many fathers. It was a crowded woodpile.

It was also, evidently, a wild night, because the next day nobody could remember when it happened. Bugs celebrated his fifth birthday in 1947, his twenty-fifth birthday in 1961, and his fortieth birthday in 1978 and then again in 1979. Apparently you can't count rabbit years the way you can the regular kind.

Bugs, like most characters, inspires that insistent question, "Who created him?" A simple answer is expected. But no simple answer works.

"It's pretty hard to pin down who created what in this business," argues Friz Freleng, a veteran of over sixty years in animation. "It's not like sitting down and drawing a strip, where all the gags and the drawings and everything are done by this one man and that's it, because animated films are not made that way. You sit around a room and you kick ideas around all day long, and one says one thing and one says another, and before you know it you've got a character there, and you don't really know who did it. People who recognized the elements that make a great character made better films than the next guy. Those who made the better pictures helped the character develop faster. Another gag, another treatment of personality, another attitude that the next guy would use, and finally it built to where it was a solid character."

"A character like Bugs Bunny has contributions by many people," Bob Clampett agreed; "storymen, animators who added things to the character, and all the directors who made the pictures molded him in those pictures."

It's logical that a rabbit with many fathers has many ancestors, and Bugs' roots stretch in all directions. The clearest family line reaches back to Tex Avery, who gave The Rabbit his famous personality. When I asked the soft-spoken Texan how Bugs came into being, he was laconic. "Oh," he said, "it just came out of a cartoon."

The Big Bang Theory of Bugs' Creation: We put a rabbit on the screen, the audience got a big bang out of it, and a star was born. The cartoon was *A Wild Hare*, which was released on July 27, 1940.

But if Bugs Bunny is an offspring of Tex Avery's, he is automatically descended from another great American character, the legendary Judge Roy Bean.

The notorious Roy Bean was not really a judge, but he said he was Justice of the Peace, and, out in Comanche Territory in the late 1800s, no one, not even the Texas Rangers, cared to argue. Bean was played by Walter Brennan in *The Westerner* and by Paul Newman in *The Life and Times of Judge Roy Bean*, but he was probably less cosmetic and more colorful in real life than he was on the screen.

The Law West of the Pecos might tell a suspect held for petty theft that he would give him a fair trial, then hang him. Presiding at a murder inquest, Bean once found forty dollars and a pistol on the victim. He fined the corpse exactly forty dollars for carrying a concealed weapon and pocketed the proceeds.

Bean's legend loomed large in the Avery family. Tex was born five years after Roy died, named Frederick Bean Avery, and told, "Don't ever mention you are kin to Roy Bean. He's a no-good skunk!"

The tall tales and the desert wildlife of his Texas environs exerted their pull on him, and he took up the two hobbies he never got tired of: drawing and hunting. When Avery reached North Dallas High School, where he drew cartoons for the yearbook, he picked up an expression that entered his vocabulary to stay, where every sentence got "Doc" attached to its beginning, middle, or end. Later, people would ask him, "Where do you get that 'Doc' stuff?" But by then it was as natural as his Texas twang.

With no thought of a Hollywood career, Fred drifted into Los Angeles right out of school, and soon found himself hanging around the docks taking odd jobs, working at the warehouse of the Safeway market, and sleeping on the Santa Monica beach at night. His skill with a pen got him work inking cartoon cels at the Charles Mintz Studio, then when Walter Lantz set up shop producing Oswald the Rabbit cartoons at Universal, he was inking and eventually animating there. Avery (now dubbed "Tex")

Preceding pages: Bugs rising: new graphics by Chuck Jones, drawn for this book.

found that the excitement of animation was getting to him. One night at the movies, when he happened to see Walt Disney's *The Three Little Pigs*, and what it did to the audience, his enthusiasm became infectious.

Story and direction were so loose in the animation business at the time, and at Lantz' studio in particular, that Avery's ability to gag up his own scenes came to be noticed, then given free reins, then relied on. "The animators all contributed gags, and Tex was really outstanding," says Lantz. Avery worked under director Bill Nolan, who was already tired of the business he'd been in practically since its inception, and soon realized he could get half a cartoon out of his hair just by turning it over to Tex with the instruction "Bring Oswald the Rabbit in on the left, take him out on the right, and do anything you want in between." A law worthy of the West of the Pecos began to infect the Lantz pictures.

In *Lumber Champ*, a character named Pooch the Pup, trying to chop down a tree, has made no apparent progress after several good swings of the axe, so the tree just sprouts a face and chimes in, "Can I take it or can I take it?" At the sporting event in *The Athlete*, the starter's gun rages out of control, shooting up the field and sending the athletes scurrying for cover. Once the gun calms down, it's up to the individual bullets to prance over to the starting line and shout "Go!"

Tex's question, to himself or to the other office gagsters who hung around his desk, was "What do you think the audience would *least* expect?" Once he had an answer that shocked his friends into laughter, it usually went on to do the same to theater audiences.

When Tex directed two cartoons at Universal, then ran out of room to advance, he went and sold his services as director to a fellow named Leon Schlesinger, and then Bugs' conception was just around the corner.

Because Tex had left two important words out of the story of Bugs' birth: Bugs Bunny came out of a *Warner Bros.* cartoon.

Left: *A Texas tall tale in a natural woodland setting: Bugs Bunny braves Elmer Fudd's superior firepower in Tex Avery's* A Wild Hare, *1940. Above: Tex Avery reviews a storyboard at the Warner Bros. Cartoon Studio with George Manuel (left) and Tedd Pierce (right).*

Four of Bugs Bunny's key directors, with their hero.

Bob Clampett: "When momentarily I appear to be cornered or in dire danger and I scream, don't be consoined—it's actually a big put-on. Let's face it, Doc, I've read the script and I already know how it comes out."

Friz Freleng: "The cocky characters, for some reason, the public seems to like. They don't like those kinds of people in real life."

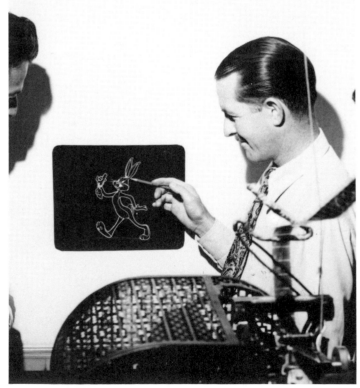

Robert McKimson: "Bugs Bunny was one of those pixie-type characters who had no compunction about doing anything . . . He's the type of character who would walk up to a lion, hear the lion's roar, and slap him."

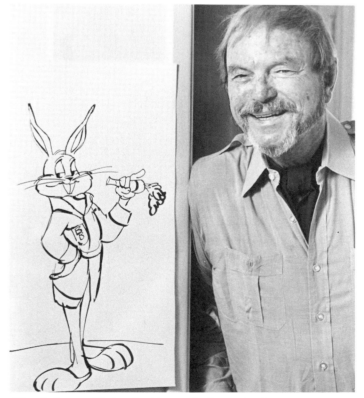

Chuck Jones: "Actually, the easiest way to draw Bugs Bunny is to draw a carrot and then hook a rabbit onto it. You'll notice the pinky (turning) up, which is very important, it indicates a kind of elegance about The Rabbit.

The Looney Tunes Bin

Bugs' own opinion of his creation comes out of a dispatch from a Warner Bros. publicist: "I guess you'd have to say that I am the combined product of over two hundred men and women of Warner Bros. Cartoons, Inc. in Hollywood."

One of the many painters of Bugs Bunny cels, Elsa Hubbell, commented in 1957, "We at the Cartoon Division are very proud . . . to know that we all have had a hand in the career of this famous rabbit." And, in one way or another, they all had. A rabbit with roots needs to find fertile soil, and the soil at the Warner Bros. Cartoon Studio had fertility to spare.

The word "atmosphere" comes up a lot when people recall their days at The Rabbit Factory: According to Mel Blanc, ". . . the studio atmosphere practically crackled with energy" Chuck Jones said, ". . . there was a tremendous atmosphere of collective creativity." Mike Maltese remarked, "It was fun going to work. The atmosphere!"

Apparently it was not an atmosphere that appealed to everybody. Leon Schlesinger, who ran the place, passed the checks out on Wednesday, usually with the lisped and slurped comment, "Pew, lemme outta here! All that'th miththing in here ith the thound of a fluthing toilet." Let him out of there they did—he had horseraces to attend to—but everyone else took their money and ran, too, generally to Laguna Beach with a gang from Disney's. Since a mass exodus out the door would have attracted attention, the windows were the usual escape route.

Maltese remembers, "That place looked old, beat-up—it was right out of Dickens. You went in the back rooms, they were *dreadful* rooms. They had composition board for walls, and we used to put our fists through it, we used to throw darts at it. Dave Monahan tried to set fire to it once, just for the hell of it, just to see if it burned. And it wouldn't burn. We did everything to that studio."

Like Oz, Xanadu, Never-Never Land, and Shangri-La, Termite Terrace has become the name for an *idea*. Specifically, it was the rattiest of the rat traps that housed the artists of the Warner Bros. Cartoon Studio (which was first called Leon Schlesinger Productions, then, after Schlesinger had sold the cartoons to Warner Bros. for a decade, he sold them the studio in 1944). Termite Terrace was a set of old wooden buildings intended to be temporary, which, according to Bob McKimson, "looked like diners." It was occupied by cartoonists for only a year or two, and then only black-and-white Looney Tunes were made there: Bugs Bunny never set foot in the place. But it was the birthplace of the unique Warner Bros. cartoon style, and generically it's become the name for the whole legendary studio, which occupied, over thirty-five years, several buildings in Hollywood and Burbank.

It was a place where you were never quite sure what you were going to see. Friday was "Theater Day." The Warner Bros. wardrobe storehouse had been raided from time to time, and anybody might turn up wearing anything. Tedd Pierce found his own Fiat parked in the hallway once, just because it occurred to a gang of the guys

Below left: Friday was "Theater Day" at Termite Terrace. Chuck Jones is visible in the feathered headdress in the rear. Below: *Typical of the gag sketches that were churned out as fast as animation drawings at Termite Terrace. Bottom: This 1937 gag shot features from left to right: John Burton, Frank Tashlin, unidentified, Bugs Hardaway, Leon Schlesinger, unidentified, unidentified, A. C. Gamer, Tex Avery, Treg Brown, and Henry Binder.*

Above: *Bugs looks over the shoulders of twin assistant animators Madilyn and Marilyn Wood in this 1952 photograph.* Right: *Bugs Bunny and some of the 75 people who were Bugs Bunny, in Michael Maltese's collage of photographs taken by Floyd McCarthy in February 1945. Top row: Virgil Ross, Warren Batchelder, Louise Beatty, Joseph P. Wilber, Dorothy Miller, Edward Selzer, Helen Miller, Arthur Milman, John W. Burton. Second row: Don Williams, Arthur Davis, Richard Bickenbach, Anatole Kirsanoff, Cal Dalton, Lloyd Vaughan, Ben Washam, Basil Davidovich, Maurice Fagin, Gerry Chiniquy, Manuel Perez, John Kennedy, P. D. Eller, Kenneth Champin, Louis Appet. Third row: Verena Ruegg, Kenneth Moore, Ann Almond, Bugs Bunny and Mel Blanc, Earl Klein, Chuck Jones, four of the sixty cel inkers and painters. Fourth row: Ken Harris, Treg Brown, Hawley Pratt, Friz Freleng, Marilyn and Madilyn Wood, Phil DeGuard, Robert Gribbroek, Marjorie Jasper, A.C. Gamer, Peter Gaenger, Auril Thompson. Fifth row: Paul Julian, Warren Foster, Robert McKimson, Edward Selzer, Robert Clampett Animation Unit, Sue Gee, Florence Finkelhor, Raynelle Day, Paul Marron, R.G. Chaney, Mildred Rossi, Carl Stalling.*

that it was likely to fit. Maltese claimed that on his first introduction to the Story Department, ". . . they were sitting around with blankets like Indians, building a bonfire in the middle of the floor." Mel Blanc sounded surprised when he said he might see "Lloyd Vaughan looking very much like he was about to take an axe to Ken Harris' helmeted head." Yet a personal request on just about every one of his visits was "Do the one about the German World War I aviator getting shot down by the British flyer," and the story crew became a flight crew.

Tex Avery came out of one poker game owing Schlesinger ten dollars, and promised it to him right after lunch. Tex was prompt, but Leon got his ten dollars in unrolled pennies, emptied out of a paper sack all over his desk. Chuck Jones was amused enough by that to return a five-dollar debt of his own in pennies, neatly encased in a jar of honey, and a friend of his who'd picked up a dinner tab found the seven-dollar differential returned by mail in one-cent stamps. When Ben Washam borrowed five dollars from Tedd Pierce and promised to return it in a few days, Pierce took him at his word and started needling him before the week was out. Washam said, "You'll get your dough—with interest, yet." And, good as his word, Washam soon handed Pierce a fine, home-cooked loaf of bread, with the inevitable five hundred pennies baked inside.

Bottles concealed in drawers were commonplace; for a long time, Cal Howard ran an entire lunch counter out of his desk. Howard didn't need the profits this enterprise garnered for him; its only value was the fun of getting away with it.

Which explains most of what went on at Termite Terrace. One animator, afflicted with an inability to sleep on the job, served sentry duty for the entire enclave, by means of a complex system of lights and wires warning the troupe of impending production managers. At the sight of the flashing lights, animators would stop goofing and start working, amd writers and directors would stop working and start goofing. Years passed without some of these managers ever seeing a writer or a director working.

By now the Warner Bros. cartoon has uncontestably carved out a niche of its own in the consciousness of film buffs, nostalgia mavens, animation fans, and the general

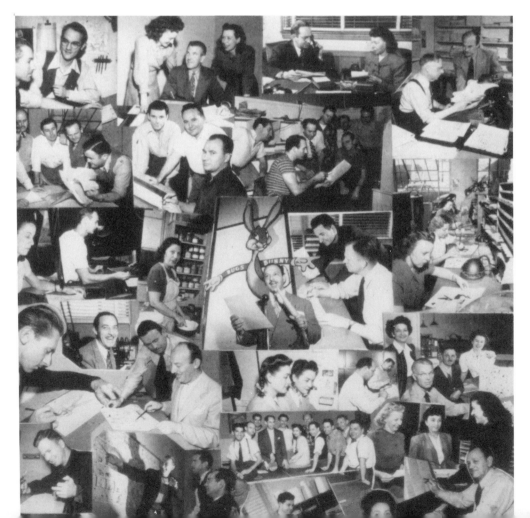

public—not a single cartoon, but collectively, en masse, as a brand name for one of the greatest series of short subjects ever made. Nowhere else in American animation, in the annals of American comedy, in fact in the world history of film, is there a series of films quite like them, blessed with a recognizable house style, a familiar yet surprising group of vivid comic characters who could stand alone triumphantly or interact dynamically, a delirious comic spirit, a ready association with pleasure, delight, exhilaration, possibly total crackup—a kind of childlike joy not limited to childhood.

"People hate to laugh unless they have a reason; they feel embarrassed," said Mike Maltese. "One thing we learned was not to be self-conscious when you're thinking up stories or cartoons or something funny. We knew, writing these cartoon stories, that the kidding around that we all did sort of broke down the barrier, and enabled us to go unashamedly, almost like children, into making absolute idiots of ourselves. An outsider would see us and say, 'Well, for heaven's sake! Grown men!' But we understood."

And the atmosphere made it to the screen.

Richard Corliss made a valuable point when he wrote in *Film Comment*, "We hear a lot about 'cartoony' feature pictures; we don't see much evidence that the hard lessons of cartoon pacing, gag-building, and the crucial *suspension of* suspension of disbelief have been learned . . . after dieting or gorging on the Warners stuff, watching almost any current live-action film is slow torture. It takes fooorrevvver for an actor to walk from the door to the kitchen table. Every reaction shot plays like an ennui festival. And don't these people have any control over their bodies? Daffy Duck can convey more with the merest shrug or saunter or slink. Who let human beings into movies anyway?"

Maltese had a single explanation for the Warner Bros. pre-eminence in the field of cartoon comedy: "The main thing with me is the characters. Let's face it, Charles Dickens' stories were nothing. His characters—Oliver Twist, Fagin, the rest of them—they were the main things. You could take a story like *Gone With the Wind* and what is it? But you get the characters—Scarlett O'Hara, Rhett Butler, Ashley Wilkes—great!"

The unforgettable comic characters of the Warner Bros. cartoons were their stock in trade, their enduring legacy. And the creation of none of them was a simple, cut-and-dried affair. Where did they come from?

Studio veterans say that it was "the con artist" in Tedd Pierce that helped to define Daffy Duck's eventual personality. Maltese recalled, "In 1944, when I was working for Freleng, we came up with Yosemite Sam in a picture called *Hare Trigger*, and I patterned him more or less after Freleng: 'WHY, I'LL BLOW YOU TO SMITHEREENS! OOOOOOOH!' Of course, we had exaggerated Friz." Cameraman Smokey Garner found his familiar refrain, "Agony! A-go-ny!" put in the mouths of animated characters like Elmer Fudd, just as Ben Washam saw his pet Arkansas expression, "Thanks for the sour persimmons, cousin," come out of Daffy's beak in *Duck Amuck*. It was gagman Cal Howard's idea to adapt Leon Schlesinger's slurping lisp for Daffy and Sylvester. (When Schlesinger himself appears onscreen in *You Ought to Be in Pictures*, that lisp-free voice on the soundtrack is Mel Blanc's.) Layout man Pete Alvarado ventures, "I think a lot of neurotic animators got rid of their aggressions" in the lunacies on the drawing board.

It was the characters who became the focus for a collective unconscious. In a Hollywood whose business it was to cater to their audience's love for recognizable personalities on the screen, a group of talented artists with an attitude problem found something that worked. Movie fans who didn't want to know from Friz Freleng or Ben Washam or Tedd Pierce or Elsa Hubbell, or "over two hundred men and women of Warner Bros. Cartoons, Inc. in Hollywood" could find something to relate to, laugh at, and remember in Bugs, Daffy, Sam, and the Roadrunner.

And it was Bugs Bunny who seemed to crystallize it all—the tensile strength, the energy, the impudence, the talent, the exuberance, the freedom, the joy, the irreverence, that was the Warner Bros. cartoon. "If you talk about the Rams of 1956,"

Top: *One of Termite Terrace's crowning achievements, Chuck Jones'* What's Opera, Doc?, *1957, is a brilliant, beautiful film but it never forgets to be* funny *at the same time. Above: Bugs captures some of what Fred Quimby called "that Warner Bros. rowdyism" in this animation drawing by Virgil Ross for Friz Freleng's* Rhapsody Rabbit, *1946. A lot of problems tended to be solved by firecrackers at Termite Terrace.*

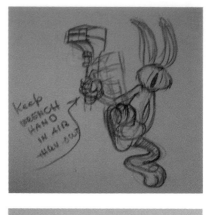

Above and top: "Joketh are funny": Some of Bob Clampett's rough sketches for his Falling Hare, 1943.

says Friz Freleng, "you can't remember the individual players, but you know it was a great team. The quarterback gets all the credit, and there are guys pushing guys around, making holes for him to run through, you don't even *see* those guys. The big hero gets all the headlines. You don't even remember the *numbers* of the guys who made the holes for him. But that's the way our business is. It was a team that developed these characters."

Leon Schlesinger, the man who had the most to do with putting it all together, has been described by Chuck Jones as "a fifth-string Harry Cohn" who permitted creativity to flourish only because he "was usually too lazy even to say no" and made no contribution to the cartoons other than to hazard, "Put in lottsa joketh, fellath, joketh are funny."

"He dressed like a vaudeville hoofer who had suddenly come into money," agreed background artist Paul Julian. "He had no aesthetic sense; he didn't know boo about anything but the money his cartoons made."

Bob Clampett gave him a little more credit: "Short deadlines, short money, but he let us make the pictures without interference. And he let us try new ideas. We would try any new idea that came to our heads. Some things didn't work, and we wouldn't use them again. He had a sense of vaudeville and a sense of theater about him . . . Leon was actually a good showman. And he was the one that [said], 'Hey, let's have the music a little faster on the main title.' On the end, he always [said], 'Let's end with one good gag and then iris fast, leave 'em laughing. And then hit 'em with the fast music.'"

The fast music they hit them with was generally the energetic work of Carl Stalling, Bugs' quiet, unassuming accompanist. Among Warner Bros. cartoon fans, Stalling's penchant for hitting us with the punchy swingtime tune "Powerhouse" whenever he's orchestrating an assembly line or a mechanical activity is as legendary as his use of "She Was an Acrobat's Daughter" to punctuate all balancing acts, "Freddie the Freshman" to jazz up any contest that resembles a game, and "California, Here I Come" whenever there's a train going *anywhere*. For Carl Stalling, all assembly lines were powerhouses, all balancing acts were done by acrobats' daughters, all games were played by freshmen named Freddie, and all trains were on their way to California.

"*Brilliant* musician," claims Chuck Jones. "He was a strange little man, but was probably the most innovative and inventive musician who ever worked in animation. The quickest way for him to write a musical score—and he did one six-minute cartoon a week—was simply to look up something that had the proper name. If somebody got in a cave, it was 'Fingal's Cave.' When a character was eating something, he'd play 'A Cup of Coffee, a Sandwich, and You,' even though it might not fit exactly. I had a bee one time, and my god if he didn't go back and find a piece of music written in 1906 or something called 'My Funny Little Bumblebee,' and *that* showed up in the picture. Sometimes it worked and sometimes it didn't—that 'Funny Little Bumblebee' thing was so obscure no one could make the connection. You had to be a hundred and eight years old even to know there was such a song."

Besides his own incidental themes, Stalling was particularly attracted to the catalogue of Raymond Scott, who wrote "Powerhouse," and whose catchy, energetic tunes tended to bear titles like "Reckless Night on Board an Ocean Liner," "In a Subway Far from Ireland," and "Dinner Music for a Pack of Hungry Cannibals." But he wasn't one to rely on a single composer; when he found out there were songs called "They Gotta Quit Kickin' My Dog Aroun'," "Go Get the Ax," "Goblins in the Steeple," "The Girl-Friend of the Whirling Dervish," "Huckleberry Duck," and "Honey Bunny Boo," he wasted no time in clearing the rights to use them.

Then Stallings' scores had to compete for the ear's attention with the highly distracting, percussive, gravity-defying sound effects of the staff's head film editor, whose name was Tregoweth Brown but who went by the short form, "Treg." Brown had been a musician, too, with Red Nichols and his Five Pennies, Benny Goodman, Glenn Miller, The Dorsey Brothers, Gene Krupa, and Jack Teagarden, and he'd also been a songwriter, iron ore miner, hobo, and chiropractor.

Brown repeated funny noises as often as Stalling repeated jazzy themes, and some of his gems became classics—especially "Trombone Gobble," the glottal stutter sounding like the gargling of a lead pipe that turns up in so many early '40s cartoons, but has been traced as far back as 1934. (Bugs uses it to race around the house, for instance, in *Bugs Bunny and the Three Bears*.) Brown was a good man on saw blades and brass sheets, though he could work wonders with just a stretched balloon or with any cheap toy whistle. He recorded new sounds for each cartoon and saved them all for future reference, filing them under descriptive titles like "Screwy Motor Noise" and "Angry Alarm Clock."

"Much . . . hilarity stemmed from Brown's outlandish imagination," Mel Blanc attested. "Why always apply the fitting sound effect, went his thinking, when something completely incongruous would be so much funnier? . . . So in addition to dialogue and sight gags, cartoons contained yet another comic element."

Though the animators and directors got good at making the characters look funny and move funny, a hallmark of the Warner Bros. cartoons is that the *soundtracks* were funny. And Mel Blanc is as responsible for that as anybody.

Mel had what Robert McKimson called a "leather larynx," and he could push it to extremes most people would be smart enough not to try. McKimson considered Blanc an expert at giving a director the voice he was looking for, usually on the first try, and, he remembered, "On some of them, he would really do a little more, he'd create something a little extra." According to McKimson, Blanc even re-recorded imitation voices of celebrities who had done their *own* voice for the cartoon, because Blanc's version was actually an improvement over the original.

Contrary to another cornerstone of Hollywood legend, Mel Blanc didn't do every voice heard in the Warner Bros. cartoons; others included Arthur Q. Bryan (the voice

Left: *Friz Freleng on Carl Stalling, pictured: "If you used a red pencil, he'd put down "The Lady in Red." If you used a blue pencil, he'd put "Am I Blue." Finally Chuck said, 'I'm not going to use a red pencil anymore."* Top: *Bugs Bunny (right) assisted his voice man Mel Blanc (left) in his rise to radio and animation stardom.* Above: *Film and sound-effects artist Treg Brown assembles a reel in this 1952 photo.*

39

of Elmer Fudd), Billy Bletcher, the great satirist Stan Freberg, females like Julie Bennett, Bernice Hansen, Sara Berner, Bea Benaderet, and June Foray, and directors and storymen like Tedd Pierce, Cal Howard, and Tex Avery. But for a while Bugs Bunny's was the only voice man to get screen credit at Warners, and at a time when the voice artists at other studios were not being publicly identified. This had less to do with altruism than it did with economics: when Blanc asked for a raise, it was cheaper to give him an exclusive credit.

But, "The cartoon writers were the backbone of this business," insisted Mike Maltese (one of the cartoon writers). "Dave Monahan, Tedd Pierce, Cal Howard, Rich Hogan, Tubby Millar, Jack Miller, and Bugs Hardaway—they're the crazy bunch. They're the ones with the wild humor."

"We had three of the best storymen in the business in Michael Maltese, Warren Foster, and Tedd Pierce", McKimson remarked, referring to the three men who eventually comprised the entire Bugs Bunny story crew. "They were all very good, *pixie* story writers, and it was interesting to watch the humor flow out of these guys."

Chuck Jones remembers that Tedd Pierce "looked like C. Aubrey Smith at twenty-two playing the role of the world's foremost authority on the dry martini." But when he was acting out a storyboard, says Bob Givens, "He was a clown!" Director Frank Tashlin agreed that Pierce "was clever, he was marvelous with those stories," and described him as "our Cary Grant . . . we were all a bunch of country boys, and Tedd . . . had a certain glamor to him: oh my God, he cut a big swath through the inking and painting department."

Together, this is the talented troupe that found ways to collaborate successfully enough to imbue Bugs Bunny with that strong sense of life. Chuck Jones remarks that when the Boston-based group Action for Children's Television consulted psychologists and child behaviorists on the impact of cartoon slapstick, they found out something surprising: "The children said they thought the characters were alive," said Jones, "but it never occurred to them that they were alive the way we were alive."

Well, obviously. Why would anyone who is alive the way Bugs Bunny is alive want to live the way we do?

Above: *Storyman Warren Foster in a 1952 photo.* Top: *The disowned progeny of a well-heeled Pasadena family, Tedd Pierce added the extra "d" to his first name when he realized puppeteer Bil Baird had dropped one of the "l's" from his.* Right: *Ken Harris searches for the spark of life to put in Bugs' expression in a 1952 photograph.*

The Masquerader

"It would have been impossible to grow up in the 1920s, seeing Chaplin and Keaton and Harold Lloyd and these great comedians on the screen, and not be influenced by them, because they were masters!"
—Chuck Jones

In *Baseball Bugs*, The Rabbit is on the pitcher's mound, when he pauses a minute, poised to spring into action—and darts us a quick coy look—then winds up and hurls the pitch. Bugs was always glancing in our direction, speaking to *us* as much as he spoke to the other characters on the screen, implicating us in every action, summing it all up for us at the end of the cartoon.

Tex Avery once remarked, "Bugs Bunny could have been anything, could have been a bird or whatnot. It's not the rabbit, it's the type of personality you put into him."

If Bugs Bunny is only incidentally a rabbit, and more fundamentally a larger-than-life screen personality who delighted children and adults both in a series of theatrical short subjects, who related to *us* as much as to the other characters on the screen, a comic hero who was in control of his physical environment, who enjoyed assuming new characterizations, "an inhabitant of the Garden who also has smarts," then it's clear that some of his roots stretch back to Charlie Chaplin's Little Tramp—and beyond into the history of the comedy short subject, into the days when they tended to be live action rather than animated, but the rest of the ground rules were still the same.

Certainly the most common explanation for a fan's devotion to the Heckling Hare is that "I grew up with him." Most of Bugs' current fans did, and certainly that's a big part of his perennial appeal: catch 'em in childhood with something they never outgrow, and you've got 'em for life. Then you've got *their* kids. The question is, who was it that Freleng, Jones, McKimson, Clampett, and all the others "grew up with"? The magic we saw as children in Bugs Bunny was a reflection of the magic that his creators knew at the hands of the silent comedians.

As Chuck Jones has commented, "There is a point at which life is breathed into a character, when it really begins to function, and that has to come about through a series, and that's why the series were so important to us. That was true of Chaplin, too. The golden age of comedy, believe me, is one of the animator's primary sources of inspiration. We rework it without even being aware of it—I suppose you could call it subliminal plagiarism."

Above: *Bugs as The Little Tramp in a Chuck Jones drawing for the 12th Telluride Film Festival, 1985.* Below: *It was Chaplin who discovered the importance of the eyes in projecting a personality on the screen.* Left: *A penetrating look from* The Adventurer, *1917.* Right: *Bugs shows he's taken lessons from the master in this cel.*

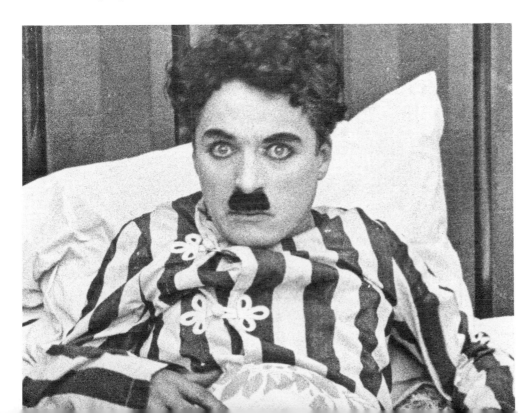

41

Before *The Birth of a Nation*, before the feature film had even taken root in America, it was Mack Sennett who established that there was a market for short comedies, that the business of exchanging guffaws for ready cash would pay off.

Sennett made a million dollars in his first year of business marketing chaos, violence, marital infidelity, and the kind of unspecified irreverence that has been grist for the comedians' mill since Aristophanes.

"I liked the Mack Sennett kind of things, I think everybody liked them," Freleng recalls. "They all ran around; they would have a bunch of people chasing an automobile that ran away, and ran over the people, and they ran into tunnels and the

Bugs appropriates a few pages from Chaplin's book. Above: *Chaplin in drag in* A Woman, *1915.* Right: *Bugs in drag in Chuck Jones'* Rabbit Seasoning, *1952.*

A great tradition is carried on: Minta Durfree on the receiving end of Mabel Normand's pastry in Mack Sennett's A Misplaced Foot, *1914; Bugs on the receiving end of Elmer's in Robert McKimson's* What's Up, Doc?, *1950.*

trains came out and they ran away from that, and they'd fall into water. They did pratfalls and threw pies and fell out of windows—it was just funny."

When Sennett signed up an English music-hall comic named Charlie Chaplin, he expected him to go through the same motions for the princely sum of $125 a week. But Chaplin felt that something, he wasn't quite sure what, was wrong.

"Little as I knew about movies," he said later, "I knew that nothing transcended personality."

Those last three words shook the screen.

Chaplin kept the irreverence, made The Little Tramp the focus for it, and established that making short comedies was not so much the business of exchanging guffaws for ready cash, it was the business of exchanging a Personality for serious capital.

Above: *The kiss as insult, used by Chaplin in* The Floorwalker, *1916, and by Bugs in a layout drawing from Frank Tashlin's* The Unruly Hare, *1945 (left).*

Charlie's popularity, particularly during the years of World War I, when his short comedies were first appearing regularly in theaters, was something stunning and without precedent—particularly stunning to Chaplin himself. Young Mike Maltese, on the Lower East Side of Manhattan, was painting a Chaplin moustache on his face with burnt cork and doing imitations on street corners—as were millions of other kids all over the country and the rest of the world. André Bazin put it simply in *What Is Cinema?*—"Never since the world began had a myth been so universally accepted."

By 1933, Charles Chaplin was the most famous person in the world, as well as one of the wealthiest and most influential. That was the year Mack Sennett closed his studio and filed for bankruptcy.

Charlie made it electrifyingly clear who it was he was communicating with. He was not communicating with a mass, undifferentiated audience. He was communicating with *you.* When Chaplin darted you a penetrating look, it penetrated.

Freleng, who was born in 1906, was among the millions of moviegoing kids regaled by the string of sixty short comedies Chaplin appeared in between 1914 and 1917, and he remembers what it meant to sit there in Kansas City, Missouri, and have The Little Tramp look at you from the screen: "I admired Chaplin very much because you could see him think, and plan, and you cared for him. In these other things, you never cared: they could get run over by a streetcar, and ten automobiles, and it wouldn't make

Ideas from the classic silent comedies were coin of the realm for the cartoon clowns. Above: One of Harold Lloyd's most famous gags, confusing a tackling dummy's leg with his own and thinking it's fractured beyond repair (The Freshman, 1925), is revised in Bob Clampett's Bugs Bunny Gets the Boid, 1942, where Bugs mistakes a skeleton on the desert for his own anatomy.

any difference. But with Chaplin, you cared if he was even *threatened* by one. I suppose he influenced a lot of people. That element that he injected into motion picture-making has been expanded."

It was Chaplin who originally forged the unlikely alloy of the Clown and the Hero, out of his pantomimic talent and the immediacy of the motion picture, who saw how both elements could be fused to create something altogether new, and whose magic haunted a generation of moviegoers—many of whom were children and some of whom would find themselves in the animation business.

And it was Chaplin also who established that it was by gestures and actions expressing attitude that a screen character existed. Jones recalls, "He'd jump up into the air and then come down and then start to run. The jump is solely a method of registering excitement and realization. He'd look like a human exclamation point, calling attention to his surprise—like saying, 'Ah! I'm surprised!'—and then he'd run. Since [the silent comedians] had no other means to express it, they'd do it with physical action, and it was beautiful to watch."

If Daffy Duck or Bugs Bunny "can convey more with the merest shrug or saunter or slink" than most actors, then Chaplin's hold on the younger generation of the 1910s and 1920s may have had something to do with it.

In fact, echoes of The Little Tramp reverberate through the mini-adventures of Bugs Bunny. The two barber chairs madly ascending to vertiginous heights in *Rabbit of Seville* are clearly out of *The Great Dictator*. The abrupt and shocking kiss Charlie plants square on the mouth of a face getting too close for comfort in *The Floorwalker* went on to become one of Bugs' favorite means of nonplusing his adversaries. When Bugs keeps track of his direct hits with a chalkboard next to his rifle barrel in *Horse Hare*, he's making an explicit reference to *Shoulder Arms*, a Chaplin film released by First National Exhibitors' Circuit, the distribution firm eventually absorbed into Warner Bros.—keeping it all more or less in the family.

The walking broomstick in *Bewitched Bunny* does Chaplin's trademark turn, with one foot in the air, at every corner; so does Bugs' little penguin friend in *Frigid Hare* and *8-Ball Bunny*. Comic transposition—or the visual pun—was a Chaplin *forte* and became one of Bugs' favorite devices; emptying an ashtray by stepping on Yosemite Sam's foot to flip up the top of his hat, so he can dump the ashes on his head, is just one example, from *Rabbit Every Monday*.

One of Chaplin's early films was called *The Masquerader*, a title that says as much as any words can about who this famous but elusive Personality was. The plot revolves around Charlie dressing up as a woman—one of Bugs' favorite tricks. But he's such a convincing woman that the effect is a little startling. In another way, The Little Tramp is like Bugs: when he's a woman, by George, he's a woman!

Chaplin's comedies were not called "classics" until the children who played hookey to see him grew up and became writers and critics. One of them, Walter Kerr, has speculated, "The secret of Chaplin, as a character, is that he can be anyone." Clearly, Charlie is the inspiration for any character who comes across as a union of opposites, or in Steve Schneider's phrase, "a character who contains within himself infinite adaptability, a character who is in essence a *complex* of characters . . . the character not as a foundation, but as a range of possibilities."

Chaplin himself seemed clear on one key point: It was the personality that effected this revolution, The Little Tramp, whom everyone loved, not the actor Charlie Chaplin, whom almost no one knew. The Tramp was really a composite personality, put together from bits and pieces of Charlie himself, the English music-hall comedian Fred Kitchen, and more traditional figures like Puck and Harlequin. Chaplin sometimes referred to his character as "a shabby Pierrot." The *commedia dell'arte* was not a distant memory in Chaplin's lifetime, but a tradition of great clowning that was seeing its last days in the music halls and pantomimes of nineteenth-century London. "I used to watch the clowns in the pantomimes breathlessly," Chaplin remembered later. "Every move they made registered on my young brain like a photograph. I used to try it all over when I got home." Great clowning, and the expression of a Personality through movement, was something Chaplin "grew up with."

In *Water, Water Every Hare,* Bugs piles one reference atop another. When he's unsuccessful in his attempts to sleep underwater, as Chaplin was in *Shoulder Arms,* he then walks to his water cooler and, still totally submerged, goes through the motions of pouring water into a cup and drinking from it, in a gag adapted from Buster Keaton's *The Navigator.*

For a while, First National was releasing the Chaplin and the Keaton comedies simultaneously, anticipating Warner Bros. later string of classic cartoons. When Baby Bugs stops Baby Elmer in mid-chase for a three-second nap in *The Old Grey Hare,* then rouses him again for more hot pursuit, it prompted Richard Corliss to remark, "Gag, movement, character, design, rhythm: it is all too much and, in Clampett's cartoons, exactly right." And it is, but it's inspired by a gag from Buster Keaton's First National short *Daydreams,* and he was perfecting a Sennett joke from *Be Reasonable.* Another of Buster's First National gems, *The Playhouse,* is the source of two classic Bugs bits: one, in *Baseball Bugs,* where the ballgame's announcer, enumerating one team's players, rattles off the name "Bugs Bunny" for every position in the field; and the other, the great effect Freleng gets when Bugs breaks into antique buck-and-wing dance numbers in *Stage Door Cartoon* and *Bugs Bunny Rides Again,* giving comically hyped enthusiasm to the kind of dance Keaton makes funny by going through the tired old motions deadpan.

Many things had followed in the wake of Chaplin's success, including the bustling one- and two-reel silent comedy business of the 1920s. Chaplin had started an entire movement, one that would keep audiences laughing throughout the decade. And the character who was "a complex of characters" discovered whole new dimensions— a series of screen personalities who were actually composite personalities, and who expressed themselves in physical movement.

The Buster Keaton on the screen was actually a composite of the real Keaton, directors like Eddie Cline, and more literary types like Jean Havez and Clyde Bruckman. The Harold Lloyd who wore horn-rimmed glasses (as the real-life Lloyd did not) was a composite of contributions from himself, producer Hal Roach, and writer-directors like Sam Taylor and Fred Newmeyer. The Harry Langdon on the screen was a composite personality put together by Frank Capra, Harry Edwards, Arthur Ripley, and Langdon himself. When Langdon decided he was funny enough to do without the other three, you never saw a career go downhill so fast.

"They were a joyous, funny, often drunken, usually wild and impetuous group," remembers Jones, who lived across the street from the Chaplin studio when he was six, "and all I wanted in the whole world when I grew up was to be one of them. This horrified my mother, who felt that the mayhem and violence of the Keystone Kops, Larry Semon, and even Chaplin . . . was hideous fare for my budding libido.

"She was right. When I did kind of grow up, my hideously budded libido found that the one-reel comedy was no longer around, but I managed to stumble into another company of comedians . . . all working in a field which was a logical extension not only of the motion picture itself, but of the old one- [and two-] reel live action comedy." Or an illogical extension. When the business of developing composite screen Personalities entered the dimension of the animated cartoon, the Personality became separated from the individual performer. The Masquerader moved into the field of animation through a complex series of moves that had begun as soon as Chaplin became an international sensation in the 1910s.

A series of Charlie Chaplin animated cartoons was made in New York at the Pat Sullivan studio—later the home of Felix the Cat. According to Sullivan's head animator, Otto Messmer, "We copied every little movement that he did. Later on, that rubbed off, and we used a lot of that kind of action in Felix. We found out that a funny walk sometimes would get a laugh without a script idea. Or the wiggling of the tail, and things of that type. Chaplin had a great influence on us."

Top and above: *"The face had to stay still, so it had to be body,"* Chuck Jones remembers about Buster Keaton. Keaton expresses dismay and disarray, despair and existential disrepair, all without using his face, in this scene with Joe Roberts in Neighbors, *1920. Bugs expresses insolence and nonchalance strictly in body language in this publicity drawing for Friz Freleng's* Sahara Hare, *1955. Below: Bugs and his penguin friend adopt a variation of Chaplin's trademark walk in publicity for Chuck Jones'* Frigid Hare, *1949.*

Because of the technical complexity of the animation process, it's easy for animators, audiences, and critics to jump to the conclusion that once you've solved the technical problems, you're ready to make a cartoon. Walt Disney was solving more and more technical problems as the 1920s went on, and the more he solved, the more he saw that wasn't the real issue.

The issue was, as Friz Freleng puts it, "You must care for any character on the screen. You must love him, or you must hate him, if he's a villain; but you must care, one way or the other, you have to feel *something* for him. To put that on the screen takes talent."

Felix was appealing, but before Mickey Mouse came along, people had no conception that it was *possible* to get so much personality into an animated character. As a lot of Chaplin had rubbed off on Felix, a lot of Chaplin and Felix rubbed off on Mickey.

"Walt was . . . really influenced by Chaplin," explained Dick Huemer, one of Disney's key storymen. "He just couldn't get him out of his system. He thought of Mickey Mouse actually as a little Chaplin. . . . Walt kept the feeling of this droll, kind of pathetic little character, who was always being picked on. But cleverly coming out on top anyway."

Disney succeeded in doing with Mickey exactly what Chaplin had succeeded in doing with The Little Tramp: focusing the audience's attention on an alter ego. As Mickey went on, the improvements in his basic design and personality made by people like Norm Ferguson and Fred Moore became permanent aspects of his character, and another composite personality was developed.

Walt used Mickey's popularity, and the cash flow it generated, to refine the techniques of animation, and suddenly cartoons were experiencing the same kind of excitement and progress that had energized short comedies around 1920.

A prototype of Bugs Bunny, Max Hare, was designed by Charles Thorson for *The Tortoise and the Hare* in 1934—essentially your basic rabbit, drawn in a way that was simple yet expressive. Like Mickey, it wasn't so much his personality that amused the audience, as the fact that he *had* a personality, and it dominated the picture.

Jones remembers that "Because of Disney, people sat up and took notice of the cartoon . . . he prepared, fought and bled for a ground where the artist could flourish and where a new art form could grow—not only at his studio, but throughout the world."

As the personalities of his characters grew more real to audiences, Disney and his artists began to feel that "believability" was more important than comedy—that it even transcended personality. A vital ingredient of what had always fascinated people about animation—the magical lack of limits, the surreal lengths to which the imagination could be stretched—was beginning to atrophy, not only at Disney's, but in animation studios all over the country. Except one.

By 1938, it was well established what the rules were in animation—what you could do and what you couldn't do. The Warner Bros. cartoonists knew the rules, they could recite them upon command, and they recognized them when they saw them on the screen in Disney cartoons and in the cartoons of his imitators. They knew it made good business sense to obey the rules. Then they broke them.

Chaplin's breakthroughs reached animation through sympathetic resourceful personalities like Felix the Cat (above) and Mickey Mouse. Right: *A recent Warner Bros. publicity drawing recreates Bugs at the time of his creation.*

The Briar Patch

Bugs Bunny was no hothouse plant. The roots of his personality stretch beyond Termite Terrace, and into much thornier soil.

Chuck Jones reminds us that his cartoons "were to go out with the Warner Brothers pictures in theaters—gentle pictures like *Little Caesar*, *I Was a Fugitive from a Chain Gang*, *Dr. Ehrlich's Magic Bullet*."

Ethan Mordden described the "gentle pictures" in *The Hollywood Studios*: "At Warners . . . the science was storytelling . . . and keep it clear and quick. I don't want it good, I want it *active*: short scenes, shorter ones, montage narration, wipes and fast cutting instead of the temperate fade, sets changed so fast that no one has a chance to see how dull they are, lit as if by bare bulb. Let Metro have its production values, Paramount its elegance. Warner Brothers is fast and plain and that is hot stuff."

The studio ambience fit the style: When Michael Curtiz didn't like Errol Flynn's reaction to the prop rocks thrown at him in *Captain Blood*, he threw real rocks himself. William Wellman was likely to sock a labor union representative in the face if he didn't get out of a shot right away, or fire a revolver at an assistant director who wasn't working fast enough.

But Bob Clampett felt, "The place was full of energy and enthusiasm. Cagney, Bogart, and other top Warner stars used to stick their heads in our windows to see how cartoons were made. We patterned a lot of things on them."

Back in the late '20s, Warner Bros. had just completed a decade of expansion. It had gotten the jump on the other studios where sound was concerned, and was

Below left: *James Cagney, Humphrey Bogart, and George Raft in a cel from* Hollywood Steps Out, *1941. The tough guy was endemic to the Warner Bros. style, making it difficult for a baby-faced innocent in a Mickey Mouse mold to gain a foothold in its cartoons. Below: Edward G. Robinson is the kind of co-star Bugs Bunny was apt to find himself up against at the Warner Bros. studio, as in Friz Freleng's* Racketeer Rabbit, *1946. Animation drawing by Virgil Ross.*

The evolution of the Warner Bros. cartoon stars. Nowhere to go but up: Bosko, above; Buddy, below.

flooding a hungry market with talkies, then using its cash to buy up theaters and all the stock in First National. Then Disney took the country by storm with Mickey Mouse. "Warners got interested in doing cartoons," Friz Freleng recalls. "Naturally, everybody was interested in it at that time, because Walt took off like skyrockets."

Leon Schlesinger made the connection between Warner Bros. and a pair of ex-Disney renegades named Hugh Harman and Rudolf Ising (who brought along their friend Friz Freleng), and agreed to act as middleman in guaranteeing that the cartoons would be delivered. Warner Bros. had been a small studio long enough, now it was pushing to be one of the big boys, and one way to do that was to release its own talkie cartoons, promoting its own music, to entertain its own customers in its own theaters.

Then the Depression took the country by storm, and Warner Bros. had to compete with the higher-budgeted films of the bigger studios. They hit on a star style that favored guns over glamor, tough guys over pretty boys, and tough girls over goddesses.

James Cagney, George Raft, Edward G. Robinson, and Humphrey Bogart were *not* going to act like the dewy-eyed heroes of the silent screen. And Bette Davis was *not* going to act like Janet Gaynor.

Looney Tunes and Merrie Melodies were created in the early '30s, and as Freleng remembers, "We were exploiting music . . . everything was music, rather than characters. We were using the novelty of animation with sound, and that's what was charming the audience. It could have been a bouncing ball, it could have been anything, it wouldn't have made any difference.

"We had to run every picture for Jack Warner, and he liked them all. I guess that's why we were as successful as we were. He'd never say a cartoon was bad. He'd look at it and he'd say, 'Yeah, that's a good cartoon'—*or* he would say, 'That's not as good as the one before.'"

But there were three Warner Bros. cartoons he *didn't* like. The development of the Warner Bros. gallery of animated comedians began with a simple action.

The only continuing character Warner Bros. Cartoons had under Harman & Ising was an unspecified creature in the Felix mold named Bosko. It was like having no character at all. After an argument over money, Harman and Ising left, took Freleng with them, and for reasons unknown took Bosko too.

Leon Schlesinger set up his own studio on the Warner Bros. lot and limped along with a character named Buddy. That was *worse* than having no character at all.

"A complete *lack* of character," Freleng calls him. Not the creation of a studio on a star search.

Fellow named Earl Duvall directed Schlesinger's first Buddy cartoons for Warner Bros., and Warner Brothers sent them back. That's when Schlesinger sent for Freleng.

"Friz, you gotta help me," he pleaded. "I've got 30,000 dollars, everything I've made in my lifetime, tied up in this." Schlesinger wasn't exactly sure what had gone wrong.

"I don't think Leon even knew what a director did," Friz says. When Freleng reworked enough animation from the three rejected cartoons to put together two that Warner Bros. accepted, this action was not forgotten.

Freleng was now senior director at Schlesinger's new shop, and his inclinations would become unofficial studio policy: "What was lacking [in Harman and Ising's later cartoons] was exactly the same thing that a lot of the cartoon studios seem to think less of, a personality," he says unequivocally. "They just thought of beautiful drawings, with a one-shot story, and then that was forgotten, and then there'd be another. But people had to hang onto a personality."

Freleng protested the dominance of Warner Brothers' music: "We said, 'Hell, you can't just keep doing this! We don't have any characters!' Then Warners said, 'OK, do what you want,' and they left us alone."

The first of the familiar Warners Bros. cartoon stars to be developed was Mr.

Porcine "Porky" Pig, postulated on Roscoe Ates, a stuttering comedian famous at the time. Porky came out of Freleng's *I Haven't Got a Hat,* but he presented serious limitations: faced with a formidable opponent like a bull or a sea serpent, there's not much he can do but get scared and run away. Adults would go out in the lobby for a smoke.

When Schlesinger signed up Tex Avery, he saw he had someone unique on his hands and told him, "I'll try you on one picture. I've got some boys here—they're not renegades, but they don't get along with the other two crews." And he palmed off on this wild man from Universal some of the most talented but least organized artists in his facility—Bob Cannon, Chuck Jones, and Bob Clampett —and put them in the *literal* Termite Terrace. The resulting chemistry of personalities started to fizz right away.

As Avery described it, "They wanted to get a 'new group' going, and 'We could do it,' and 'We gonna make these funny pictures.' We encouraged each other, and we really had a good ball rolling. Schlesinger was smart. He didn't disturb us, and he knew nothing of what went on over there. We worked every night."

"The climate was correct," according to Jones. "At the other [building], Ray Katz, the office manager, and Leon Schlesinger, and some of the other front office people were constantly parading the halls. But Termite Terrace was a good 200-300 yards away, and when anybody came, you could see them, so everybody would pretend to be working. And they never understood that we were enjoying ourselves, which was against the law!

"The enthusiasm was real. When you felt like it, you worked overtime, whether you had to or not. If you got a piece of work you really enjoyed, you would spend the extra time on it cheerfully—it never occurred to you not to."

Clampett, too, remembered it well: "That's when we first started, little by little, trying out the more offbeat gags . . . easing them in, sneaking them in, until we were sure of it . . . A lot of the things we would think of and laugh at, but then not use in the films right away, because it was risky."

Out of many things—the lunatic surrealism of the old pre-Disney cartoons (carried into the sound era by the Fleischer brothers), what Clampett called the "sane insanity" of the Marx Brothers, the grace and wit of the current Screwball Comedies—a new approach began to develop in the cartoons of the Tex Avery unit that would eventually be called the Warner Bros. cartoon style.

Avery and his crew developed a rash style of comedy that startled audiences into guffaws: a style in which quacking geese were known to break into sterling tenors, cuckoos from clocks found it in them to proclaim, "Time marches on!" and any character described as "a snake" would eventually find himself slithering. You could cast asides to the audience, heap scorn on the names in the credits, or even, as actually happens in *Daffy Duck and Egghead,* shoot a warm body from the audience in cold blood.

Disney would have been afraid this hurt believability. But with animated characters this *heightened* their reality. Avery's characters were not barnyard mammals and geese out of a '30s cartoon, but fast-talking, wise-cracking sharpies out of a '30s comedy. He began to move the Hollywood cartoon away from what he called "fuzzy bunnies."

This first became apparent in the Looney Tune *Porky's Duck Hunt.* A hunter himself, Avery thought it would be funny if one of Nature's Own turned the tables on his oppressor, and did they love it! He created a screwball duck who *didn't* get scared and run away when somebody pointed a gun at him, but leapt and hopped all over the place like a maniac. Now the studio had not only a concept but also a character: henceforth, its Looney Tunes would be looney and its duck would be Daffy.

"When it hit the theaters," Clampett remembered, "it was like an explosion."

In May of 1936, Schlesinger instituted the unit system at his studio, solidifying his staff, now 125 people, into three units, each under a director. Then Clampett and Jones became directors and acquired units. Each unit developed a style of its own, set by its director.

Above*: Porky Pig, in a characteristically flustered pose, in publicity for Frank Tashlin's* Porky's Double Trouble, *1937.* Below*: Daffy Duck, in a Bob Clampett animation drawing from Tex Avery's* Porky's Duck Hunt, *1937.*

"At Disney's, the directors didn't make the pictures, Disney did," Clampett explained. "But under Leon's system, we directors were the 'Disneys.' Once Leon found the directors he had confidence in, he began going to the races more often."

"Tex started making better cartoons, and we all started imitating each other," says Freleng. "We finally found a path."

In early 1940, the show-business weekly *Showmen's Trade Review* said the Merrie Melodies were "Featuring 'gags' that send patrons into roars of laughter." David Golding wrote in *Boxoffice Barometer*, "Challenging the Disney dynasty are the animators under Schlesinger's guidance."

Still done on a shoestring—like on the main lot, style was cheaper than technique.

"We couldn't afford expensive animation like the Disney Studio," said Maltese. "We had to rely on story."

Avery went on trying to figure out what the audience would *least* expect. So a baby chick called plaintively for its mother—in a shout that strained the capacity of the sound system; an innocent "little deer" popped up into a Mae West impression; a frog was shown in closeup "croaking"—shooting himself point-blank in the head.

It wasn't a far cry from this to a little grey rabbit who stared into the barrel of a gun—and chewed on a carrot and said, "What's up, Doc?" out of the side of his mouth in a Brooklyn accent.

This called for a different kind of rabbit than you find in Texas. That kind isn't likely to chew carrots in the wild—unless they have opposable thumbs like Bugs Bunny.

There may have been other rabbits cooking in the Avery think tank: rabbits who have opposable thumbs and are capable of anything, who could fit this zany new cartoon style, have been around for generations. Bugs' origins probably have less to do with real rabbits than with a hare named Zomo. Like jazz and rock and roll, Bugs has at least some of his roots in black culture.

Zomo is the trickster rabbit out of Central and Eastern Africa, who gained audience sympathy by being smaller than his oppressors and turning the tables on them through cleverness, thousands of years before Eastman invented film. A con artist, a masquerader, ruthless and suave, in control of the situation. Ready to put anything over on his bigger, usually dumber, antagonists. Specialized in impersonating women.

Zomo bet he could steal milk from a cow, then flattered the cow, told her she was strong enough to split a tree. The cow charged the tree, crashed into it, embedded her horns in the trunk. Zomo got his milk.

Africans, brought to America as slaves, carried these trickster tales to the Old South. Zomo merged with another Heckling Hare, Nanabozho of the Native Americans, became Br'er Rabbit. Now when the cow was stuck in the tree, Br'er Rabbit brought his wife and kids to get milk.

Stuck in *Br'er Fox's Tar Baby*, Br'er Rabbit told the fox he could "bobbycue," hang, drown, or skin him, but "fer de Lord's sake, don't fling me in dat briar-patch." So Br'er Fox flung him in the briar patch, and Br'er Rabbit chattered back merrily, "Bred en bawn in a briar-patch, Br'er Fox—bred en bawn in a briar-patch!"

Growing up on a Georgia plantation in the 1850s, Joel Chandler Harris heard these tales from slaves. As an adult he set them down on paper, putting them in the mouth of "Uncle Remus." The Br'er Rabbit stories ran in the *Atlanta Constitution*, then came out in book form in the very popular *Uncle Remus, His Songs and Sayings* in 1880, and *Nights with Uncle Remus* in 1883. Harris said intelligence won out over brute force. Explicitly. The moral of the story.

Disney put Br'er Rabbit on the screen in *Song of the South* in 1946. By then it was Bugs Bunny who was "Bred and bawn in a briar patch!"

The Heckling Hare. Couple thousand years old. Slouching toward Termite Terrace. To be bred and bawn.

Above: Bugs and his mannerisms were anticipated by Zomo the trickster and his descendent, Joel Chandler Harris' Br'er Rabbit (pictured) long before cartoons were ever animated. Below: Bugs' insouciance in chewing on a carrot in a moment of stress may have originated in this scene from Frank Capra's It Happened One Night, *1934.*

Wabbits, Wabbits, Wabbits!

The word "bugs" came to mean crazy sometime in the early 1920s and was almost immediately applied to Ben Siegel, a mobster whose murderous rages earned him the name "Bugsy," though only when he wasn't around to hear it. Then Chicago's killer George Moran was tagged "Bugs" for the same reason. So if you were "bugs," it was expected that you were pretty tough, as well as pretty wild.

Both meanings fit Ben Hardaway, top sergeant to the Battery D, Second Battalion, 129th Field Artillery in World War I. Known as the Dizzy D, this was a pretty bugs group of fighting Irish and German Catholics, all hailing from the same tough neighborhood in Kansas City, Missouri, and tales of the havoc they wreaked struck panic into the hearts of veteran and recruit alike. There is little record of any of this violent activity being directed against the enemy, but they did run through four commanders very quickly, getting one dishonorably discharged for failing to control them and sending another to the psychiatric ward.

"Bugs was very clever in figuring out gags," remembers Lowell Elliott, who worked with Hardaway at the Walter Lantz Studio, "but he needed some sort of framework to hang them on."

Porky's Duck Hunt gave him that framework. Hardaway dreamed up the idea of putting Daffy's frenzy and virtually his voice in the body of a rabbit, and the picture came out in 1938 under the patently derivative title of *Porky's Hare Hunt*.

"That's just Daffy Duck in a rabbit suit," says Freleng about this cartoon. "Bugs Hardaway worked on formula. That's all he knew."

But it's one of those formulas that works: the idea of putting a rabbit, rather than a duck, at the business end of a hunt situation is a great cartoon concept, one with thousands of years of tradition behind it and built-in appeal. And Hardaway introduced in this picture the idea of The Rabbit faking a sympathy-ploy death scene, and proclaiming, "Of course you realize this means war" (Groucho Marx's line from *A Night at the Opera*—and in a voice that is spookily close to Groucho's). While Daffy could hop on water and get Porky's gun to work, this screwy rabbit can work more miracles than that: he pulls himself out of a hat, uses his ears for propellers to become a premature helicopter, and makes the dog chasing him disappear.

The only problem with this cartoon is that it's a donut—its hole is right in the center. The rabbit's personality is a hodge-podge of characteristics with no character. He is white at this point, closer to Goofy than to Daffy, with two prominently ungainly buck teeth and a Mortimer Snerd voice. He spends more time working up fury than he does engaging our sympathies. Hunted by Porky Pig, he asks him if he's got a hunting license; presented with the document, he tears it in half and proclaims, "Well, you haven't got one now!" He sails from tree to tree like a bird. He is at no time under the influence of rational thought. He is a Loony Tune, but he isn't Bugs Bunny. Carl Stallings plays "Hooray for Hollywood" as The Rabbit goes on his rampage, as if the studio was expecting great things of this character. But they already have Daffy and he's a genuine lunatic; this guy's an imitation. He doesn't even have Buddy's one saving grace: the quality of being forgettable.

Nevertheless Norman H. Moray, in charge of production and sales of short subjects for Warner Bros., sent word from New York that people were asking theater owners when the next rabbit cartoon was coming. There were no plans to do another one, and *that* rabbit had pretty well worn out his welcome in one picture. So there was something of a search for a new rabbit.

A character *looking* just like the rabbit in *Porky's Hare Hunt* appears in Chuck Jones' *Prest-o Change-o* about a year later, but he's quieted down and become as obsessed with magic as a lost Teller looking for his Penn. So vases appear in the air and drop on the heads of two curious puppies who haven't done anything to him; a door turns into a chest of drawers with the rabbit emerging from drawers at random to bean dogs. The image of a Heckling Hare as a Harpo-like magician who can pro-

Above: *Joseph Benjamin "Bugs" Hardaway in a 1940s photo.* Below: *The pesky rabbit in Hardaway's* Porky's Hare Hunt, *1938, pulls himself out of a hat, then establishes that he's not cowed by superior firepower.*

Rabbits who weren't Bugs Bunny were quite a fixture in Warner Bros. cartoons of the late '30s. Below: The clever rabbit in Frank Tashlin's Porky's Building, *1937, in a model sheet drawing, can lay bricks with his ears. Top right: The looney tunes rabbit of Bugs Hardaway's* Hare-um Scare-um, *1939, is shown in a cel. Above, right, and opposite: The same rabbit then appeared, in a more sedate mood, in Chuck Jones'* Elmer's Candid Camera, *1940—seen here in a frame from the film (above) and in two production cels (right and opposite) autographed by Leon Schlesinger.*

duce props effortlessly whenever he *needs* them would have to wait.

When Bugs Hardaway decided to make *Porky's Hare Hunt* all over again with a different hunter and a rabbit, he went to Max Hare's designer, Charlie Thorson, now working at Schlesinger's, and asked him to design him a new model sheet. It came back, labeled "Bugs' Bunny," and the rabbit, now one year old, was turned prematurely grey. Then Hardaway went to work on the cartoon he called *Hare-um Scare-um*, giving his rabbit the same voice and the same kinds of gags as before. Obviously, he was missing the point.

"Bugs' Bunny" is no less a dervish than his predecessor, but he is now a magician the way Bugs Bunny would be: he produces a ketchup bottle from nowhere and splashes its contents everywhere; he reaches into a "pocket" in his fur that was never visible before, and pulls out a "hot shot buzzer" when his whim dictates. *Showmen's Trade Review* called the cartoon "Excellent" and remarked upon the "Many unique gags." And, for audiences of 1939, he seems to have been doing what he was supposed to do.

But he eats celery instead of carrots. In terms of the core *personality*, he is no ancestor to Bugs Bunny. "Hardaway's Bugs would stand in a crouched, ready-to-leap fashion, as somebody who's afraid and prepared to get the hell out of there," Jones points out. "The Bugs that evolved stood upright, a guy who's not going to go anyplace— sure of himself."

Then came 1940 and, first, *Elmer's Candid Camera.* Chuck Jones put this second rabbit at the other end of a camera rather than a gun. And he slowed the rabbit down to the point where his actions could be registered by the human eye. For the first time, this rabbit has his feet on the ground.

This string of four rabbit cartoons preceding Tex Avery's *A Wild Hare* has often been described as if it were the "evolution" of Bugs Bunny. The Warner Bros. cartoonists find this pretty funny.

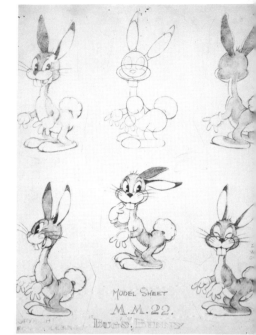

Above: *Model sheet by Charles Thorson from Bugs Hardaway's* Hare-um Scare-um. *That apostrophe in his first name is not on every copy of this famous model sheet.*

"Bugs Hardaway . . . had no part in it," Robert McKimson felt. "He had a completely different character."

"I don't think there was any relationship between those characters, really," Friz Freleng insists. "I don't think Tex was affected by that at all."

Bob Givens, who designed Bugs Bunny and Elmer Fudd for *A Wild Hare,* has no doubt about it: "Bugs isn't Hardaway's bunny. Tex said, 'I'm going to have a rabbit and a hunter,' so I did Bugs and Elmer. Tex gave it the personality and Mel gave it the voice, and that was it." The rabbit Givens came up with is a tall, angular animal, not the round, squat bunny Hardaway had been using.

As usual, Tex paid careful attention to the other cartoons, then went ahead and did what he felt like doing. And he pulled a new rabbit out of a hat.

Once again, the Warner Bros. cartoonists reached back to *Porky's Duck Hunt,* the film that started it all. Instead of Porky's stutter, Elmer Fudd says he is "hunting wabbits" in a childish wisp. And instead of a screwball duck who isn't scared when he sees a gun, it's a wayout rabbit. But now the whole thing has a different spin.

Images from A Wild Hare: *Layout drawing, frames from the completed film, and the original title card (rarely seen today, since the film's Blue Ribbon reissue got a new title affixed to the negative—and got the film inadvertently retitled* The Wild Hare *in the process).*

In *A Wild Hare,* Bugs Bunny isn't frenzied, he's collected. He's not burning himself out in a single cartoon, he's implying there's more fun to come. He's funny not because he's demented, but because he's got it all under control. He's not appealing for sympathy, he's telling *us* what's what, point blank, to our face. He isn't a fuzzy bunny, he's a Heckling Hare, bred and bawn in the briar patch. The wiseguy Warner Bros. version of the character who was many characters. What we least expected and what we most hoped to see.

As in *Porky's Hare Hunt,* he chomps on a carrot, but he does it in the open, when his predator is looking, in open defiance of the death threat he poses.

Avery took a tremendous risk in trying to stage a death scene in a comedy cartoon without cuing us in right away that it's all a sham, but it works, and it points up who this character *is.* We watch in disbelief as he pretends to be dying, and somehow the idea is an oxymoron, it makes no real sense. This guy is life itself; it's a contradiction in terms for him to have a death scene.

"We decided he was going to be a smart-aleck rabbit, but casual about it," Avery recalled, in some of his rare, guarded words on the subject, "and [his] opening line in the very first one was 'Eh, what's up, Doc?' And, gee, it floored 'em! They expected the rabbit to scream, or anything but make a casual remark—here's a guy with a gun in his face! It got such a laugh that we said, 'Boy, we'll do that every chance we get.' It became a series of 'What's up, Docs?' That set his entire character. He was always in command, in the face of all types of dangers."

This expression may have been a combination of Avery's high school memories and the famous line "What's up, Duke?" from *My Man Godfrey,* as Clampett has suggested. The line clicks, but the gag was a bunny rabbit peeking out of his rabbit hole and coming out with any kind of hip expression at all, a Bowery Boy plopped down in the middle of a Silly Symphony.

Elmer's answer to that opening question is "There's a wabbit down there," and right away Bugs has figured out that Fudd is not only dumber than he is, he's much less secure. He seems to *know* when he covers Fudd's eyes and says, "Guess who!" that Elmer's going to recite the names of various women he hopes have caught up with him—and not just women, but glamorous women celebrities: "Wosemawy Wane? Owivia de Haviwand?" (Carole Lombard was one of the contestants in the 1940 original, but

after her death in an aviation accident in 1942, she was replaced in the Blue Ribbon reissue by Barbara Stanwyck.)

For all his manic invention, Hardaway's Bunny was one of those demented "rube" characters who might appear in any studio's cartoon after *Porky's Duck Hunt*—Goofy with his ears up. What Avery came out with was a *sophisticated* version of the woodland creature who wasn't afraid of the hunter, a Daffy Duck who was a sharpie. This simple but all-encompassing difference would last decades: where Daffy heckles Porky like a creative but irritating mosquito in the left ear, Bugs hones in for the jugular.

"When we saw that on the screen, we knew we had a hit character," Freleng remembers. "He was the most timid of animals, yet he had courage and brashness. The whole gimmick was a rabbit so cocky that he wasn't afraid of a guy with a gun who was hunting him. We recognized right away that this was a better personality than the other would be, because you couldn't like the other character."

"Disney understood that kids warm up to rounded forms," remarks Steve Schneider. "Think of the structure of Bugs: He is long and lean and pointy and phallic, long ears, with razor-sharp teeth that bite. This was a character that was not based on circles, but on blade shapes, projectiles. Even his eyes are sharp, rather than round."

"We didn't feel that we had anything until we got it on the screen and it got quite a few laughs," Avery recalled. "After we ran it and previewed it and so forth, Warners liked it, the exhibitors liked it, and so of course Leon Schlesinger ran down and said, 'Boy, give us as many of those as you can!' Which we did."

And for twenty-five years thereafter, the boys from Termite Terrace would come back to *A Wild Hare* and wonder, "What is it we did right?"

3

THIS IS YOUR LIFE, BUGS BUNNY

Above: *Animation drawing from Chuck Jones'* Super Rabbit, *1943.*

Super Rabbit, 1940-1944

Out of many characters, The Rabbit had arrived.

The years of World War II proved to be the years of Bugs Bunny's adolescence: It was during this period that Bugs was *stretched*, as a cartoon and as a character, to reach the flexibility that would be one of his hallmarks.

A Wild Hare has the basic comic concept intact, but it looks tame today, because the Warner Bros. cartoonists had to keep *topping* it. You thought *A Wild Hare* was funny? Wait'll you see *The Heckling Hare*. You thought *The Heckling Hare* was funny? Wait'll you see *Fresh Hare*.

When Joseph Priore assessed the short subjects field for the trade magazine *Boxoffice Barometer* at the end of 1942, he concluded, "There was evidence in every company's lineup of cartoons [of] a fresh brand of humor and comic treatment. The Disney stuff this year was not up to its previous high standard. This is a war year. People want entertainment . . . The cartoon subjects from the Schlesinger studios, in the opinion of this reviewer, had more on the comedy ball."

That sentiment was shared, sometimes by people at Disney.

"Those were wonderful days," remembered Bob McKimson. "The pictures were coming out funny, and everybody was thinking funny. Most of the guys weren't making much money, but they were having an awful lot of fun."

Warner Bros.' whole style picked up: Only recently has Friz Freleng come to realize, "An unbelievable change took place in only three or four years. The films we made in 1938 are as different from the ones we made in 1942 as night and day." More than these few years seem to separate Avery's *Porky's Duck Hunt* from Jones' *My Favorite Duck*, Avery's *Little Red Walking Hood* from Freleng's *Little Red Riding Rabbit*. Forties cartoons were a new entity, a genre all to themselves, easily distinguishable from the '30s cartoons of Disney, Warner Bros., or anybody else. A new style was developing: most of it was Avery's doing, most of it was taking place right there at Warner Bros., and most of it was focused on The Rabbit.

But the new character had no name at first. Neither he nor Elmer had been tagged specifically in *A Wild Hare*, and now that Jack Warner himself was getting letters about The Rabbit's popularity, a search began for an appropriate name.

Jack Rabbit, or Jack E. Rabbit, was the personal choice of Tex Avery himself, since he had spent so much time hunting jackrabbits and, as he put it, "I thought it would please my Texas friends."

Finally "Bugs' Bunny" came back from the old *Hare-um Scare-um* model sheet as a result of the name search, and Rose Horsely, Schlesinger's publicist, right away decided it was "so cute!" But this particular hare was the creation of Tex Avery, whose major aim in professional life was to steer clear of "fuzzy bunnies," and he was horrified by the suggestion. "That's sissy," he said. "Mine's a *rabbit*! A tall, lanky, mean rabbit. He isn't a fuzzy little bunny."

To Avery, "Bugs Bunny" sounded like a Disney character. But that was the idea. Alliteration, in a pattern set by Mickey Mouse (and possibly Charlie Chaplin), followed up by Donald Duck, Betty Boop, and even Daffy Duck and Porky Pig, was the established style. Horsely had Leon Schlesinger's ear, and, in the words of Avery's later cartoon *Uncle Tom's Cabaña*, "That wasn't all she had, neither." Schlesinger thought a moment, then said, "OK. Bugs Bunny. We'll go with it."

The Heckling Hare was bred and bawn and christened. The name originally cooked up for people like "Bugsy" Siegel and "Bugs" Moran now belonged to the most popular cartoon character in America. It first appeared on screen in the titles for *Elmer's Pet Rabbit*.

For today's audiences, Bugs is more than a little unrecognizable in some of these cartoons from the early '40s. The development that was taking place is graphically presented in Bob Clampett's 1944 cartoon *What's Cookin', Doc?*: Bugs in the framing sequence, campaigning for an Oscar, fully fleshed out, brash, big as life, dynamic and

In Friz Freleng's Fresh Hare, 1942, Bugs takes great glee in leaping in the air as a preliminary stage to burrowing deep underground.

irresistible; then he puts one of his "better scenes" on the screen, and there he is in *Hiawatha's Rabbit Hunt* in 1941, rat-faced, tentative, even his voice a pale shadow of its familiar self, the star of *A Wild Hare* not sure what to do next. His growth from one figure to the next happened through a steady accumulation of elements: the voice and the look that best expressed that personality; the name and the gag style that best fit it.

What the Termite Terrace gang had in 1940 was your basic Warner Bros. wise-guy rabbit—cool like Bogart, snide like Edward G. Robinson, feisty like James Cagney. And at first, the Warner directors seemed determined to make Bugs a smart-aleck at every turn and at any cost. He talked sassy, he stuck out his tongue, he razzed the audience, and he did whatever we didn't expect. Once he'd gotten that out of his system, he could relax and become a little bit more of an audience-pleaser.

This development went on film after film, season after season, and director after director. Right away, Chuck Jones and Friz Freleng were directing cartoons featuring the studio's new discovery, and a year later Clampett joined in the fray. As each director added new levels to this character, it was picked up by the others and became a part of the mix. Bugs was picking up new attributes like a Christmas tree collects trimmings, and in this way he became an emblem of the collective personality that was Termite Terrace. It was in these five years that Bugs became like The Little Tramp, like Harry Langdon, like Mickey Mouse, an integrated, composite personality.

Robert McKimson, who was then animating in Bob Clampett's unit, later confessed that "Bugs Bunny, after five or six pictures, was thought to be exhausted. But we came up with new ideas so that he lasted . . . Over the years you run into so many different twists to these things, that you forget that they were very funny at one time. But after a while even the funniest things get to be jaded."

The new ideas came out of what Mel Blanc called "collective inspiration. The visual rendering of a character enabled me to settle on an appropriate voice, which in turn helped the animators to refine physical characteristics. Together, writers, artists, and voice-men imbued a mere sketched animal with a distinct personality." Gradually the flat, street-kid voice got Jerry Colonna-ized into something bright and sparkling, a pleasure in its own right. (The resemblance to film and radio comedian Jerry Colonna is especially pronounced in Bugs' guest appearance in *Porky Pig's Feat*; he's practically doing an imitation.) Bugs picks up the habit of saying, "Soitn'y!" like the Three Stooges' Curly. He picks up, in fact, a little bit of everything—radio, vaudeville, Chaplin, both Disney and Fleischer—but puts it all together in a concoction that felt new.

"I think every comedian had some impact," admits Friz Freleng. "And we probably thought we made it up ourselves! I think people were affected by the war, without really knowing it, because everybody was out to produce, produce, produce. Things got more exciting, the pace picked up, the tempo of everything picked up."

Below : *Animation drawing from Bob Clampett's* Wacky Wabbit, *1942.*

Left to right: *Animation drawing from Chuck Jones'* Hold the Lion, Please, *1942; Animation drawing from Friz Freleng's* The Hare-Brained Hypnotist, *1942; drawings from Freleng's* Jack-Wabbit and the Beanstalk, *1943.*

It was the fact that he was a hip, aware cartoon character that struck his audiences funny. So, as time went on, he became super-hip, super-aware—and that's when he became super-funny. Bugs could do the most outlandish things, and the audience would not only accept it, they'd cheer for more. In a great series of Mike Maltese-written/Friz Freleng-directed cartoons, Bugs can be seen getting hipper and funnier by degrees:

He became funniest as a creature of infinite resource, a magician rabbit like the one in *Prest-o Change-o* and *Hare-um Scare-um*, in moments like the one from *The Wabbit Who Came to Supper*, when the clock chimes twelve and Bugs tries to convince Elmer it's New Year's Eve, throwing confetti in the air. Where did that come from? Nowhere. He simply closes his fists, and when he opens them confetti pops out. He yells, "Happy New Year! Yippee! Hurray!" and Elmer falls for it, even though it's July. And so would we, if we were lucky enough to be in the same room.

Bugs, madder than the March Hare and saner than Alice, knows he's in a cartoon. He always had a trick, and he always had the prop that was necessary to pull off that trick. Whatever it was—a sledgehammer, a stick of dynamite, an anvil, a cannon—he needed it, he got it! Where did it come from? Nobody wanted to know, they just wanted to see him pull off his fast ones. And his fast ones kept getting faster.

In *Fresh Hare*, with Mountie Elmer chasing Desperado Bugs in the snowy North Woods, the tempo picks up enough to make the previous Rabbit cartoons drag by

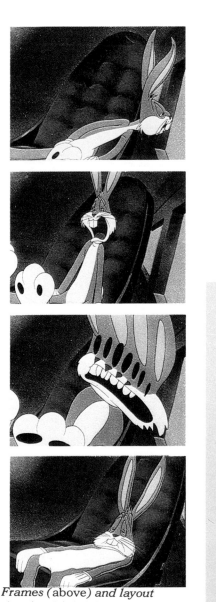

Frames (above) *and layout drawing* (right) *from Robert Clampett's* Falling Hare, *1943.*

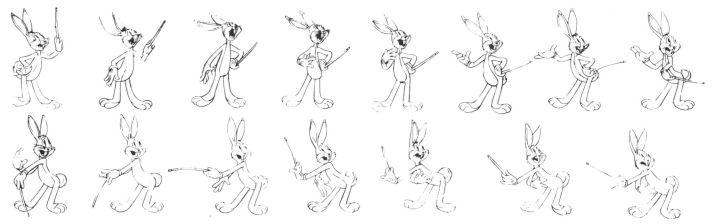

comparison and set the standard for the Bugs Bunnies to follow: quick set-up, quick payoff, then on to the next gag.

By the time of *The Hare-Brained Hypnotist* in October of 1942, the standing joke of Elmer as a hunter in the forest being heckled to the point of madness by a brash and cocky Bugs is being toyed with, reversed, and virtually lampooned as if it were any other film convention and up for grabs. Elmer tries messing with Bugs' head and attempts to capture him through hypnotism, but Bugs zaps the trance back to Fudd. Finally, Bugs hypnotizes Elmer into believing he's a rabbit, but Elmer just takes on the personality of the nearest rabbit, and that's Bugs Bunny. Bugs being heckled by Bugs has the effect of turning him into a straight man, and he blusters and sputters in traditional straight-man style, exclaiming, "Who's the comedian in dis picture, anyway?"

"I would expect certain scenes from certain animators," Friz comments about his talented crew. "I used to use Gerry Chiniquy for dancing, because he could analyze a dance. We'd work together: I'd come in, and I'd do the dance, and we'd study it and sketch it out, between the two of us. Virgil Ross was really a character animator. Art Davis was great for big action scenes in the broad, Eastern style."

Freleng's Bugs, like Freleng, is impulsive, spontaneous. In *Hare Trigger*, he dashes offscreen before he's finished his dialogue, and the dust in his wake has to finish it for him. He doesn't really need to be provoked into a fight: he's ready to take on all comers from the word go. But he's making it all up as he goes along. The inherent joke is that we know Bugs can't lose, so the inevitability of the other fellow's defeat is rhythmically presented, like a dance. Sometimes, as in *Stage Door Cartoon*, it *is* a dance.

"I love music," Freleng says. "I can't read it, but I can feel it. Music inspires my visual thinking. I time my cartoons to music, and I find it helps me. Everything is done rhythmically."

But along with the rhythm came an innate sense of the harmonies of life, a wholeness and naturalness to the action in a Freleng film through which even the dementia dominant in the Warner Bros. cartoon took on an inherent rhythm and interior logic. When Bugs pleads with Elmer to let him back in the house in Freleng's *The Wabbit Who Came to Supper*, he stops abruptly in the middle of his appeal and tells us, "Hey! This scene oughta get me the Academy Award!" It's not the first time he steps out of character, but his timing and delivery are so *natural*, so *convincing*, that the line has the surprise effect it's supposed to.

Maltese remembered that "Freleng would say, 'Let's knock 'em dead!'" And he usually did. Mastering the technique of getting laughs on a shoestring, Freleng became the undisputed master of the Repeated Action for Comic Effect. When Bugs breaks *repeatedly* into a buck-and-wing dance in *Stage Door Cartoon*, it's repeatedly hilarious, just as it is when Bugs repeatedly maneuvers down the row of seats in a theater in the post-war *Hare Do*, keeping up a non-stop stream of pseudo-apologetic chatter—"Excuse me, Pardon me, Pardon me, Excuse me . . ." The animation, as well as the joke, can be savored on every repetition.

Below*: Director Friz Freleng (left) and storyman Michael Maltese (right) collaborated on a series of cartoons that developed Bugs' character and gag style.*

Above*: Frames from Friz Freleng's* Stage Door Cartoon, *1944.*

Above: *Robert McKimson's first model sheet of Bugs Bunny, drawn up after the tremendous success of* A Wild Hare. *Right: In 1943, working as lead animator in Robert Clampett's unit, McKimson made the simple but effective revisions in his 1942 model sheet (right) that created the definitive Bugs Bunny (below right).*

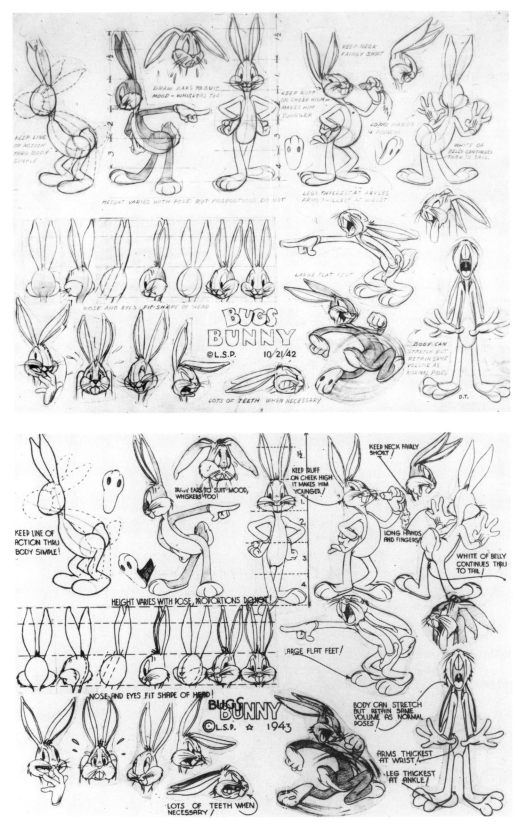

As for Jones, he admits to feeling somewhat at sea with the character until he made *Super Rabbit* in 1943, which he calls "one of the first cartoons where I got a real feeling for Bugs, and the way he would later develop, for me at least. You could see he was really enjoying himself, which I enjoyed. It was a matter of understanding the Bugs Bunny in me."

Another of Bugs' early pictures, *The Wacky Wabbit*, became a milestone for another reason. "We showed Elmer going across the prairies looking for gold," Maltese recalled. "The Rabbit comes up and he says, 'Eeeeeh, I t'ink I'll break up a dull afternoon by heckling that poor character.' And then he starts heckling Elmer, just for the *sake* of heckling. Now, all the gags that followed were funny, but this thing just died. We discovered then that what makes this guy lovable is that he's gotta be picked on."

"We started out with Bugs going hunting for trouble," as Freleng explained it to *The New York Times* in 1945. "That wasn't successful because it wasn't true to type. He never starts the scrapes he gets into anymore. He's full of mischief, but he always starts out minding his own business."

It was Wildman Bob Clampett, who directed *Wacky Wabbit*, who took Bugs to brand new limits all around. Clampett made it clear that this was a cartoon character with teeth, and that's the way his artists animated him.

Clampett is also the man who put the screwball bounce into the meat-and-potatoes style of animation that previously prevailed even in the zany cartoons of Tex Avery. Bob Clampett was not afraid to apply insane distortions to a character, even a precious, precocious character like Bugs Bunny. He'd turn him white, flatten him, fold him up like a rug, spin him around like a propeller, and melt him like butter, ending up with the wildest Rabbit this side of *Hare-um Scare-um*. When Clampett followed up Avery's *Tortoise Beats Hare* with his own *Tortoise Wins By a Hare*, it's chiefly the animation on Bugs that sets the two apart. The angles on Bugs go to all extremes, and his extremities go to all perpendiculars, as he expostulates inelegantly with Cecil Turtle, and races against elegant backgrounds of blurred peach and burnt umber.

For Clampett, much of the Warner style derived from the single moment in *Porky's Duck Hunt*, which he animated himself, in which Porky complains about Daffy retrieving Porky's dog from the water, when Porky had been looking forward to this happening the other way around. "That's not in the script," exclaimed the Pig, to the vast amusement of audiences to this day. Clampett's explanation of Bugs' character goes back to that same concept: "Some little guy would give him trouble, like in the first Tortoise and Hare race, where suddenly the little tortoise has got his number, or like the little gremlin in *Falling Hare*. But, as you notice, at the end, he's saying again to you, 'Look, it was all in the script.' So he's always in control."

It was as an animator in Bob Clampett's unit that Robert McKimson added many of the embellishments to the character that finally *defined* Bugs Bunny for millions of fans—to the point where all previous incarnations of the Heckling Hare are unrecognizable, unacceptable. "I drew the way he looks," as McKimson later put it. "We made him cuter, brought his cheeks and head out a little more and gave him just a little nose."

Almost as soon as they started working with the character, the Clampett unit, with McKimson in the lead, gave Bugs a larger muzzle than the first model sheets called for, and his face began to look less ratlike. Then they structured the nose differently, and the teeth were naturally anchored to the same bone structure, in a more appealing facial design. By the time Clampett made *Bugs Bunny Gets the Boid* in 1942, he had arrived at what we might call the Classic Bugs Bunny. By late 1944, the same design was reaching the screen in the cartoons of the other units. Once Freleng made *Stage Door Cartoon*, released near the end of that year, the McKimson look was universal.

Jones has explained why this was important: "The eyes slant in, which gives him a sort of elfin look—hopefully. Bugs Bunny has a tiny nose resting on a stubby form.

BUGS BUNNY

Starring in "MERRIE MELODIES" SEZ:—

"Thanks, Doc—I mean you Exhibitors for cookin' up all those votes for me in the BOXOFFICE poll of the ten best shorts series."

Created by

LEON SCHLESINGER

Producer

"MERRIE MELODIES" and "LOONEY TUNES"

Released by WARNER BROS.

BOXOFFICE BAROMETER

Above: *The Warner cartoons started doing better in the annual trade polls than they ever had. The* Showmen's Trade Review *poll of motion picture exhibitors ranked the Merrie Melodies sixth on their list of top short subjects in 1939, but by 1943 they had shot up to first. In 1942, in both the* Boxoffice *and the* Showman's Trade Review *polls, the exhibitors voted the Merrie Melodies cartoons into second place. This trade ad was run in response to the* Boxoffice *results, but in the case of* Showman's Trade Review, *the theater owners elected Bugs to his own spot, which turned up in the Number Five position. Finally, in February of 1944, the Warners Short Subjects salespeople saw the light and, without breaking up the existing series, Merrie Melodies and Looney Tunes, began selling the Bugs Bunny cartoons to theaters as a separate category they referred to as "Bugs Bunny Specials."*

Above: *June 1943 comic book, issue No. 20.* Below: *In-house wartime sketch.*

If your rabbit, say, has a three-inch-high head, in this scale, then 3/16 of the mouth on either side of the nose defines the mouth. The cheek overlaps the mouth. We noticed that cheekiness was true of babies and an actress named Sonja Henie: she just had too chubby cheeks to make a broad smile. So, incorporating that unlikely idea into Bugs, you must be able to express his reactions with those little tiny 3/16ths. When he's sad, it turns down; when happy, up."

Bugs was the cartoon version of the loud-mouthed but lovable Brooklynese smart-aleck who turns up in the cockpit, in the barracks, or on the battlefield in every World War II movie, as inevitable as the flag and, apparently, just as effective in rallying the spirits of a beleaguered nation. The idea that the battle was winnable was a very popular one during World War II.

Like Chaplin, Bugs made a short film for the war effort. The Bugs Bunny Defense Bond short, usually referred to as *Any Bonds Today?* ran no longer than two hundred feet of film, or just over two minutes in length, and, hurried through the production process, broke records by being completed in three weeks. When Bugs sang the title song, its rousing spirit seems to have put his voice into definitive focus for the first time. The film was rushed to Henry Morgenthau of the United States Treasury Department on Monday, December 15, 1941—initiated prior to, and completed after, Pearl Harbor.

And, like Chaplin, Bugs experienced his first bursts of popularity during the emotionally charged wartime period. It was during World War II that Bugs Bunny earned his spot as sort of a national mascot.

As author Richard Schickel, a moviegoer at the time, recalled the effect, "The Bunny's personality perfectly suited his times. He was a con man in the classic American mold, adept in the techniques and ethics of survival, equally at home in the jungle of the city and in Elmer Fudd's carrot patch. In the war years, when he flourished most gloriously, Bugs Bunny embodied the cocky humor of a nation that had survived its economic crisis with fewer psychological scars than anyone had thought possible and was facing a terrible war with grace, gallantry, humor, and solidarity that were equally surprising."

Bugs' likeness was contributed by the studio for various divisions of the armed services as part of the war effort: it appeared, for instance, on the equipment of the 385th Air Service Squadron, on the first Liberator Bomber that struck at Davao in the southern Philippines, on every vessel and piece of equipment of the Motor Torpedo Boat command, and as a morale builder on the country's biggest hospital ship, the *U.S.S. Comfort.* Bugs was considered an unofficial member of both the Seventeenth Weather Squadron and the Fourth Parachute Battalion, and an *official* member of the Seabees. He was actually given a service record by the Marine Corps.

In 1969, Bob Clampett told Mike Barrier, "The boys were all in uniform . . . and they particularly loved Bugs Bunny for his lack of inhibitions . . . Bugs Bunny has been loved for over a quarter of a century now, but he has never been loved the way he was during those war years . . . It is most difficult now to comprehend the tremendous emotional impact Bugs Bunny exerted on the audience then. You must try to recapture the mood of a people who had seen the enemy . . . blitzkrieg defenseless civilians, sink our fleet in a sneak attack, and threaten our very existence.

"It was during those war years . . . that the Bugs Bunny cartoons . . . passed Disney and MGM for the first time to become the Number One short subject."

Theater owners were specific in their claim that Bugs was perking up their attendance figures. "I played this on the coldest Saturday of the year," wrote Cleo Manry of the Buena Vista Theater, in Buena Vista, Georgia, of Avery's *All This and Rabbit Stew*, "and my patrons said the laugh they got out of it was all that kept them warm." Bob Clampett's *Wabbit Twouble* prompted the owner of the Alfred Co-Op Theater in Alfred, New York, to tell the *Motion Picture Herald*, "Bugs Bunny is in it, so I had extra attendance and a hilarious audience. I billed this on almost equal terms with the feature."

During World War II, the studio received countless requests for drawings and letters attesting to The Rabbit's popularity among servicemen, including: "Dear Bugs Bunny: How come we don't see more of you in the far-flung Pacific? I think it is only natural for you as an aspiring star to be out here with us. This request comes on behalf of many thousands of servicemen who hold your inimitable countenance in high esteem," from two sailors on board the U.S.S. McNair. And " . . . even outranking Betty Grable in popularity was your character Bugs Bunny, who receives far more whistles, cheers, and applause than anyone else," from Sgt. M. Chaitt of Cochran Field in Macon Georgia. When the carrier Lexington went down, its seamen reported with a great sense of loss that two Bugs Bunny cartoons went down with it. They even remembered which two: Hiawatha's Rabbit Hunt and The Wabbit Who Came to Supper. Right: Reconstructed cel from animation drawing from Bob Clampett's Falling Hare, 1943.

The Utah Celery Company of Salt Lake City offered to keep all the studio's staffers well supplied with their product if Bugs would only switch from carrots to celery. Later, the Broccoli Institute of America strongly urged The Bunny to sample their product once in a while. Never took. Mel Blanc would have been happy to switch to any of these vegetables, since carrots made his throat muscles tighten and the words couldn't come out, but it was no go. Carrots were Bugs' trademark. The only concession they ever made was to move the carrot-crunching sounds and dialogue to the last spot in the recording session.

No one got more pleasure out of Bugs' success than storyman Mike Maltese, a scrapper from New York's Lower East Side with an incisive eye and a quick tongue, who had collaborated with Bugs' father, Tex Avery, on the cartoon *The Heckling Hare* before he began his string of hits with Friz Freleng. Many feel that it was in this picture that Maltese and Avery together imbued Bugs with the aggressive, independent New York spirit that broadened the outline only suggested by *A Wild Hare* into the character we've come to know. For the first time, Bugs' Brooklyn accent seemed to be rooted in part of his authentic nature.

The Heckling Hare also involved Bugs in one of the wild experiments for which Avery was becoming famous in the cartoon business, when the dog hunting Bugs, then Bugs himself, fell off a cliff for a wild finish. The two characters plummet to earth, screaming their little heads off, clutching each other in terror, rotating wildly through space, exploited with every dramatic angle possible, becoming more and more intense, dragging on for what seems like an eternity—until finally it occurs to you that this *is* an eternity. Then it looks just preposterous enough to be funny.

Bugs and the hunting dog finally sprout brakes, for a thoroughly unlikely safe

Above: *Almost as soon as* A Wild Hare *had created its sensation, Schlesinger was paid a visit by Oscar LeBeck from Western Publishing. On the strength of its deal with the Walt Disney Studios and the success of a single comic book,* Walt Disney's Comics and Stories, *distributed by Dell Publishing Co., LeBeck had been told that Dell would be happy to distribute comic books based on the characters of any Hollywood animation studio he could make a deal with. Issue No. 1 of* Looney Tunes and Merrie Melodies Comics *carried the story of* A Wild Hare. *Above is issue No. 12, October 1942.* Right: *Some 1940s Bugs memorabilia. Bugs Bunny merchandise was licensed, almost as soon as* A Wild Hare *hit the screen, through the Leon Schlesinger Corporation, set up in September of 1937 to handle toys and commercial tie-ins for all of the studio's characters.*

Left: *Animation drawing from Chuck Jones'* Bugs Bunny and the Three Bears, *1944.* Below: *Frames from Tex Avery's* The Heckling Hare, *1941.*

landing, topping Avery's wild climax with a wild conclusion. But the fall was originally intended to be topped by yet another one, with the characters sighing in relief, then taking two steps and falling off one more cliff, hurtling through space for the second time and calling out, "Hold onto your hats, folks, here we go again!" as the picture irised out in mid-tumble. That catch-phrase was the well-known punchline to a then-current joke of dubious reputation, and accounts vary as to whether it was the adult connotation of the line or the depressing effect of ending a cartoon on its two principals hurtling toward certain death, but *something* caused Jack Warner to object to *Heckling Hare*'s original ending. Leon Schlesinger had little patience for arguing such fine points when the head of the studio took offence: the last forty feet of the cartoon were excised before its theatrical release, and in the present version (still widely seen on television), the action abruptly fades out a few seconds after the rabbit and the dog have landed solidly on terra firma at the end of their first fall.

As with his Rabbit's name, Avery didn't take kindly to such imposition. At noon on Tuesday, July 1, 1941, Tex walked out of the studio. Schlesinger then hit him with a four-week suspension. Two months after the walkout, it was announced that Avery was heading his own unit in the cartoon department at MGM, where he earned about half again his Schlesinger salary. In the interest of a larger paycheck, Tex abandoned his child. The reconciliation would be a long time in coming.

Avery settled in for a thirteen-year run at MGM, where, according to him, "They said, 'Look, give us another Bugs Bunny.' And, brother, I never came up with one."

There's no such animal.

The Bugs Bunny Spirit, 1945-1949

The major advantage that a cartoon studio has over other comedy stables is that talent may leave to go on to bigger things or better deals, but you never lose your *stars*. Avery may go to MGM, but Bugs won't.

By the mid-1940s the Warner gang *knew* they were leading the pack in the short cartoon field. It was during the last of the war years, and in that first flush of national relief, pride, and excitement that followed World War II, that Bugs Bunny reached what was perhaps his prime. Whether directed by old hands Jones, Freleng, and Clampett, or freshmen Bunny directors Robert McKimson, Frank Tashlin, and Arthur Davis, Bugs was as vital, spontaneous, and pure, out-and-out funny during these years as he would ever be. In 1945 and 1946, Bugs never took a misstep: *Hare Trigger*, *The Unruly Hare*, *Hare Conditioned*, *Hare Tonic*, *Baseball Bugs*, *Hare Remover*, *Hair-Raising Hare*, *Acrobatty Bunny*, *Racketeer Rabbit*, *The Big Snooze*, *Rhapsody Rabbit*, *A Hare Grows in Manhattan*—a consecutive run of hits rolled off the Termite Terrace assembly line.

Hare Conditioned, which finds Bugs as an elevator operator, calling out, "Sixth floor—rubber tires, nylon hose, bobby pins, girdles, alarm clocks, bourbon, butter, and other picture post cards," prompted one theater owner to comment, "We need more and more of these funny cartoons with Bugs Bunny, which are fast stealing the top spot away from the features." *Herr Meets Hare*, a piece of slapstick war propaganda that pits "Buggsenheimer Bunny" against none other than Hermann Goering, and features his first impersonation of Brunhilda, was rated "Excellent" by *The Exhibitor*, and *Film Daily* commented, "Bugs Bunny does it again." It was such a sensation in East Coast theaters that it prompted letters from the New York office and was voted one of the Ten Best Short Subjects of 1945 in the annual *Boxoffice* poll.

Like Douglas MacArthur and Dwight D. Eisenhower, Bugs was greeted by a peacetime America as a war hero, and residual waves of stored-up affection continued to be lavished on him.

In his cartoons, Bugs became something of an expert at having conniptions (showing his Clampett influence), throwing himself from one expertly designed pose of cockeyed convulsion into another in a fraction of a second, twitching in fright at the sight of a monster in *Hair-Raising Hare*, leaping into a seizure of "Rabbititus" in *Hare Tonic*, topping each spectacular paroxysm with another even better in *Hare Remover*, throwing his fits all the way to the moon in *Haredevil Hare*.

In the 1940s, Mike Maltese described his job in these words: "The storyman says there are no more zany seven-minute ideas and proceeds to write one anyway." In a later interview, he got closer to the bone of the experiential reality of the equation: "Everybody, right down the line, had somebody handing him some work that he had to do. But the writer went into the room and said, 'Oh, my God! What's funny?' And this you learn how to live with through the years, through death, illness, trouble in the family, and everything else. What I used to do was sit in a room and say, 'Well, what'll I do?' And I'd sit there. And the inspiration I got was the idea that if I didn't come up with anything, I wouldn't get paid. Economic pressure was the spur, known as a baby at home and the rent and all that: Get Funny. And I can't say exactly how it works, but ideas begin to come to you."

So lampoons of the Bugs-and-Elmer routine continued: parodies of Bugs and Elmer, as performed by Bugs and Elmer. It became the Warner Bros. cartoonists' way of keeping Bugs fresh and flexible, of keeping themselves fresh and flexible, when they approached Bugs year after year, and keeping their cartoons on the same track without wearing out the same groove.

Elmer gets fed up with the whole routine in *The Big Snooze*, wailing, "I get the worst of it from that wabbit in evwy one of these cahtoons!" and tears up his contract with Mr. Warner, much to Bugs' dismay. "Think what we've been to each other!" Bugs protests. "Why, we've been like—like Rabbit and Costello! Damon and Runyon! Stan

Above*: Chuck Jones' layout drawing for his* Hare Tonic, *1945.* Top: *Insolence and self-mockery merge in this elegant animation drawing from Jones'* Hare Conditioned, *1945.*

and Laurel!" But to the tune of "Someone's Rockin' My Dreamboat," he invades Elmer's dreams with more rabbits than Fudd can count, proliferating, translucently, one layer upon the other, all coming out of an adding machine. "I'm multiplyin', see?" The Rabbit explains.

A secret formula whipped up by Elmer in Frank Tashlin's *Hare Remover* is the cue for every variety of role reversal, attitude reversal, costume reversal, and prop reversal between Elmer, Bugs, an "experimental dog," and a wild bear who wanders into the fray. The formula turns the dog into a Mad Fiend who eats grass, but when Bugs' fit is over, it hasn't made him any madder than usual—just mad enough to give Elmer a taste of his own medicine and turn *him* into a second grass-eating Mad Fiend. Fudd's mad enough to give his derby to a bear, making Bugs think the bear is Elmer Fudd. When the bear eats Bugs' carrot, Fudd thinks the bear is Bugs Bunny. When the bear gets tired of baiting Elmer, Bugs does a bear-faced imitation and Elmer buys it, making the bear think they're both bananas.

Through it all, Elmer's manic-depressive mood swings make him the victim of every plot twist, as he goes from elated at capturing Bugs ("I caught the wabbit! I got him! I got him! I got the wabbit! Ha-ha! Boy! My! My! My! My expewiments will continue! I needed a wabbit and I got him! Huwway! Huwway!") to a fit of his own in dismay over the failure of his formula to affect "The Wabbit" ("Ooooh! It don't work! It doesn't work! I'm a tewwibwe scientist! Oh, this is tewwibwe! I twied my best and A-a-a-a-a-ah! it won't work!")—which ought to earn him about double for his comedy acting whatever rewards his formula would have netted him.

Below: *Bugs helps Edward G. Robinson with his coat in* Racketeer Rabbit, *in animation drawing by Virgil Ross from Friz Freleng's 1946 cartoon.*
Above: *Bugs rocks Elmer's dreamboat in this publicity drawing for Bob Clampett's* The Big Snooze, *1946.*

Above: *Model sheet from Art Davis' Bowery Bugs, 1949.*
Right: *Cel from Friz Freleng's Hare Splitter, 1948.*

Arthur Davis directed a solo Bugs Bunny in 1949 called *Bowery Bugs*, taking the opportunity, as one of the West Coast studio's native New Yorkers, to present Bugs in what some people feel was his *real* natural habitat. Bugs seems to know the territory well, performing nearly a record number of con jobs in this cartoon, appearing as a bustled lady, a moustached ne'er-do-well, a cop on the Brooklyn Bridge, and the Swami Rabbitima—sending Steve Brodie jumping off the Brooklyn Bridge howling, "Everybody's a rabbit!" and spending very little screen time as Bugs Bunny.

McKimson's is the Bugs who would walk up to a lion and slap him, which is basically the tone of the initial confrontation in his first Rabbit picture, *Acrobatty Bunny*, as Bugs stares straight into the beast's Jaws of Death, rings a chime on the nearest sabre tooth, and calls for Pinocchio. McKimson's Bugs is a rabbit strongly inclined to

Below: *Publicity drawing from Frank Tashlin's* The Unruly Hare, *1945. Tashlin makes his characters more flexible in their subtle moments than the average animation director, and more psychologically precise in their explosive ones, so the characters who are visibly role-playing are more convincing on* both *levels than most cartoon directors can manage on one.*

sneer, and part of his director's skill was his ability to keep The Rabbit from being unattractive while he preserved his independent streak. It's also McKimson's Bugs who blows up the Easter Bunny in *Easter Yeggs* and badgers the ape in *Hurdy Gurdy Hare* till he confides to us, "I'll bet this kid won't take much more of this guff!"

And it's McKimson who directed the outrageous *Rebel Rabbit*, which has Bugs turning off the water at Niagara Falls, rupturing the Washington Monument, filling in the Grand Canyon, giving Manhattan back to the Indians, cutting Florida adrift, stealing the locks from the Panama Canal, and tying railroad ties into a Windsor knot.

70

Though McKimson seems to have seen Bugs this way, he didn't go in for outrageous stunts himself—unless you happened to consider his particular form of precision graphics outrageous enough to suit you.

When McKimson and his brother Tom showed up for their first day of work at Warner Bros., they marched in together, almost in step, in flashy matching polo outfits topped by camel's-hair coats and berets, sat down at their desks, and set to work at exactly 8:00 a.m. "This was all very spectacular," marveled Bob Clampett, who witnessed the entire scene, "like a Busby Berkeley routine."

Physically, McKimson resembled Hal Roach comedian Charlie Chase, to the point where that nickname attached itself to him at the studio. Bob and his brother "were considered capable and dependable," in Clampett's words, "and they never seemed to

Above: *Animation drawing from Chuck Jones'* Mississippi Hare.

indulge in the foolishness around them." When he was an animator, he had a solid reputation for producing a lot of very polished work very quickly, almost as if he could envision the completed drawing on the page and was simply tracing with his pencil what his eye could already see. After suffering a serious automobile collision during his animating days, however, McKimson returned to work a changed man. He claimed he could actually see things *more* clearly, and then began turning out drawings at nearly *double* his already prodigious rate. "It's a strange thing," he admitted, "but it happened to me."

The solid professional work that Bob McKimson cranked out at lightning speed in the 1930s hadn't yet developed the warmth and personality of McKimson's great Bugs Bunny animation for Tex Avery and Bob Clampett in the 1940s; that was a sophistication that developed through experience, and when it did, it affected the visual style of the entire studio.

The group dynamics at Termite Terrace received a backhanded bolstering in 1944, when Leon Schlesinger sold the entire Warner Bros. Cartoon Studio directly to Warner Bros. for a reported one million dollars.

Right away, however, the parent studio felt someone had to be put in charge of this lunatic asylum and chose, almost at random, an executive named Edward Selzer. If it was the wrong choice, no one was going to worry about it but the cartoonists. But by now their collective Bugs Bunny spirit was strong enough to rout opposition.

"When Warner Bros. took over, we kept our independence; we fought the Front Office," Mike Maltese remembered. "We had our own way of doing things, we were used to working as we pleased . . . So we all had a meeting at Sorrentino's Restaurant in Burbank—Friz and Chuck and the rest of us—and we said, 'We're gonna have to fight.' We made up our minds that if Eddie Selzer made any suggestions about cartoons or stories, we'd all look at the ceiling. All of us. Then finally he understood, and he left us alone."

Below: Jean Blanchard's model sheet of Bugs for the Robert McKimson Unit, late '40s, demonstrates the sassiness that he instilled in the character.

It was during this period that the studio instituted a new practice for trying out storyboards in front of a combined audience that included the directors and storymen from the competing units, allowing everyone a chance to gag up and help develop any existing cartoon concept. Of course, this had always gone on—and continued to go on—informally between the units, so that Mel Blanc was impressed that "members of McKimson's staff felt free to pitch ideas to one of Chuck Jones' men, and vice versa. Such communal spirit was vital to Warner Bros.' success."

Maltese claimed back in the 1940s, "The competitive spirit here helps toward a better product. Especially if it's a cooperative competitive spirit. Each department realizes that the next department's work must be as good to have their own appreciated on the screen. A matter of one hand washing the other."

But, as Jones describes the new process, it appears to have had an incalculable effect on the development of the Bugs Bunny spirit: "Either the writer or the director would come in with a concept, and . . . we'd have what we called, for want of a better word, the period of the Big Yes, which meant that for two hours you could only say Yes . . . you could only contribute to the idea, and that meant that all negatives were out: 'I don't like it.' 'There must be a better way.' 'I don't like to criticize, but . . .' 'I've heard that one before.' 'I don't know.' Or: 'Oh, for Christ's sake, Chuck.' All are roadblocks impeding the advancement and exploration of the value of an idea and are forbidden.

"People who all their lives had said nothing but negatives were unable to keep still, so therefore they had to say something . . . It's surprising, you can even get creative stuff out of people you wouldn't normally expect to. And we converted a number of people who had been cynical into giving people."

"As I look back, it seems to me that some of our best pictures emerged out of our constant fight against negativism."

"The success of Bugs and his sundry antagonists encouraged the directors to try combining other characters," Mel Blanc remembered. The message was clear to the Warner Bros. cartoonists: it was Personalities that ruled the roost in the short comedy business, it was star characters that dictated the economics in the cartoon business, and, in the low-budget business of making Warner Bros. cartoons, it was a pair of characters who could oppose each other dynamically that was your ticket to success. It was around this time that the studio began to pit Tweety against Sylvester, Henery Hawk against Foghorn Leghorn, the Roadrunner against the Coyote, Daffy or Sylvester against Elmer—whatever screwball combo had the potential to set each other off in

Above: Title card drawing by Robert McKimson for his first Bugs Bunny cartoon, Acrobatty Bunny, *1946. Below: Chuck Jones on the Big Yes session, where no negative comment of any kind was permitted: "The 'Yes' session lasts only for two hours, but a person who can only say 'no' finds it an eternity. Negative-minded people have been known finally to inflate and burst with accumulated negatives and say something positive, because it is also true that a person who heretofore can only say 'no' is also a person who must say something." At this 1952 session: Michael Maltese at the storyboard; seated first row: Chuck Jones, Friz Freleng, Edward Selzer, Selzer's secretary. Second row: Tedd Pierce, Robert McKimson, Warren Foster, Production Manager John Burton.*

an explosive chemistry that would tickle the audience's funny bone. The Warner Bros. cartoons became a series of two-character battles in a milieu in which passersby are conspicuously absent.

If these various conflicts had one element in common, it was the phenomenon Mitchell Cohen pointed out when describing the Warner Bros. cartoons in *The Velvet Light Trap:* ". . . a premise that the hostile, aggressive force will be defeated by an intelligence that . . . will turn the destructive passion into self-destruction." The Bugs Bunny spirit was already infectious, now it was contagious. And the child became father to the studio.

Pursued by Fudd through a theater lobby in *Hare Do*, Bugs defeats Elmer simply by knowing that if you're in a cartoon, throwing on the "Intermission" signal will jam the lobby so full of smoking people that your pursuer will be immobilized—*every* time, reliable as a faucet, no matter how many times you try it in the space of a single minute. This knowledge alone is enough to defeat his adversary.

But just having a trick is not enough. In the later *Big House Bunny*, Bugs eludes Yosemite Sam by running to the top of the prison's gibbet, pressing a button conveniently installed on its side, and receiving a smooth elevator ride to ground level. Sam tries pressing the very same button, and *in the first frame* of the next shot, has his neck already enclosed in the noose, the floor being yanked from under his feet, and his entire body hurtling toward a finish sure to prove fatal to any live-action figure.

There's the gag Bugs first pulls in *Acrobatty Bunny* and then again in *Sahara Hare*, where he uses a toy mouse to frighten away the elephant recruited by his antagonist, and the pachyderm not only leaps up in fright, but grabs the villain with its trunk and uses him as a live weapon, slamming the ground with him in a panicked but ultimately futile attempt to beat the harmless mouse to death. Sylvester the Cat, apparently learning the trick from Bugs, tries this strategy in *Tweet Zoo*, but the elephant just leaps in the air in fright and comes down on *him*.

Below*: Ostensibly a theater lobby, but in reality another stage set for one more flummoxing of Fudd by Bugs Bunny in Friz Freleng's* Hare Do, *1949; layout by Hawley Pratt, background painted by Paul Julian.*

Bugs knows something Sam doesn't, and as time went on all the other Innocent characters at Warners knew it too. Bugs never said what it was he knew, but he never doubted that he knew it. At the end of Freleng's *High Diving Hare*, with Bugs tied up at the end of a diving board hundreds of feet in the air, and Sam securely on the diving platform, sawing the board away, the Warners cartoonists pull off one of their most famous and most outlandish conceits, one that Freleng had used to Tweety's advantage in his Oscar-winning *Tweety Pie*, and that would resurface in *Don't Give Up the Sheep* and *A Star Is Bored*: Sam saws the board clean through, and the *platform* collapses to the ground, while Bugs and diving board hang suspended in mid-air.

"I know dis defies de Law of Gravity," Bugs confesses, "but, uh, you see, I never studied Law!"

There grew an implicit understanding between the Innocents (Bugs, Tweety, the Roadrunner, etc.) and the Universe-at-Large—often there is *no physical explanation* why their schemes should succeed and their adversary's consistently fail—that characters like Sylvester and the Coyote just can't get the hang of. It may be an erratic, intractable Universe, changing as the weather, but there will always be those who are in harmony with it, and there will always be those who are bucking the grain.

After a while, this works the way it does in the old samurai films, like *Sanshiro Sugata*, or what Yoda says to Luke Skywalker in *The Empire Strikes Back*, or the lessons from the '70s television show *Kung Fu*: To be a warrior, you've got to comprehend the flower, you've got to understand The Force.

Bugs explains it best at the end of *Rabbit Every Monday*, when Sam's got him locked in his stove with orders to "Quit stallin' and start roastin'!" The Rabbit keeps emerging from the stove with requests for things like a bottle opener, cracked ice and more chairs, and "Be a pal and see if you can't scare up a few more ashtrays, kiddo, huh?" And party noises emerge from the depths of the stove every time the door is opened. It's when Bugs pleads invitingly, "Ain'tcha comin' in, Mac? The goils have been askin' for ya" that Sam is hooked—he spruces himself up and leaps willingly into the stove. Bugs hops out, latches the door, and thinks he's pulled another fast one.

But that's where it becomes apparent that calling Bugs a winner is meaningless until you understand what it is he's winning *at*. Having a change of heart, he decides to release Sam, but finds, much to his astonishment, that a balloon floats out from the open door, that a party really *is* going on inside that tiny stove (the way a party is always going on in one of these cartoons: in a stock shot from a Warner Brothers feature).

Bugs doesn't need an invitation: he dives in and joins the festivities. When we last see him, he's wearing a party hat and twirling a noisemaker, reassuring us, "I don't ask questions—I just have fun!" Which, really, is all the reassurance we need.

It was a Zen thing: every Warner Bros. cartoon was eventually about achieving Harmony with the Universe. Every Warner Bros. cartoon eventually had the Bugs Bunny spirit.

Below: *The gibbet becomes an elevator for Bugs Bunny, but not for Yosemite Sam, in these frames from Friz Freleng's* Big House Bunny, *1950.* Above: *The same logic plunges Sam to a doom from which fate spares Bugs in Freleng's* High Diving Hare, *1949.*

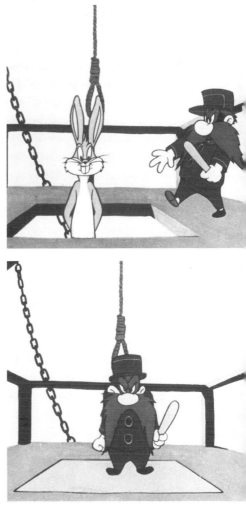

The Rabbit in the Grey Flannel Fur, 1950-1958

As Bugs carried on into a new decade, the Warner Bros. short-subject salespeople kept on requesting Bugs Bunnies, and the units kept churning them out.

But in 1949, several new shifts in the wind were affecting the movie business, the animation business, and, inevitably, Bugs Bunny.

One of these changes was the breaking off from the animation establishment represented by Disney, Warner Bros., and the other major cartoon studios, of an independent movement, ensconced in a studio of its own by 1948, called United Productions of America. Based on a more impressionistic, less storybook, style of graphics than the Disneyesque form then in vogue, UPA revolutionized the look of all studio animation throughout the 1950s and into the '60s. As Chuck Jones has remarked, "That kind of *severe* movement sometimes is much more effective than flowing movement."

Freleng, too, adapted to the new style, as did most of the existing animation crews. But he felt, "When you create a character that becomes standard, you can't change him for a style. With Bugs Bunny you had a dimensional set-up. Once we created an image for that character, we had to stay with it."

So, as Bugs goes on, his surroundings do *more*, and he needs to do *less*.

Another of the changes resulted from the Supreme Court consent decrees of 1948, which separated the Hollywood studios from their theater chains, breaking up the integrated booking system that had kept the cartoons supported by the studio. Arthur Davis' unit was shut down, and he returned to the position of animator in the Freleng unit. For a period of ten years, Freleng, Jones, and McKimson directed the entire output of the studio.

From 1948 to 1956, television loomed as a growing threat to the film industry, without yet being opened up as another outlet for the Hollywood product. To further set Bugs' 1950s cartoons apart from those of the energetic '40s, Warner Bros. eventually sold their pre-1948 color cartoons to Associated Artists Productions, for syndication on television, preserving their post-'48s for later network release by themselves. This has meant that the Bugs Bunny films seen for years first on ABC, then on CBS, then on ABC again, on Saturday mornings, have looked and felt like a somewhat different breed from the older (actually younger) cartoons seen on various stations in various cities at various times on weekdays. There have been, essentially, two schools of Bugs Bunny cartoons, available in different times in different ways.

It's apparent in the 1950s that the Warner Bros. cartoon writers and directors

Above: Layout drawing by Chuck Jones for his Ali Baba Bunny, *1957.*

Below: Animation backgrounds entered a stylized, impressionistic period in 1950. This characteristically inventive one was painted by Phil DeGuard, from Ernie Nordli's layout for Chuck Jones' Broom-Stick Bunny, *1956. Opposite: The "funny feeling" that comes over Bugs whenever he's near gold, as animated by Virgil Ross in Friz Freleng's* 14 Carrot Rabbit, *1952.*

resorted more than once to repeating themselves. In some cases, they were re-working old routines, developing existing ideas, reinterpreting the existing mythology. And in some cases, they were simply repeating themselves.

The more they repeated, or even pulled variations on, their old gags, the more creative their treatments of those gags had to become, until gradually—in a world in which the audience knew the outcome of the joke before they even saw the set-up—the treatment *became* the gag, the rhythmic, impeccably-timed rendering got to be eagerly anticipated in its own right. The Warner Bros. cartoons continued to stay fresh by maintaining the self-mocking quality they had established in the '40s.

In the 1950s, with the post-war Baby Boom transforming his previous audience from rowdy kids in uniform to mature adults with responsibilities, Bugs found his new audience extended to include those "responsibilities." The nation was filling its nurseries and schools to capacity with children, and they were all becoming Bugs Bunny fans. The studio's key artists and directors—essentially the same people who had been drawing the Looney Tunes and Merrie Melodies for Leon Schlesinger in the '30s—had reached a more advanced age, and Bugs himself seemed more settled, less scattered in the '50s cartoons. Friz Freleng has admitted, "We used to get into meetings every once in a while and say, 'Look, we're losing Bugs. He's not as bright and mischievous as he was. Let's bring this kid back.' As we were getting older, he was getting older without our realizing it."

Older and, in some ways, wiser. The Bugs Bunny who prances elegantly through

Below: Frames from Jones' Broomstick Bunny, *layed out by Nordli, show the influence of the UPA accent on design to express character. Above: Chuck Jones directs "characters" Bugs (Mel Blanc) and Witch Hazel (June Foray).*

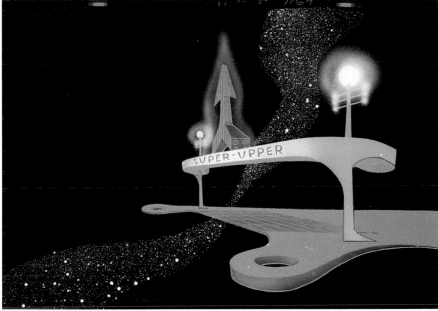

Left: The background paintings for Jones' Hare-Way to the Stars, 1958, were painted by Philip DeGuard, from layouts by Maurice Noble, on thin black paper rather than the stiffer cardboard normal for animation backgrounds, resulting in a completely different texture and a convincing feeling of outer space on the screen. Chuck Jones: "We just built a kind of transparent city, suspended in space, rather than a planet. That was Maurice's idea, to use those hunks of what looked like transparent plastic." Maurice Noble: "The idea of space became more and more developed. I'd do a sketch, and pretty soon we had floating cities, and jet-propelled taxicabs and all this. Space evolved. Out of the graphics, sometimes, would come another facet of the cartoon: a gag, or staging or even a complete dramatic switch in the middle of the cartoon. Then Chuck would go back and introduce it into the story as he developed and layed out the animation." Following pages: Cel and matching background, with overlays painted by DeGuard, layout by Noble—from Chuck Jones' 3-D cartoon Lumber Jack-Rabbit, 1954. In June of 1953, the Warner Cartoon Studio was disbanded, as a response to Jack Warner's conviction that the entire film industry was going to swing over to 3-D just as it had swung over to talkies after The Jazz Singer. Once they'd belatedly hired their cartoonists back again, the Warners allowed Lumber Jack-Rabbit, a rather mild Bugs Bunny cartoon, to be photographed in 3-D process and released to theaters with only one conspicuous 3-D effect: the Warner Bros. shield zooming out through its concentric circles and practically into the audience's lap.

delightful cartoons like *Hare Do, Hillbilly Hare, Rabbit Every Monday, Hare Lift, Bugs and Thugs, Sahara Hare, Ali Baba Bunny,* and *Hare-Way to the Stars* has gained in polish and *savoir faire* what he may have lost in adolescent high spirits. Whether playing an animated Dean Martin to Daffy Duck's Jerry Lewis, or up against what at first appears to be more threatening opposition, Bugs was now capable of coaxing his opponents into burning themselves out without lifting much more than a delicate pinky to add a grace note to their self-destruction.

This is the period that might be called Bugs' Maturity, and that was best handled by Chuck Jones.

Jones, who had something of an obsession with failure, had blown his brief chance at an acting career at the age of twelve, when he mugged too conspicuously in a Fred Thomson Western, and never quite got over the fact that at six months his brother Richard turned in an unacceptable performance in another movie and so "managed to fail as a baby." When he began to direct cartoons in 1938, he was dismayed by the ability of Tex Avery and Friz Freleng to create terrific effects and incredible cartoons that he could never have created, and so effortlessly, so naturally and instinctively, without having to analyze them to death. He didn't know how they did it, and neither, apparently, did they.

Jones remembers, "Eddie Selzer always told me that I wasn't in the same class with Friz, and so did Leon. Openly. I thought so, too. I'm a *nave* character, as Bugs would say."

Finally, and after great anguish and further analysis, he came up with the solution: make cartoons that *they* could never have made. By the time the '50s came along, that was exactly what he was doing.

Jones suffered creative agonies at the drawing board; they were apparently visible on his face, and others on the Warner Bros. Cartoons staff got used to seeing them, to the point where Treg Brown remarked, "If he could transfer to paper what is going on with his facial muscles he'd have the world by the tail." But what finally emerged from his tortured analysis, to become a Jones byword and a much-quoted apothegm, is "I believe that when you make films, however much agony goes into them, they should look loose and free . . . only the love should show." The reason Avery and Freleng hit their stride before he did is that they already *knew* that without having to *say* it.

Chuck found hilarious ways to express vulnerable moods; he did incredible things with eyes: a look of horror in which the character's eyes come to resemble a pair of neighboring saucers, each harboring a pea, or in which they become kidney beans of terror, fried eggs of dismay, lamb chops of mute appeal. "Chuck is a highly sensitive man, that's what makes him the artist he really is," claimed Michael Maltese, storyman for Jones almost exclusively after 1949. "That's why when one of Chuck's characters gets hurt you don't feel that they're really hurt. It's like he's going to make them better right away."

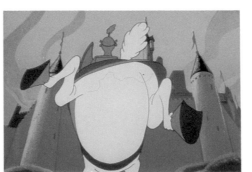

The chemistry between Maltese and Jones was apparent to everyone in the studio. Jones also collaborated brilliantly with layout men Robert Gribbroek and Ernie Nordli, with the inventive Maurice Noble, and with trusted animators Ken Harris, Ben Washam, Abe Levitow, and Lloyd Vaughan to create a dynamic, functioning unit of people who knew how to develop each other's ideas. As animator Phil Monroe remembered his days with the Jones unit, "Our unit was all of a single mind, more or less. We all went to art school and we all tried to better ourselves and to develop under Chuck. As a result, Chuck was known as kind of a boy scout leader—we socialized a lot together, which the guys in other units didn't do, and had a lot of fun together."

Of his other animators, Jones remarks, "Ken Harris was one of the greatest action animators who ever lived. Benny Washam was a good action animator, too, whatever was needed, but he was brilliant at dialogue."

The progression of Jones' visual style is a progression from *more* to less *being more*; the production values of his films get simpler as he proceeds, and each movement gets more expressive. This reaches perhaps its natural limit in *Bully for Bugs* when a matador expresses mood, atmosphere, character, and conflict, simply by flaring a nostril.

"Chuck always had a tendency to get profound," Maltese remembered. "He'd say, 'Yes, this is so . . .' and take off his glasses. I'd say, 'Come off it, Charlie, or I'll kick you in the ass.' Underneath it he was a crazy cartoonist like the rest of us."

"Chuck was a sophisticated kind of guy, and he started educating Bugs," comments Freleng. "He started using words that the average 'dese' and 'dose' guys don't even know, and he started injecting those into the character himself. We had to pull back from that, reminding Chuck that we had to get back to the 'dese' and 'dose' characters. We had to remind each other, in storyboarding and the exchange of our thoughts, to get back on the track [of] what Bugs really was."

Opposite: *Bugs' vulnerability, as interpreted by Chuck Jones in this brilliant sequence from* Knight-Mare Hare, *1955. With his hair dryer still on his head, Bugs finds himself challenged to a duel in medieval England. Unable even to lift the sword he's been tossed, he seems to be surrendering to the inevitable, but as usual calls upon his reserves for one more trick.*
Above: *Cel and background from Chuck Jones'* Barbary Coast Bunny, *1956.* Below: *The matador flares a nostril in* Bully for Bugs, *1953.*

Right: *Chuck Jones' layout drawing of Bugs and Elmer's dance in* What's Opera, Doc?, *1957, is matched nearly exactly by animator Ken Harris in a frame from the finished film. Animator Lloyd Vaughan: "Chuck is very specific about these characters; they look very loose and everything, but they have a lot of planning to them. He has very definite ideas that he wants put in his drawings. He gives us a broad layout, but the little acting innuendoes and things that go in there are pretty much up to the animator." Jones: "The director does three or four hundred drawings for a cartoon, character layouts, with key positions, and from that the animator works. But mine are* still *drawings; the animator's not beholden to use any of them, and shouldn't even try. There are animators who always worked between my extremes, and that wasn't what I wanted. Ken Harris would change it. He'd use it as an idea, but the action would flow thorugh and go beyond it." Maurice Noble: "I really wonder how these animators can go through this accumulation of drawing after drawing that counts up to a funny scene. These funny, funny things that Ken Harris puts together—and yet he's a Terrible-Tempered Mr. Bang, kind of an explosive character. And one would never connect him with this zany animation he would put out." Bottom right: Background painting from the cartoon by Philip DeGuard from layout by Maurice Noble.*

Lloyd Vaughan, one of Jones' long-time animators, has described Jones' directorial method by saying, "Chuck is very specific about these characters; they look very loose and everything, but they have a lot of planning to them. He has very definite ideas that he wants put in his drawings. He gives us a broad layout, but the little acting innuendoes and things that go in there are pretty much up to the animator."

Where varying interpretations of Bugs Bunny are concerned, Jones' feeling was that "Friz's were usually a little more physical. When you think about *Sahara Hare*, and the others, it seemed to me that there were things that happened quickly; Bugs would cleverly do something at the last moment. My Bugs, I think, tended to think out his problems and solve them intellectually a little bit. Also, I insisted upon perhaps a stronger provocation. To me he was a quiet-living rabbit and would never ever engage in anything except perhaps a few pranks, and he'd have fun in jokes and stuff like that, but he would *never* engage in conflict without provocation—*extreme* provocation. In some cases, like *Long-Haired Hare*, he was provoked three times."

What Jones was trying to do with Bugs is most readily apparent in *Homeless Hare*, when The Rabbit finds himself, rabbit hole and all, scooped up by a voracious steam shovel, giving him a vertigo he first attributes to a wild night. The Maxie Rosenbloom of an equipment operator who's made this inadvertent catch listens quietly to Bugs' plea that "Dis is my home. So, uh, put it back where you found it, will ya, please?" and responds with an "Of course I'll put it right back!" that is just a touch *too* sincere.

But the polite bunny takes him at his word, assures him "No hard feelin's," and prepares to snuggle back into his cozy rabbit hole—when the bottom drops out of the

steam shovel and his life, and he's dumped with a marked lack of ceremony into a gravel heap. With the next load of earth plopped on top of him.

All of which is terribly amusing to Mr. Equipment Operator, who enjoys a good, hearty laugh over it on his way out of his cockpit, and is prepared for no more than a momentary irritation when he hears Bugs' "Yoo Hoo! Hoicules! Here's a message for ya!" from high atop the conglomeration of girders.

The message is attached to a brick, and both are dropped directly on his face with a clank, in a point-of-view shot that ought to *hurt*. But the resentment this guy's managed to inspire in only a few seconds, combined with his Rock of Gibraltar face that looks like it could survive worse and probably has, only serve to make the *ferocity* of Bugs' challenge incredibly funny.

The message reads simply:
OKAY HERCULES
YOU ASKED FOR IT
BUGS BUNNY

The rest of the wild, hyperbolic cartoon action proceeds from this set-up: the guy has girders dropped on him, gets catapulted into space by Bugs on the construction elevator, gets dropped into wet cement and dry girders, gets slammed through planks, and, finally, via an elaborate Rube Goldberg machination that Bugs initiates with a single hot rivet, finds a ten-ton boiler dropped on his head—and our vindictive pleasure in seeing all this being visited upon him is totally derived from the innocence and vulnerability Bugs has shown in his opening scene. When The Rabbit has done his worst, his last line to his adversary is "Well, Toodles, do I get my home back, or do I have to get tough?" He gets his home back.

Jones enjoys pitting Bugs against formidable beasts like this equipment operator, the grisly crushers of *Rabbit Punch* and *Bunny Hugged*, and the bull in *Bully for Bugs*—impossible forces that often get the best of him and seem, for a time, beyond even his powers to overcome. When he does, in the end, triumph, his victory is doubly sweet.

Jones' Bugs is carefully motivated and works carefully himself: less impulsive than The Rabbit as seen by the other directors, he has to work it all out. But he draws on reserves deep inside himself, reserves that *Bugs* never agonizes over for a minute.

Above left: *Some 1950s Bugs Bunny memorabila and sheet music. In July of 1949, the Warner Bros. Service Corporation in New York was established specifically for the purpose of handling the licensing of Bugs Bunny and the other Warner characters for toys and other merchandise. Western Publishing's comic book business reached its height in the mid-'50s; Bugs was appearing in his own* Bugs Bunny *series, as well as the* Looney Tunes *and* Merrie Melodies, Porky Pig, Daffy Duck, *and the short-lived* Elmer Fudd *comic books. With his own strip running daily and on Sundays, with children's books and Capitol's records, Bugs was a pervasive element of American culture before he ever appeared on television. There were Bugs Bunny Coloring Contests (opposite) in many cities (the winners received a trip to Hollywood and a visit to the cartoon studio), and a papier-mâché statue of The Rabbit fourteen feet high was built to help celebrate Easter in Kansas City. Above: This 1953 poster demonstrates one more technique from the inventive Warner Bros. sales force.*

Wideo Wabbit, 1959-1964

Bugs was a noticeably older rabbit as he passed his eighteenth year (and gaining fast, about to celebrate his twenty-fifth birthday only two years later). The old gags were beginning to look frayed around the edges, and new ones were not coming along to take their place.

Robert McKimson, who saw it happen, said, "It's toward the end of the '50s and into the early 1960s, just before we closed down, that things got too subtle, with everything underplayed. He became too much of a suave character. You know, you have to progress, and this underplaying was a different way of doing things. Sometimes you don't always progress in the right direction."

It was because of that awareness that "you have to progress" that the Termite Terrace gang was able to keep Bugs hopping, to keep him funny, and to allow him to continue surprising us, for two decades. If that resulted in a mis-step or two somewhere along the line, it only proves that they were human, and proceeding on instinct rather than formula.

But the theatrical cartoon was heading into treacherous waters, where a single mis-step spelled death—heading, actually, in the direction of the two-reel comedy, another victim of neglect by theater owners, who refused pay the higher prices that quality demanded, and their patrons, who took them for granted as long as Hollywood was turning them out and they were getting something for nothing.

Animation crews who had made the adjustment to budgets that seemed less than ideal were now forced to try to adjust to budgets that were even less than that. The cartoons became even shorter than they had been before. Motion was a luxury to be indulged in only in moments of extreme duress. Characters who had been convincingly three-dimensional for two decades were now quite evidently drawings, sliding back and forth across more artwork.

What mattered most was that comedy conveyed through character and expressed through a delicate inter-working of tempo, mood, animated action, and vocal histrionics began to falter and lose its step. A fine line was crossed, somewhere between reversing, or even sending up, the old routines, and replacing them with cardboard substitutes. The result was not so much Bunny Ha-Ha as Bunny Peculiar.

What was happening in Bugs' case was really the disintegration of his collective personality. Termite Terrace had gained and lost personnel at a steady pace since 1940,

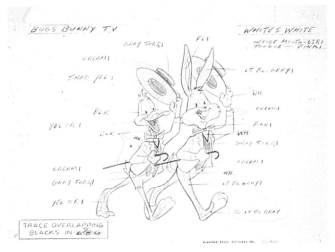

Top: "So what's a rabbit to do?" Bugs seems to be asking in this cel from Friz Freleng's Shishkabugs, 1963. Center: Drawing by Robert McKimson from Dr. Devil and Mr. Hare, 1964. Above: Frame from Freleng's Apes of Wrath, 1959. Above right: Color chart of Bugs and Daffy for The Bugs Bunny Show, which first aired in 1960.

but some of the losses suffered in the late '50s were crippling. The defection of Warren Foster and Michael Maltese to the novelty (and higher salary) of television animation, the loss of Tedd Pierce, the death of Fudd voice Arthur Q. Bryan, the retirement of Carl Stalling, then the death of his arranger, Milt Franklyn, after he'd taken Stalling's place—all these events within the space of a couple of years took their inevitable toll.

"The day of one character chasing another, like Tom & Jerry or Elmer Fudd after The Rabbit, is kind of passé," Freleng remarked in the '60s. "The reaction used to be great, but your theater audiences today are different. The young kids see television and don't go to theaters. They used to line up for the Saturday matinee; they don't even have it anymore. And the older people stay home and watch television. That's why we've got an entirely different kind of audience."

By this time Bugs had become, in effect, a television personality, having premiered as host of his own prime-time network television show in October of 1960, and having given the phenomenal hit *Gunsmoke* a run for its money in its evening slot. It was television that Warner Bros. seemed to see as the future of animation, and, for the moment, it meant that they would recycle their backlog endlessly and cease production.

The last Bugs Bunny theatrical cartoon, *False Hare*, was directed by Robert McKimson from a story by John Dunn and released on July 16, 1964—twenty-four years, to the month, after the release of *A Wild Hare*.

Above: *Pose from model sheet from* The Bugs Bunny Show. Below: *Big Bad Wolf and his nephew try to pass themselves off as rabbits in this color chart for Robert McKimson's* False Hare, *the last theatrical Bugs Bunny cartoon, 1964.*

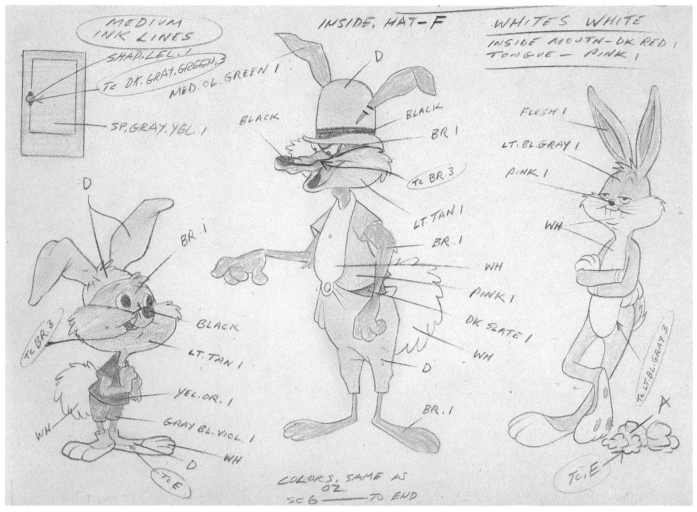

The Unsinkable Bugs Bunny, 1965-1990

"There are just no good parts for rabbits anymore. But then what can you expect? There are no rabbit screenwriters, no rabbit directors. If you ask me, I think the studios are afraid of us now that we're not willing to settle for mere carrots."

—Bugs Bunny, quoted by Gregg Kilday in *The Los Angeles Times*

It was during this period that Bugs Bunny became The Rabbit Who Refused to Die.

The trend in '60s animation was away from the series that had served as entertainment for all ages and all levels of sophistication since 1940, and away from the characters who had been prancing across the screen since just about that time, toward . . . Something Else. *Anything* else, it sometimes seemed, just so long as it wasn't The Cartoon as we'd gotten used to it, as Disney had created it, as Tex Avery had brought it to comic life, and as brilliant practitioners like Freleng, Jones, Jack Hannah, Ward Kimball, Bob Cannon, Paul Julian, and Bill Hanna and Joe Barbera had kept it alive.

Animation critic Michael Barrier noted in 1969, "There's an urge to grind Bugs Bunny and Donald Duck into the dust, not merely to do something that doesn't much resemble Bugs Bunny or Donald Duck."

Most of the medium's characters fell by the wayside at this point. Some enjoyed a brief television career, then faded even from that retirement home.

As it gradually dawned on people that real cartoons were fading from the screen and being replaced by static, talky horrors (sometimes resembling cartoons for the blind, in their inclination toward *describing* every action prior to, after, during, or instead of, its actual performance), a powerful nostalgia developed for the Golden Age they had unwittingly experienced. Something we had grown up with had died!

Bugs' appeal worked, at first, against any comeback attempts. Because he was Warner Bros. star character, management preferred to leave him out of the low-budget efforts the studio produced, or caused to be produced, between 1964 and 1969. The Warner Bros. Studio itself changed hands several times during the ensuing years, and consistent policies were hard to come by. "We get one set of rules to go by," Bob McKimson remarked in the 1970s, "and all of a sudden they sell the studio and we've got another set of rules and another set of people to cater to."

But Bugs lived on as a figure of nostalgia. When his voice artist established the Mel Blanc School of Voice and Commercials, it was chiefly known by its short title, Bugs Bunny Tech. Bugs sold Kool-Aid, in commercials made by Friz Freleng at DePatie-Freleng Enterprises and by Tex Avery at Cascade Productions. Avery enjoyed working with The Rabbit again, but dealing with a celebrity of this magnitude was a little awkward. He was continually astounded by the eternal popularity of his creation. Coming home after a day of work on the Bugs Bunny commercials, he would pass out used Rabbit cels to the kids in his neighborhood. But the existence of a supply only increased the demand, and he found himself besieged by requests for cels long after he'd given away his last one. When he asked one little girl what happened to the batch of cels he'd already given her, she piped up, "My brother takes them to school and sells them for fifty cents apiece!"

Bugs Bunny as a Name, rather than an animated character, appeared in revues staged by Rodger Hess with titles like "The Bugs Bunny Follies," "Bugs Bunny in Space," and "Bugs Bunny Meets the Super-Heroes," in such locations as Madison Square Garden, the Chicago Opera House, and as far afield as Melbourne, Australia, and Caracas, Venezuela.

But then, just as animation was becoming a Lost Art, it began to be appreciated for its own sake. Chuck Jones, who had been producing and directing successful animated television specials since 1970, and had been campaigning during most of that time for the rights to the now-retired Warner Bros. characters, finally received per-

Above: Cel from a Tex Avery Kool-Aid commercial of the late '60s or early '70s. Below and bottom: New animation from recent CBS specials produced by Hal Geer and directed by David Detiege: Bugs Bunny's Thanksgiving Diet, *1979 and* Bugs Bunny's Mad World of Television, *1982.*

Friz Freleng with Bugs at Warner Bros. Animation in early 1980s.

Chuck Jones, at the Museum of the Moving Image, London, 1988.

Above: *Newly-created limited edition cels, based on original sketches or frames from previous productions, have great value as collectors items and are sold through art galleries. Clockwise from top left: by Chuck Jones, Robert McKimson, Friz Freleng, Robert Clampett.*

mission to create two Bugs Bunny half-hours, *Carnival of the Animals* in 1976 and *A Connecticut Rabbit in King Arthur's Court* in 1978. After their success, the viability of the television special as a vehicle for classic clips with freshly animated wraparounds was tested and proved by the Warner Bros. studio itself in a long-running series of new bottles containing vintage wine, starting with *Bugs Bunny's Easter Special* in 1977, and running up to 1989's *Bugs Bunny's Wild World of Sports*. Brand-new seven-minute episodes directed by Friz Freleng and Chuck Jones, and animated by some of the old Warner gangsters, appeared in *Bugs Bunny's Looney Christmas Tales* in 1979, and *Bugs Bunny's Bustin' Out All Over* in 1980.

Although Bugs had never starred in any feature films while he was one of the leading performers in short subjects, he became the lead attraction in a number of compilation features which consisted basically of his best cartoons (what *Variety* called "the WB vaulties"), thanks to the success of MGM's compilation feature *That's Entertainment*.

The first of these, Larry Jackson's *Bugs Bunny Superstar*, was released by United Artists in 1975 and contained no new cartoon footage. But in Chuck Jones' *The Bugs Bunny/Roadrunner Movie* in 1979, Bugs appears as a charming host (in his own home, yet), something after the fashion of the Edward R. Murrow program *Person to Person*, which he'd spoofed when it was new as *Person to Bunny*, and talks us through some retrospective glimpses of his, and Jones', brighter moments. This let loose a succession of Bugs and Daffy features, pouring out regularly for a while to theaters, cable channels, and videocassette outlets, with titles like *Friz Freleng's Looney Looney Looney Bugs Bunny Movie* and *Bugs Bunny's 3rd Movie: 1001 Rabbit Tales*.

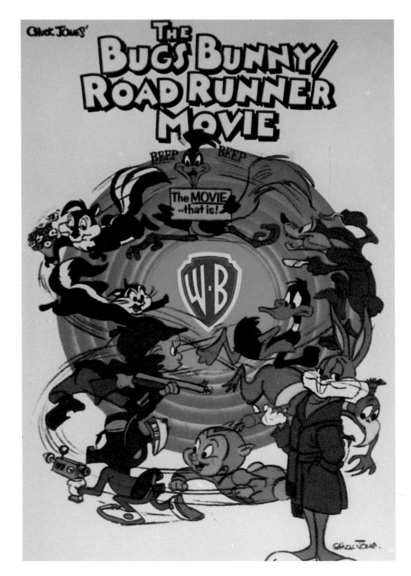

Above and right: Publicity for recent Bugs Bunny compilation features released by Warner Bros. Opposite: Bugs now has a legacy: original oil painting by Chuck Jones based on his own fund-raising poster for New Orlean's Children's Hospital, 1980.

Above: *Studio politics: the Bugs-Daffy rivalry continues to this day in the hallways of Warner Bros. Animation in Burbank, California in this mural created by Richard H. Thomas, Brenda Banks, and Alan Bodner.* Below: *The current Bugs Bunny newspaper comic strip, written by Brett Koth, combines a contemporary look with a design based on the classic theatrical cartoons.*

Bugs was once again an active bunny, returning to life and charming his hordes of admirers anew. And getting more active and more charming ever since. As the Video Age has unfolded, Bugs' progress has been toward a more and more active life, with new specials, surprise appearances, and new theatrical cartoons once again being prepared for the big screen, to compete with the vintage material being discovered and re-discovered by a wider audience every day.

Bugs' chief supervisor today is Edward Bleier, President of the Animation Division for Warner Bros. in New York, and he was an ABC network executive when The Rabbit first went on the air in his evening time slot in 1960; he was in charge of Saturday morning programming when Bugs switched to that time period, and he built the network's Saturday morning schedule around "that Oscar-winning rabbit" and his cronies; going to work for Warner Bros in 1969, "It was a simple switch," he says, "to the opposite side of the desk." It's been his job since then to make sure that Bugs has stayed active—or, as he puts it, "to protect the legacy and make the most of it; but also to do what I could to create new material, to keep Chuck and Friz and Mel gainfully employed, and also to develop a new generation of talents."

Bugs has nearly always been in the company of Freleng, Jones, and many of the other artists who originally nurtured him (such as Bob Givens, who designed him for *A Wild Hare* and went on contributing to the design aspect of many of the later compilation features). But increasingly his life has been governed by the abilities and enthusiasms of a younger crew of writers and directors who had one special qualification for working with the Heckling Hare: they grew up with him.

Kathleen Helppie-Shipley, Bugs' immediate supervisor on the West Coast, remembers becoming acquainted with the character on his Tuesday night prime-time show, when it was still frequently possible to see cartoons in theaters. Hiring talented artists from the same age group with the same experience of the Warners menagerie and the same affection for it—fans-turned-animators like Darrell Van Citters, Terry Lennon, and former animation historian Greg Ford—she is currently attempting, in her words, "to bring the characters into the '90s—not just update them, slap a guitar on Bugs: he was hip and contemporary in the '40s and '50s, and we're maintaining the character integrity and translating that to the '90s.'"

The Bugs Bunny daily newspaper comic strip, operated by its syndicate since the early '40s as a separate enterprise from the cartoons, was eventually brought under the direct supervision of Van Citters at the Warner Bros. Animation Division, for an overhaul in which its graphics were improved and its humor made "more personality-driven" than it had sometimes been in the past.

And, as new projects are planned today, that is where the conentration has remained: keeping Bugs true to the character audiences know from a daily exposure and making him fresh for new generations who don't live in the '50s; keeping his verbal humor as acute as his sight gags, so that his appeal works on two levels and hits all ages simultaneously.

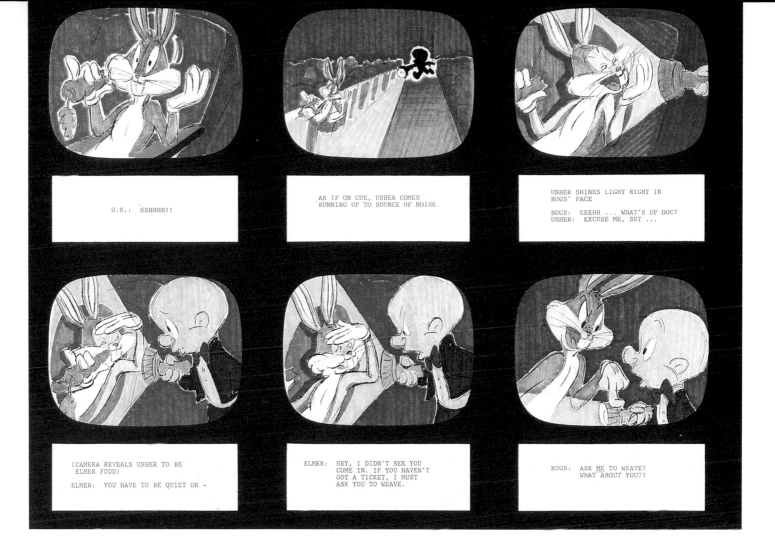

O.S.: `SSHHHH!!`	AS IF ON CUE, USHER COMES RUNNING UP TO SOURCE OF NOISE	USHER SHINES LIGHT RIGHT IN BUGS' FACE BUGS: EEEHH ... WHAT'S UP DOC? USHER: EXCUSE ME, BUT ...
(CAMERA REVEALS USHER TO BE ELMER FUDD) ELMER: YOU HAVE TO BE QUIET OR -	ELMER: HEY, I DIDN'T SEE YOU COME IN. IF YOU HAVEN'T GOT A TICKET, I MUST ASK YOU TO WEAVE.	BUGS: ASK ME TO WEAVE? WHAT ABOUT YOU?!

But Bugs originated as a character in a series of theatrical short subjects, and in today's world, with no demand for a steady stream of such items, new activity for the character is continually in the process of being channeled into other venues, such as public service videos, feature film cameos, and appearances on network television. Talks are under way to get Bugs back to the prime-time television spot he appears to deserve, and, says Bleier, "I have no greater ambition than to find the right idea for a theatrical feature. We can't simply *do* a theatrical feature, because the cartoons are so ubiquitous; we have to find something that is sufficiently different and compelling to *be* a theatrical feature. We're looking, and we're looking hard."

Sometimes, out of the talent and enthusiasm involved, the ideas grow faster than the realities of the marketplace can encompass them. "I frustrate everybody," Bleier admits, "because they still want to do even more production. And I keep saying, 'I'm finding new markets. . . .'"

Through ongoing production that Bugs has clearly influenced (the Roger Rabbit films, for instance, and the upcoming *Tiny Toons* series, featuring the next generation of Warner cartoon characters) the Bugs Bunny legacy survives and endures.

But more importantly, despite all odds, Bugs Bunny himself survives and endures. "When I started working with him," confesses Bleier today, "I liked him; he was very good. But I had no idea that I was working with an American folk classic."

Yet that has become, year after year, the increasingly inescapable fact. Bugs Bunny, one character or many, foole or hero, cartoon or cartoonist, has survived the death of the medium that spawned him, to go on giving us pointers in being the best that we can be.

The Heckling Hare. Couple thousand years old. Ready to carry on for a couple thousand more.

Above: *Storyboard drawings by Darrell Van Citters from the upcoming* Ballot Box Bunny.

4
BUGS BUNNY AND "FRIENDS"

CHUCK JONES
1989

Bugs and Elmer

*Elmer Fudd, in a model sheet
from* Hare Tonic, *1945*

Most people who have a speech impediment the size of Elmer's learn what words to avoid to keep from sounding ridiculous. But, since Elmer had Maltese, Pierce, and Foster writing for him and making him look ridiculous was their job, he seemed to be going *out of his way* to put words in his mouth that would trip up his tongue. So it's not enough that he's got to shout, "You wascawwy wabbit!" at Bugs at every opportunity; in *Stage Door Cartoon* he grows erudite enough to refer to him as "You tweachewous miscweant." And his threat to Bugs and Daffy in *Beanstalk Bunny*, "I'll gwind your bones to make me bwead" has enough trouble striking terror into the heart, without his topping it off, once he's found a pepper mill that should do the trick, with the pleasantry, "This oughta gwind their bones vewy nicewy." Elmer, like Bugs, was truly born and fully fleshed out in *A Wild Hare*, and so shares Bugs' Jubilee celebration with him. Polls have shown that Fudd is still a popular character, scoring higher with adults than most of the child-oriented imaginary characters like the Muppets and the *Sesame Street* bunch.

In Friz Freleng's estimation, "Elmer Fudd wasn't really a villain. He was a pitiful character. There was no credit to a guy who could outsmart Elmer Fudd. You wondered why you didn't hate Bugs for doing what he did to him. You had to invent new opposition for Bugs, because Elmer was just a victim of a smart rabbit." By 1942 the Warners Toonsmiths used him in reversals or spoofs of the familiar rabbit-hunter situation, as they did in *The Hare-Brained Hypnotist, The Old Grey Hare, Hare Remover, Rabbit Fire, Hare Brush*, and *What's Opera, Doc?*

Without changing the basic nature or concept of the character, Elmer's directors and animators developed him into a creature capable of great elasticity, especially in *Hare Remover* and *Hare Tonic*. He eventually reached the point where his *derby* could become as expressive as Bugs' ears if the occasion warranted it, hopping, bouncing, and twirling around when his face and body were incapable of communicating all of his inner turmoil.

Preceding pages: *Because every story requires conflict, and every Warner Bros. cartoon story required being pared down to two characters, max, all of Bugs' "friends" are characters trying to do him in, as Chuck Jones illustrates in a drawing created for this volume.*

The role reversal that was an integral aspect of the hunter-prey charade as enacted by Bugs and Elmer. Elmer in current publicity art from Warners Bros. Animation; Bugs takes on protective coloring in a cel from Friz Freleng's Hare Brush, *1955.*

In their search for bigger and more ferocious antagonists for Bugs, the writers and directors would abandon Elmer for an entire year at a time, only to bring him back again for another round of indignities, because, like Larry "Bud" Melman, he was such a lovable buffoon.

When Elmer was coerced into getting on a stage and performing in *Any Bonds Today?*, it was the start of a new lease on life for the character. In films like *A Corny*

Elmer in one of his moments of true glory, in Chuck Jones' What's Opera, Doc?, *1957; Above: Layout drawings by Jones.* Right: *The scenes as they appear on film, as animated by Ken Harris.*

Concerto, Stage Door Cartoon, What's Up, Doc?, and *Rabbit of Seville*, it was as a performer that he was at his most ludicrous, and, therefore, at his maximum usefulness to the studio. Finally, that became his *only* function, and, in cartoons like *Wideo Wabbit* and *Person to Bunny*, his roles became limited to performance situations in which he only belonged because he didn't fit, and Elmer became an unlikely Mr. Show Business, like Durwood Kirby, Ringo Starr, and Ed McMahon. And Babwa Wawa.

Left: *Drawing by Robert McKimson.* Above: *Elmer's apparent welcome for Bugs turns out to be part of a trap in Robert McKimson's* Easter Yeggs, *1947. Background painted by Richard H. Thomas from a layout by Cornett Wood.*

Left: *"Why did you hit me in the face with a coconut custard pie with whipped cream?" fellow Warner star Humphrey Bogart demands of Elmer in an animation drawing by Virgil Ross from Friz Freleng's* Slick Hare, *1947.* Above: *Scene from* Bugs Bunny's Bustin' Out All Over, *1980.*

Bugs and Daffy

The idea of teaming Bugs and Daffy, possibly the two greatest creations in the history of animated cartoons, was at first unthinkable, then incongruous enough to be funny, now a standard bit to be trotted out whenever a gag is needed. With Porky, Daffy is one of only two major Warner Bros. cartoon stars to be established *before* Bugs, rather than, like most of them, in the wake of his success. Daffy started life as the target of a hunter's rifle, just as Bugs did, and became a comedian through a totally unexpected reaction to that fact. Daffy went on to become the lunatic fringe of his own cartoons, just as Bugs became the moral center of his.

Before comic fireworks could be set off by a confrontation between them, one of the characters would have to undergo a reversal of comic sympathy, to go from being the character we laughed *with* to being the character we laughed *at*.

And it was inevitable, in the combined process of development and deterioration that constitutes the life of a cartoon character, that it would be Daffy who would change, that he would become a parody of himself. As Tex Avery saw Daffy Duck in the late '30s, he was the expression of raw, vital energies. As Friz Freleng and Chuck Jones see him in the '50s, he's just a maladjusted mallard. When the Termite Terrace

Right and opposite*: The Bugs-Daffy relationship is neatly summed up in these two cels from Chuck Jones'* Duck! Rabbit, Duck!, *1953. Daffy's background painted by Philip DeGuard from Maurice Noble's layout.* Left: *The first meeting: Bugs and Daffy encounter each other on screen for the first time in Frank Tashlin's* Porky Pig's Feat, *1943.*

Below: "Ain't I a stinker?" chuckles Bugs as he bedevils Daffy on the drawing board in Chuck Jones' Duck Amuck, 1953. Right: "What a way for a duck to travel—underground!" grouses Daffy in Jones' Ali Baba Bunny, 1957, more or less ignoring the fact that it's no way for a rabbit to travel, either. Top right: Daffy hoists his own petard in a frame from Friz Freleng's Show Biz Bugs, 1957.

delinquents of the '40s cooled down to respectable heads of households in the '50s, Daffy became a victim of the policy of containment that dominated the decade: This lunatic must be confined.

And it was equally inevitable that Bugs' imperviousness to criticism, the fact that he can do no wrong, should itself become a source of comedy at the studio. The

Daffy proves himself a thorn in Bugs' side in two animation drawings from Chuck Jones' TV specials. Below: Carnival of the Animals, *1976.* Left: A Connecticut Rabbit in King Arthur's Court, *1978.* Above: *The Bugs-Daffy "feud" continues: a still from Greg Ford and Terry Lennon's CBS Special,* Bugs Bunny's Wild World of Sports, *1989.*

unstoppable success of their star character was a point of pride to the cartoonists, but like everything else, it was fodder for the laugh-making apparatus.

So for these two to enter into any kind of conflict, it became necessary to make Daffy jealous of The Rabbit's success, to turn him into a black Iago duck. The Bugs-Daffy relationship is one that, like W.C. Fields' famous hatred for Charlie Chaplin, started out in terms of the highest admiration (in *Porky Pig's Feat*), and progressed easily and quickly into a feud. Like another famous Fields feud—his long-running battle with Charlie McCarthy—it was good for business. Daffy's plots against Bugs could even backfire and trip *him* up, with no participation from The Rabbit whatsoever. Didn't matter. Daffy would still snarl and mutter, "So that's the way he wants to play, huh?"

"He is a creature of infinite error," says Chuck Jones of Daffy. "You have to draw him frame by frame, because with each frame he makes a different mistake. Daffy can be fawning and overbearing at the same time, which isn't easy! He rushes in and fears to tread at the same time. To me, he's the most complex character of all. I suspect that I am much more like Daffy than I am at all like Bugs. Within us dwell dreams and realizations. Daffy is a realization, Bugs is a dream. So you have recognition in one character and aspiration in the other."

Bugs and Daffy and Elmer

When Chuck Jones and Mike Maltese had their Big Yes meeting for *Rabbit Seasoning* in November of 1950, they worked up the following dialogue for Bugs and Daffy to exchange after they had dived into Bugs' rabbit hole for cover:

DAFFY: I wonder if Elmer is still around.

BUGS: I know a way to find out.

DAFFY: Well, do it.

BUGS HOLDS DAFFY UP THRU HOLE. THERE ARE SHOTS. DAFFY COMES BACK INTO HOLE AND SAYS: I asked for that.

As the same sequence emerges in the completed film, it's amplified in the following way:

BUGS: (Whispers) Take a peek up and see if he's still around.

DAFFY: (Whispers) Righto!

DAFFY HOISTS HIMSELF UP UNTIL HIS HEAD IS ABOVE GROUND LEVEL. SHOTS ARE HEARD. HE DROPS BACK INTO THE HOLE.

BUGS: Is he still dere?

DAFFY: (Dazed, his beak blasted into a magpie schnoz, in a Mel Blanc frazzled voice) Sthtill lurking about!

BUGS: I tell you what: *You* go up and act as a decoy and lure him *away*!

DAFFY: (No longer sure what's being said) No more for me, thankth! I'm drivin'! (Drops)

The first exchange was funny enough. As the scene finally reaches the screen, the basic comedy of the original idea is maintained, embellished with new jokes and new shadings on the original joke, so that three or four gags are going on at one time. This is the basic reason for the long-standing affection these cartoons have acquired over the years: the way that Bugs' attitude, Daffy's ineptitude, and Elmer's naivetude highlight, overlap, intensify, and ricochet off each other.

Rabbit Seasoning is the second entry (bracketed by *Rabbit Fire* and *Duck! Rabbit, Duck!*) in a splendid series of cartoons written by Maltese and directed by Jones, chronicling the attempts by Daffy Duck to convince Elmer Fudd that it's rabbit season and that he'd better blast Bugs before his time runs out. Through machinations he initiates but can never quite keep track of, Daffy repeatedly winds up being the target himself, and has to keep retrieving his beak from the wrong side of his head. Somehow, this always prompts him to decide that it's Bugs who is "desth*pic*able." It is the most famous authentic trilogy in the history of American studio animation.

As Bugs and Daffy shove the barrel of Elmer's gun back and forth at each other, their gestures reveal their differences: Bugs is so definite about his position when he insists the season is "Duck" that his index finger judiciously applied is enough to steer the barrel appropriately; as Daffy yells "Rabbit!" he has to *leap* at the gun in a panic and shove it away with both fuss-and-feathered hands.

Through insights like this, what becomes apparent is that Bugs is rooted in the forest, secure in his place there. Daffy is still trying to figure himself out. Each wants to be the object of whatever season it *isn't*, but Bugs never loses sight of who he *is*. When Daffy does, he's dead.

Writer Richard Thompson sees the series this way: "Both Bugs and Daffy are con men and talkers, but Daffy talks too much . . . Bugs stands back from a situation, analyzes it, and makes his move; Daffy becomes emotionally involved, loses his distance, and blows it."

The rooted Bugs soon figures out that there must be some root cause for Daffy to bring all this fire and brimstone upon himself, that maybe there's something in him that *likes* this punishment. ("Shoot me again, I enjoy it!" Daffy screams in semi-confession at one point. "I love the smell of burnt feathers and gunpowder and cordite!") Bugs quickly realizes that the easiest option is to get The Duck to prompt his

Above: Scenes from Jones' Rabbit Seasoning: Bugs and Daffy try to play mind games on each other. Daffy, as usual, gets the shotgun blast he had in mind for Bugs.
Opposite: Scenes from Chuck Jones' Rabbit Fire: Bugs and Daffy try to convince Elmer that it is, respectively, duck season and rabbit season; then, that they are, respectively a duck and a rabbit; then a female hunter and a loyal hunting dog. Finally, it turns out to be Elmer season.

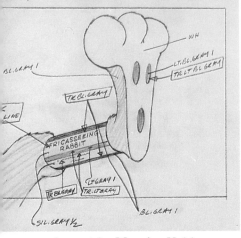

Layout by Maurice Noble

own destruction. Just a little finagling, and he'll have Daffy screaming, "I *demand* that you shoot me now!" And as long as Elmer's around, he'll get his wish.

The comedy of Elmer, used simply as a dupe, is that he seems unable either to comprehend or to enter into the debate, and becomes a sort of reliable idiot automaton, firing on cue—like a computer that puts "gzortenplatt" up on the screen because the buttons for those letters were pushed. If Bugs can convince Elmer it's baseball season, he'll run off shooting at a baseball.

In these conflicts, as Roger Bullis put it, the forest eventually "seems more like a vaudeville stage," in which "the forest creature ends up pursuing the unsuspecting hunter . . . The woods has turned into a Never-Never Land where the hunter shoots when told to do so by the hunted creatures, where the animals delight in semantic contests, and where giant elephants appear at a moment's notice."

Below: Scenes from Chuck Jones' Duck! Rabbit, Duck!, 1953. The proliferation of seasons grows truly Byzantine, with Elmer finally convinced by Bugs, as the most implausible game warden in the history of charades, that, in spite of snow on the ground, it's really baseball season and he should be hunting baseballs. Daffy finds to his chagrin that it's actually duck season, and comes to the conclusion that this makes Bugs "deshpicable."

Left: *Cameraman Ken Moore photographing* Duck! Rabbit, Duck! *in 1952, with a pile of Daffy Duck cels at the ready. Personality animation is still, in spite of years of technical advances, an irretrievably frame-by-frame process, with the animator making the key drawings for each movement—after scores of story, concept, and layout sketches have already been made and exposure sheets and/or bar sheets filled out, to indicate the way the writer, the director, and the layout person envision the scene, and model sheets have been prepared to demonstrate the way each character should look in a variety of poses. The action will still not look smooth until the in-between drawings have been made by the animator's assistant(s), linking up the key drawings in a completed movement. These drawings are sometimes filmed, producing a pencil test, which can be projected and studied to ensure that the action is smooth and convincing; but this stage is often bypassed when the production is short on time and/or funds. The animation drawings are finally traced in ink on transparent sheets of acetate (celluloid at one time, giving rise to the name "cel"), then painted in color, or opaqued, on the reverse side. After that, they are ready to be photographed, one at a time, usually at the rate of two frames of film per cel over painted backgrounds, as Ken Moore is doing here. There will be a quiz on this tomorrow.*

Bugs and Yosemite Sam

"The only two things a pirate'll run fer is money and public office," says Sam in *Daffy Duck's Movie: Fantastic Island.*

In a move to counteract the insistent insipidity of Elmer Fudd, to find a character explosive enough to engage in combat with the unfazable rabbit, Michael Maltese, Friz Freleng, and Hawley Pratt designed Yosemite Sam with an eye to making him as *small* a character with as *big* a voice as they could imagine, all noise and a yard high.

Maltese remembered, "I was going to call him Texas Tiny . . . Wyoming Willie . . . Denver Dan. We were deliberately going for a location to make it Western. So I called him 'Yosemite Sam.' I had never been to Yosemite, but 'Yosemite Sam' *sounded right*. He could almost steal the picture from Bugs. His temper was larger than he was . . ."

With characteristics attributed variously to Freleng and to The Terrible-Tempered Mr. Bang from the old "Toonerville Trolley" comic strip, Sam was an instant success. "We didn't try to make him likable," says Freleng, Sam's exclusive director for most of Termite Terrace's operation. "We did just the opposite; we made the meanest character in the whole world. But they liked him in spite of that. Guys like Yosemite Sam snapped up your picture, because Sam was such a violent character, and he didn't have to stop and think and plot, like Elmer did." Freleng also confirmed what Mel Blanc always claimed about Sam's voice being the "roughest, toughest" voice in his entire repertoire: "When he yells like Yosemite Sam, boy, he can tear the walls down!"

Sam underwent perhaps less evolution than any other major character in cartoon studio history. As he appeared in his first film, *Hare Trigger*—roaring at Bugs, "I'm Yosemite Sam! The meanest, toughest, rip-roarin'est, Edward Everett Horton-est hombre, what ever packed a six-shooter!"—so he would remain, essentially unchanged, for the next forty years of his life. (Although his origins may precede his name and the proper color scheme: the Southern sheriff in *Stage Door Cartoon* is mighty close to the eventual Sam.)

Once Bugs heard his opening line (or whatever variant was dreamed up for the adventure at hand), he sized up his opponent and figured out the most expedient line of attack. Sam would rage on, red hair ablaze, putting on a magnificent show; but as his dialogue revealed, as well as any explosion that blasted away his hat and singed his moustache (as in *Buccaneer Bunny*), there was very little underneath all that shrubbery.

Right: Sam's first model sheet.

Animation critic Greg Ford has described it best: "Yosemite Sam was risible and fallible by virtue of his *over*-aggressiveness, outwittable and outsmartable by virtue of his easily galled and consternated, anything-you-can-do-I-can-do-better desire to prove his gumption and gusto; in *High Diving Hare*, Bugs Bunny can hornswaggle Yosemite Sam again and again to do those dare-devil, death-defying dives from the platform's dizzying heights by simply daring him to 'step across this line' ('Ah'm a'steppin',' Sam would foolhardily say, and down he'd go)."

When Jailer Sam locks Prisoner Bugs in his cell in *Big House Bunny*, it takes little convincing on Bugs' part to sell Sam on the idea that he's locked Bugs *out* and himself *in*. He's quick to reverse the situation—but too quick to pay attention to the fact that he had it right the first time.

Sam too has been a victim of the studio's penchant for self-satire, in scenes like the opening of *Rabbitson Crusoe*, where his serrated, unpolished voice is heard on the soundtrack, narrating the story of his shipwreck and survival on a South Seas island in the kind of florid seventeenth-century prose appropriate to Defoe's original hero, doing what might politely be described as the most unsuccessful James Mason impression on record.

Seemingly designed to show off the combined wonders of the Technicolor process and the RCA soundtrack, Sam came equipped with two built-in absurdities. Mel Blanc pointed out one of them: "He's a little cowboy from Yosemite—which is in California—but he talks like a Texan." The other came about because he was conceived as a Western holdup man, and was given a black mask shading his eye area, with both eyeballs jutting wildly out from the shadows. But to keep the character from being trapped in the Western milieu, Friz and his story men in subsequent pictures put him on a pirate ship, south of the Mason-Dixon line, in the middle of the Sahara desert, in a medieval castle, and even in ancient Rome—and wherever Sam went, there went his Lone Ranger mask, however preposterous, incongruous, or anachronistic; the little guy'd look naked without it.

Above: Sam realizes the girl he was about to marry was Bugs Bunny in these great animation drawings by Virgil Ross for Friz Freleng's Hare Trimmed, *1953. Above left: Sam is his usual genial self in this publicity pose.*

Above: *Cel from Friz Freleng's* Wild and Wooly Hare, *1959, married to a background from a different film*. Right: *Though Yosemite Sam started life as a Western outlaw, he seems to be best remembered as a pirate, as he appears here in* Captain Hareblower. Opposite top: *Sam in a cel and background from a recent production*. Opposite bottom: *Nearly forty years after they first met, Sam is still able to move Bugs to tears. A scene from Friz Freleng's feature-length compilation* Bugs Bunny's 3rd Movie: 1001 Rabbit Tales, *1982*.

Bugs and Marvin Martian

As Bugs' opponents were getting larger, noisier, more and more vicious, blood-thirsty, savage, and insane, it occurred to Chuck Jones and Michael Maltese that there might be humor to be gained from the *least* noisy but *most* destructive creature imaginable. Out of this thinking emerged the Martian who was eventually tagged Marvin, an alien equipped with firepower enough to blast the planet Earth out of his way on a whim, and with the strength and endurance of string cheese. Marvin never gets bombastic or pretentious about the bomb he plans to detonate and destroy Life As We Know It. He gets no surge of power contemplating the havoc he is capable of wreaking; he only fusses when his "Illudium Pew-36 Explosive Space Modulator" (which he over-articulates, as if we were likely to confuse it with a similar device) isn't right where he put it—in a voice apparently borrowed from the scientist who fed Bugs his vitamin-fortified carrots in *Super Rabbit*.

A *pedantic* Martian is the great concept here. Bugs is usually forced to conquer this extraterrestrial foe without the aid of impressive hardware or software, without the use of anything digital or anything with silicon in it. He fights back as the Brooklynese version of the Heckling Hare always did—with a sense of humor, *joie de vivre*, and his spunky variety of Yankee ingenuity. And by turning his own weapons against him. Bugs has defeated Marvin as soon as he's upset his concept of the universe. Bugs Bunny's cartoons with Marvin raise the possibility that when we encounter alien life forms, we may have a thing or two to tell them, whether they are a more "advanced" race than we are or not.

From Chuck Jones' Hare-Way to the Stars, *1958. Right: Bugs remarks conversationally that there's no sense in finding a way to get back to Earth if it's not going to be there anyway, before he absorbs the full impact of what he's talking about. Above: Marvin's reinforcements. Layout by Maurice Noble, background painted by Philip DeGuard.*

Left: *Poses from* Hare-Way to the Stars *model sheet. Above: Bugs and Marvin continue to develop their relationship, in a cel from Jones'* Spaced Out Bunny, *1980, merged with a background from his* Haredevil Hare, *1948, painted by Peter Alvarado from a layout by Robert Gribbroek.*

113

Bugs and Wile E. Coyote

When trickster tales were told by the Southwest American Indians, it was the Coyote, not the Heckling Hare, who starred. But there was one important difference in the way the stories worked: in American Indian folklore, as in Warner Bros. cartoons, the Coyote had a tendency to get caught in his own traps.

Wile E. Coyote is so clever that, when Bugs puts a combination lock on his rabbit hole in *To Hare Is Human*, the Coyote erects a window near the spot, so that he can break in and pick the lock.

Chuck Jones' contests between his two favorite characters create not the comic combustion of a duo like Bugs and Yosemite Sam, but the static tension of a chess tournament between mismatched players. Bugs' repeated "Checkmates", delivered with express train speed and nitroglycerine force, highlight the comic counterpoint that is going on in this competition: between self-assurance and self-importance, between being centered and being self-centered, between a cool head and cold logic. This contest is no contest.

As Bugs notes, "Even a genius gets the message after a while."

Above: *Wile E. Coyote is not quite certain how to react when Bugs greets him with "Daddy! You're back from Peru!!" in this Chuck Jones layout for his cartoon* Rabbit's Feat, *1960. Right and opposite: Background layouts by Maurice Noble and Corny Cole for Jones'* Compressed Hare, *1961, showing the respective abodes where Bugs and the Coyote call upon each other while developing strategies. "Are you in, genius? Are you in, capable? Are you in, describable?" muses Bugs when he lays eyes on Wile E.'s pretentious mailbox (below opposite). The sketch of Bugs' more modest shingle (above opposite) is the basis for the background painted by Philip DeGuard and William Butler (right).*

114

A Chuck Jones drawing of Wile E., from a Roadrunner cartoon

Bugs and the Tasmanian Devil

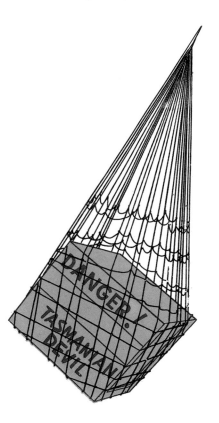

According to the 1989 Walker poll, the most exciting of the Warner Bros. characters is Bugs' most mindless, most ferocious antagonist, the Tasmanian Devil (or, as he came to be known, "Taz Boy," from a fan's letter). "Taz" owes his existence to two things. The first is the search for ever more mindless, ever more ferocious antagonists for Bugs. If Yosemite Sam is a better answer than Elmer Fudd, then the next logical step is a growling beastie, viciousness unadulterated by awareness. The second is the quest for more and more remote, unpredictable cartoon characters, the attempt to get away from the endless cats and dogs and mice.

As Bob McKimson remembered the genesis, "That was when Sid Marcus was writing for me, so we were kicking around different types of characters, and I said, 'About the only thing that we *haven't* used is a Tasmanian Devil.' He said, 'A *what?*' He didn't even know what they were. And so we just started talking about it and came up with this character." The reason that McKimson *did* know what a Tasmanian Devil was had to do with the fact that he "worked a lot of crossword puzzles, and these things came up every once in a while . . ."

This was the kind of quest that resulted, in the Jones unit, in the creation of the Roadrunner and the Coyote, and like those characters, "Taz Boy" has a name that is incidental, subordinate to his species. Baroque enough that there should *be* such a cartoon character as a Roadrunner or a Tasmanian Devil; a name would just be excess baggage.

When Mel Blanc began to develop a voice for this new character, he asked, all innocence, "What does he sound like?" and was told, "Nobody has ever heard one." So he was compelled to ad-lib some kind of guttural gravelly gargle, once transcribed as "—eccawchkupkekupke—." Blanc testified that the experience of doing this one "doesn't make me jump with joy, I'll tell you that!"

In a way, this sense of a primordial destructiveness made Bugs' most ferocious opponent his biggest pushover, as well as the most graphic illustration of Joel Chandler Harris' dictum that brains would always win out over brawn. Because "Taz Boy" falls for any ploy Bugs Bunny can think up. In *Dr. Devil and Mr. Hare*, Bugs shows "Taz" an abstract painting and says, "Look at this mirror." He wilts. There is no trick too obvious, no disguise too transparent, no gag too old to bring the Tasmanian Devil to a complete and utter halt, his drooling growl transformed into a look of absolute confusion, his Yosemite Sam ferocity instantly reduced to the most total be-Fudd-lement.

Elements from Robert McKimson's Tasmanian Devil cartoons. Above: *This cel from* Bill of Hare, *1962, demonstrates that this is not an animal to be treated casually.* Right: *A model sheet indicates the comically fierce visage of the predator.*

Left: *This cel from the first of the "Taz" pictures,* Devil May Hare, *1954, illustrates what happens when the brainless brawn tangles with the Heckling Hare; trying to cope with having an inflatable life raft inflate inside him, complete with oar.* Below left: *Layout from* Bedevilled Rabbit, *1957, is more specific about who should observe caution. This includes rabbits.* Below: *A McKimson drawing of Bugs and Taz.*

. . . and Other Friends

Witch Hazel: Bewitched Bunny, *1954;* Broom-Stick Bunny, *1956;* A Witch's Tangled Hare, *1959.*

The Gremlin: (not Vendel Vilkie), Falling Hare, *1943.*

Clyde Rabbit: His Hare Raising Tale, *1951;* Yankee Doodle Bugs, *1954*

Junior Bear: Bugs Bunny and the Three Bears, *1944.*

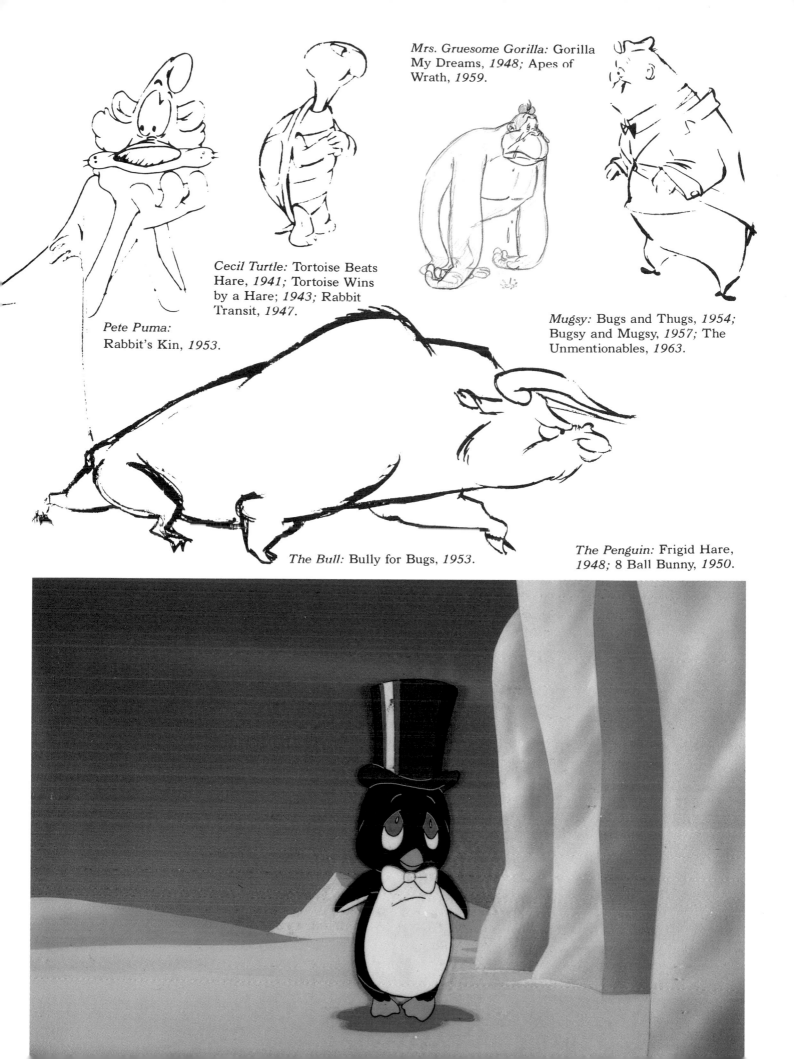

Mrs. Gruesome Gorilla: Gorilla My Dreams, *1948;* Apes of Wrath, *1959.*

Cecil Turtle: Tortoise Beats Hare, *1941;* Tortoise Wins by a Hare; *1943;* Rabbit Transit, *1947.*

Pete Puma: Rabbit's Kin, *1953.*

Mugsy: Bugs and Thugs, *1954;* Bugsy and Mugsy, *1957;* The Unmentionables, *1963.*

The Bull: Bully for Bugs, *1953.*

The Penguin: Frigid Hare, *1948;* 8 Ball Bunny, *1950.*

5
BUGS BUNNY'S GREATEST HITS

Note: I have chosen sixteen films, which for me capture just about everything that is great about Bugs Bunny as a character. This list has been compiled through careful consideration, the screening of every Bugs Bunny film at least once, and consultation with the present staff of Warner Bros. Animation as well as several outside experts. But, finally, it is my list. For every fan of Bugs Bunny there would probably be a different list of "Greatest Hits."

The fact that this list is being published in a book does not mean that its maker presumes it is the *only* such list possible, or that its maker is unaware that there are plenty of Bugs Bunny cartoons left over which have engendered more than their share of admiration and affection. One could just as easily include, for instance, *Racketeeer Rabbit, Gorilla My Dreams, Acrobatty Bunny, A Wild Hare, Long-Haired Hare, Tortoise Wins By a Hare, Bugs Bunny and the Three Bears, Stage Door Cartoon, Hare Trigger, Hare Tonic, The Big Snooze, High Diving Hare, A Hare Grows in Manhattan, Sahara Hare, Duck! Rabbit, Duck!, Broomstick Bunny, Rabbit Fire, Ali Baba Bunny, Beanstalk Bunny*, and any one of about fifty other pictures. The Bugs Bunny cartoons are probably best remembered as the greatest and most prolific *series* of cartoons in the history of animation, and I have singled out a few isolated examples which, for me, indicate how great certain entries in that series could be. Description is my aim, not prescription. By leaving out what is perhaps *your* particular favorite Bugs Bunny cartoon I have not attempted to imply that your judgment is warped, or that you don't know Bugs Bunny.

I have said only, "I love *these* cartoons, I think they're great films, and here's my best explanation why." And I'm sticking with that.

Previous pages: *Background painted by Richard H. Thomas from layout by Cornett Wood for Robert McKimson's* What's Up, Doc?, *1950.* Left and right borders: *Frames from the Bugs Bunny title scene appended to all of Bugs' cartoons from the mid-'40s on.* Above and opposite: *Just a few of Bugs' memorable misadventures not included in this particular selection of Bugs Bunny's best.* Above: *Chuck Jones'* Rabbit Fire, *1951.* Opposite top: *Chuck Jones'* Long-Haired Hare, *1949.* Opposite bottom: *Friz Freleng's* High Diving Hare, *1949. Only the author's intransigence has kept these and other fine cartoons out of the pantheon.*

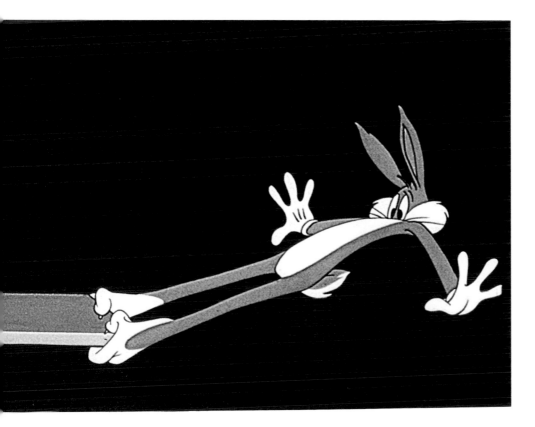

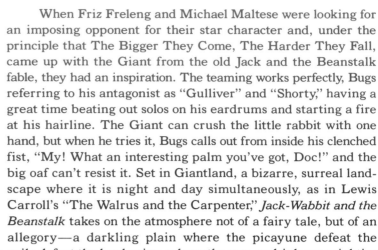

Supervision by I. Freleng;
Animation by Jack Bradbury; Story
by Michael Maltese; Musical
Direction by Carl W. Stalling.
Released in the Merrie Melodies
Series June 12, 1943.

When Friz Freleng and Michael Maltese were looking for an imposing opponent for their star character and, under the principle that The Bigger They Come, The Harder They Fall, came up with the Giant from the old Jack and the Beanstalk fable, they had an inspiration. The teaming works perfectly, Bugs referring to his antagonist as "Gulliver" and "Shorty," having a great time beating out solos on his eardrums and starting a fire at his hairline. The Giant can crush the little rabbit with one hand, but when he tries it, Bugs calls out from inside his clenched fist, "My! What an interesting palm you've got, Doc!" and the big oaf can't resist it. Set in Giantland, a bizarre, surreal landscape where it is night and day simultaneously, as in Lewis Carroll's "The Walrus and the Carpenter," *Jack-Wabbit and the Beanstalk* takes on the atmosphere not of a fairy tale, but of an allegory—a darkling plain where the picayune defeat the mammoth, where the agile defeat the lumbering, where the pen-and-ink are mightier than the sword, where the meek figure out ways to inherit the earth.

It's not as if Bugs' victory is cut and dried. "I'm so smart sometimes it almost frightens me," he boasts when he talks the Giant into a duel, realizing that his opponent's twenty paces will take him halfway around the world and well out of his own harm's way. But some earth-shaking tremors tell Bugs he's miscalculated: the twenty paces are enough to walk the bozo *all* the way around the circumference of the globe, and he's patiently counting out the last few steps as he looms on the opposite horizon.

Whether Bugs can defeat this behemoth just by being a quicker thinker is pointedly the object of the game. "You think you're pretty C-A-T smart, don't ya?" the Giant taunts Bugs, trapping him inside what is for him a normal-sized drinking glass. But Bugs, hermetically sealed in this container, spontaneously generates not only the glass cutter that will save his life, but the showcards that will make it look like entertainment—the last one reads, "Back in 15 minutes," a span the lummox prepares to time out with precision on his wrist-grandfather clock while The Rabbit makes his getaway.

It's not hard, even at this remove, to see how a cartoon like *Jack-Wabbit and the Beanstalk* could have provided an accessory delight to an audience then engaged in a struggle for survival against an enemy claiming to have an inherent physical superiority, to be a race of Supermen.

*Frames from the finished film.
Below: Bugs, faced with superior
strength and firepower times
100, gets the best of the Giant
and has him enjoying it. Below
right: He can hardly conceal his
getaway from an inverted glass,
so he turns it into a sidewalk
demonstration of his handy-
dandy glass cutter.*

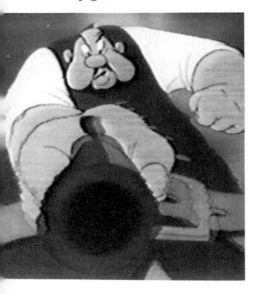

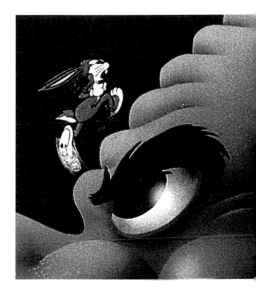

"Comparable to Disney's," said a Chicago exhibitor, when he played this cartoon in 1943. This was meant to be a compliment, but the remark contained a hidden irony. The obvious precedent for this cartoon is the still-famous Mickey Mouse adventure of 1938, *The Brave Little Tailor*, in which Mickey, as the tailor who gets in trouble by boasting, "I killed seven with one blow," finally conquers his giant by stitching him inside his own clothes with the tools of the tailor trade: a simple needle and thread. In 1938, it was inconceivable that the wiseguys of Termite Terrace could ever compete with the exquisite animation, impeccable story construction, and magnificent fairy-tale atmosphere of something like *The Brave Little Tailor*.

By 1943, the star power of Bugs Bunny had made such quibbling academic. With personality rather than technique, with sight gags and wisecracks rather than fairy tales, with agility rather than bulk, with brains rather than muscle, Bugs brings down his Giant.

Above and left: *About to be crushed in the Giant's fist, he reads his palm and teases him about the secrets contained in his heartline. He causes his adversary to furrow his brow, then uses it as an escape route to the scalp, where he loses himself in the foliage.*

Below: *Model sheet of the Giant.* Right: *"So long, joiky! Send me a postcard from Alba-koike!" Bugs calls to the Giant in the scene from which this cel is taken.* Opposite: *Another cel from this production, in which Bugs gloats, "You know, I'm so smart sometimes it almost frightens me," prior to being frightened, instead, by the Giant's next approach.*

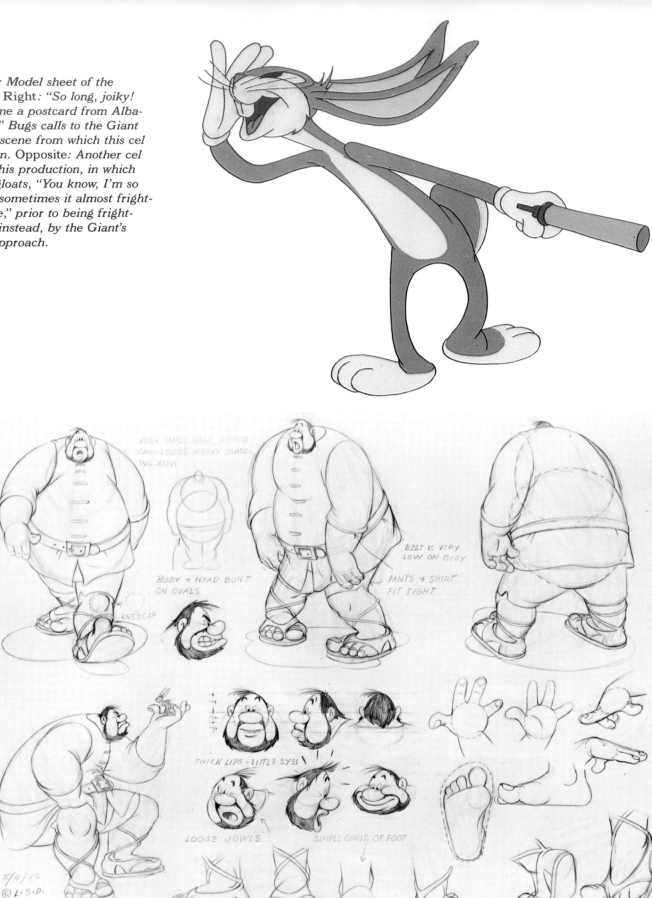

"CORNY CONCERTO"

Featuring Porky Pig and Elmer Fudd. Supervision by Robert Clampett; Story by Frank Tashlin; Animation by Robert McKimson; Musical Direction by Carl W. Stalling. Released in the Merrie Melodies Series September 18, 1943.

Above: *Elmer Fudd, doing his best impression of Deems Taylor hosting* Fantasia, *with a five o'clock shadow and a recalcitrant shirt front. Below: Animation drawing by Rod Scribner for the final scene; its corresponding frame in the final film is on opposite page, lower right.*

Recognized as a standout in its day, singled out as a favorite ever since, this unique picture features Bugs in only its first half, but that small "Tales from the Vienna Woods" episode is nevertheless a unique and remarkable entry in The Rabbit's long career.

This delirious lampoon of *Fantasia* is saturated with that most elusive of essences, Comic Atmosphere. Elmer Fudd, with a five o'clock shadow rendering him a cross between Deems Taylor and Emmett Kelly, urges us to "wisten to the wippwing whythms of the woodwinds, as it wowws awound and awound—and it comes out here!" In pure narrative terms, the events transpiring in the episode are predictable and true to formula. But as danced out by Bugs, Porky, and Porky's hunting dog, they form an impudent comic ballet, in which they and the "Stwauss" music render each other incongruous, absurd.

Clampett never directed animation more outrageously rubbery, more self-mockingly hyper, more satyric. When Porky and his dog camouflage themselves in a bush while stalking Bugs, the bush becomes a new character, tiptoeing stealthily in perfect imitation of the hunters, in perfect synch with the music, in perfect defiance of the order of nature. Perfect. When the hunting dog snaps to pointerly attention, he vibrates into place like jello hardening in time lapse. The green and purple backgrounds seem to grow more abstract as the scene progresses. When a squirrel in a green tree ends up with Porky's rifle and takes aim, it rolls into position like a trunk aimed by an elephant, and his intended victims feign a preposterous pose of fawning mock-fright that approaches believability from the wrong direction. When Bugs pulls off one more phony death scene, he *deflates*.

The resulting balance between an out-of-control *looseness* of movement and a razor-sharp *precision* of atmosphere is awe-inspiring, the kind of achievement in animation that was never going to happen at Disney's and has rarely been matched anywhere else. Today, when any full animation is considered quality stuff, we're not likely to see the brilliant *comic* animation in *A Corny Concerto* equalled, much less surpassed.

Above and opposite page: *Frames from the final film.* Upper left: *Aiming the blunderbuss.* Upper right: *Judging from this pose, Bugs Bunny & Co. have either just been shot or just been asked to pretend they have. This and the ensuing scenes were animated by Rod Scribner.* Bottom: *Boobs in the wood. Bugs' bra and tutu have no source other than the music.*

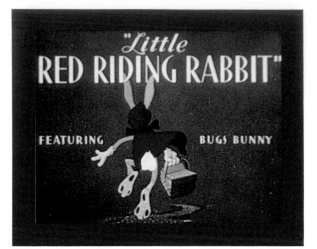

Supervision by I. Freleng; Story
by Michael Maltese; Animation
by Manuel Perez; Voice
Characterizations by Mel Blanc;
Musical Direction by Carl Stalling.
Released in the Merrie Melodies
Series January 4, 1944.

*Opposite: Frames from the
finished film. As the action
progresses, Red shows Bugs the
rabbit she's got in her basket;
Bugs tries to con the Wolf into
believing he's an informant, spill-
ing the beans on where the real
Bugs Bunny is hiding, and in one
case, turns out to be right; the
Wolf gets his own bum's rush
right in the middle of the one
he's trying to give Red; Bugs
converts the Wolf from an offen-
sive to a defensive posture, and
soon has him right in the swing
of things; and, concealed inside
the Wolf's nightie, Bugs makes
creative use of some burning
embers.*

*Right: Animation drawing of the
Wolf stealthily making his way
into Grandma's house.*

One more fairy-tale lampoon, but this one, given Maltese's wit, Freleng's timing, and the interplay of no less than three vivid and memorable characters (somewhat of an extravagance in the dire straits of Warner Bros. economics), has emerged as a perennial favorite among Warner cartoon fans and, seen with an audience, always knocks 'em dead.

Bugs is the bunny that wartime bobby-soxer Red Riding Hood is taking to Grandma's as a gift—"Ta *have!*" as she makes redundantly apparent. But Granny is working the swing shift at Lockheed and, in fact, never even appears. The Wolf (who runs through the bulk of the footage wearing Grandma's nightie) is one of those gravelly-voiced, thick-headed scoundrels Bugs has such an easy time with. Between the Heckling Hare and Red Riding Hood, who keeps wanting to ask questions like isn't the Wolf's nose awfully big for her Grandma's face "ta *have,*" the fearsome Beast is being needled to death. The degree of the Wolf's patience with Red is indicated by his answer to the nose remark: "OK, Yeahyeahyeahyeah, sure-sure, Iknow, thanksalot, goodbyegoodbyegoodbyegoodbye!"—all an accompaniment to a bum's rush to the door.

But he's apparently being caught up in The Rabbit's high spirits; Bugs uses his old ploy of mimicking his adversary in order to turn the tables and get the adversary to mimic *him*, and soon has him singing "Put On Your Old Grey Bonnet" with evident glee (a potential recruit for the Evident Glee Club). When Red spoils his fun with another "Hey, Grandma," his irritation at losing the rhythm is as clearly visible as his delight in getting back into the swing of "Your Old Grey Bonnet." It takes him more than a couple of beats to wake up to the fact that Bugs, his ostensible quarry, has vanished.

But that's OK. Bugs Bunny comes back to point out Bugs Bunny's hiding places, jumping from one to the other, whistling frantically, pointing like a monkey, jump-cutting from hiding place to hiding place (a bold bit of film technique that, like most of the Warner innovations, saved money), creating a great effect of speed—too much speed for Bugs, apparently: in one of the hiding places he's actually caught hiding!

The intrusion of wartime references into a classic fairy tale looks a little self-conscious today, but it fits in well with the notion of a wisecracking rabbit, as well as a breathlessly paced, high-comedy cartoon. It's another way of saying it's the middle of the twentieth century and the old rules don't apply anymore—including the resolution of the tale. Bugs jams the Wolf into a punishing position, suspended over a shovelful of burning embers, his arms loaded down with half the furniture in the house, then gets interrupted one *more* time by his Martha Raye of a Red Riding Hood, and his patience snaps. In the kind of turnaround Jean Renoir pulled off in *Boudu Saved From Drowning* and Ingmar Bergman would later use to great effect in *Virgin Spring,* Bugs rescues the Wolf by putting Red in his place, then enjoys a carrot with him for the finale. This looks like the beginning of a beautiful friendship.

The audience's burst of enthusiastic laughter at this conclusion makes the comic statement clear: It's only in fairy tales that the Good Guys don't have a little Beast in them.

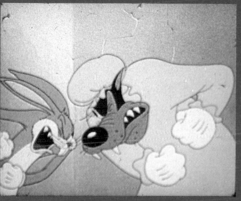

The "OLD GREY HARE"

Featuring Elmer Fudd. Directed by Robert Clampett; Animation by Robert McKimson; Story by Michael Sasanoff, Voice Characterization by Mel Blanc; Musical Direction by Carl W. Stalling. Released as a Bugs Bunny Special in the Merrie Melodies Series October 28, 1944.

This must be the only Bugs Bunny cartoon in existence in which Bugs never once appears in his usual form. Bob Clampett piles a flashback onto a flash-forward (as if just *one* of those conceits weren't enough for a seven-minute cartoon). Bugs appears first as an elderly, infirm rabbit, fit for an Old Rabbit's Home, in what is supposed to be the year 2000, then as an infant rabbit being *remembered* by the elderly rabbit, but nowhere does he appear as the familiar Bugs Bunny. The elderly rabbit himself is one of the jokes, modeled after the look adopted by young Midwestern farmhands of the Gay Nineties when they were old country yokels in 1944, rather than any look the senior citizens of 2000 A.D. could be expected to adopt. And his "What's up, Pruneface?" greeting to Elmer assumes that Dick Tracy's villains are still items of recent memory in the year 2000.

It's all part of Bob Clampett's general technique of piling absurdity atop absurdity, in what is one of his most popular, and probably his greatest, Bugs Bunny cartoon. It's also part of Clampett's ability to *stretch* the character, the extremity of the age range provided by this single cartoon being all Bugs really needs to give us a full perspective on his being, a sense of his living a total life. Even in old age, we learn, Bugs is more active and spry than most teenagers, and the extremes of his animation are genuinely *extreme*.

It's also part of a general pattern of formula reversal that had been at work at the studio since *The Hare-Brained Hypnotist* in 1942, providing turnabouts, parodies, off-the-wall interpolations, unlikely variations on any established theme, whatever it took to avoid staleness and redundancy.

But it only goes to reinforce the existing relationship between Bugs and Elmer. When Elmer shoots Bugs with his "Buck Rogers Lightning-Quick Rabbit Killer," it's just a prelude to getting himself shoved into the grave Bugs has dug (ostensibly for himself), buried alive, then blown up with a bomb that rattles the final That's All, Folks title. *The Old Grey Hare* is also probably the only Bugs Bunny cartoon to make a comment on old age, and it's all too true: when Elmer loses what Bugs represents for him, he's as good as dead.

Above: Frames from the completed film.

Below: *Model sheet showing the extremes of the aging process for both Bugs and Elmer. Opposite and left: Layout drawings.*

133

Directed by I. Freleng; Story by Michael Maltese; Animation by Manuel Perez, Ken Champin, Virgil Ross, and Gerry Chiniquy; Layouts and Backgrounds by Hawley Pratt and Paul Julian; Voice Characterization by Mel Blanc; Musical Direction by Carl Stalling. Released as a Bugs Bunny Special in the Looney Tunes Series February 2, 1946.

Below and opposite far right: Model sheet drawings showing the design for your basic Gas-House Gorilla. Below right: The Gorillas demolish the Tea Totalers as they conga around the bases.

In a movie scene populated by *Field of Dreams*, *Bull Durham*, *Eight Men Out*, and *The Natural*, it's obvious that baseball means more on the American screen than a game played with a ball and a stick. It's become everything from a visual metaphor for the nature of the American character, to a ritual test of manhood, to a path to immortality. Like the American West, the baseball diamond has charted out a cinematic territory of its own.

So it's a natural for the Great American Cartoon Star to take his turn at bat in the Great American Game, and just as natural for him to turn out one of his wildest pictures.

The game between the Gas House Gorillas and the Tea Totalers is, perhaps inevitably, leaning toward the former, with an imposingly wide margin. In a gag that got laughs all over the studio when director Freleng acted it out for supervisor Ed Selzer, the Gorillas just step up to the plate and knock balls out of the park, one after the other, until they form a long conga line all the way around the diamond. Bugs, wearing a straw boater and holding his carrot in a hot dog bun, tosses the Gorillas a heckle that he could beat them single-handed, and they take him up on it.

After that, it's Bugs Bunny in every position in the field, proving The Rabbit is quicker than the eye—and when he's not, he's got a trick to convince you he was. As usual, once he's up against the brutes, all's fair, and once he's dazzled them with his footwork, his unearthly slow pitch leaves them stunned. Anyone with an ear can pick up Maltese's touch in the dialogue, especially when Bugs invites us to "watch me pace dis pat'etic palooka with a powerful, paralyzing, poifect, pachydoimous, percussion pitch."

In the final inning, each outrageous moment tops the one before it, with Bugs handling it all like a veteran. One of the Gorillas swings with a tree trunk at Bugs' pitch, sending the ball somewhere in the direction of the stratosphere, and sending our hero out of the ballpark and down the street in the nearest cab. But a wrong turn tips him off, along with the traditional "Your Driver" ID card, boldly emblazoned with the face of one of the Gorillas (right along with his proper name, Social Security number, and all that jazz), and Bugs is out of there and into a bus (reading a newspaper—hate to waste a second). Appropriately enough, it's the Umpire State Building he's got to elevator to the top of before he's *nearly* close enough to catch that mother, and its flagpole he's got to climb before he's a hare's-breadth away. He throws in his glove to make the catch for him, his success called by the game's umpire, who is clinging to the side of the Umpire State Building like he lived there, and by the Statue of Liberty, who chimes in with a radio tagline, and whose decision we must assume is final.

This cartoon was completed and shipped to New York by the studio in June of 1945, before the end of World War II, but not seen on theater screens till February of 1946, after peace had been declared. America was home from the war, glad to have its baseball and its Bugs. It's a glorious double-header.

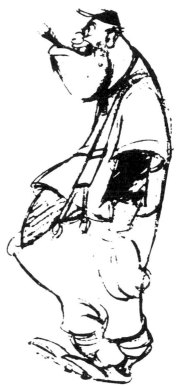

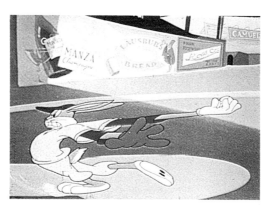

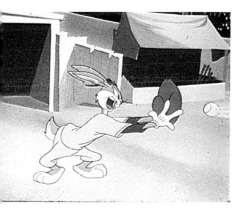

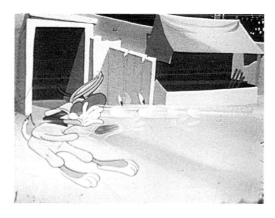

Bugs heckles the Gorillas with the claim that he could lick them single-handed, and they rise to the bait. Once put on the spot, Bugs throws himself into the game—as well as throwing himself a couple of nasty pitches. On the bottom row are displayed a few of the tricks that finally turn the tide of battle.

Following pages: Bugs goes to great lengths—and heights—to win the game, with the help of the Statue of Liberty.

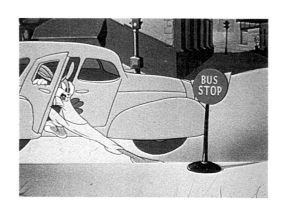

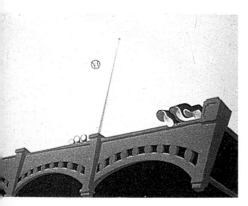

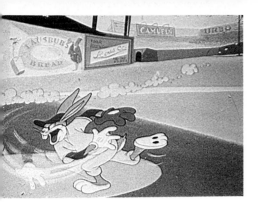

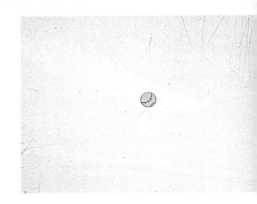

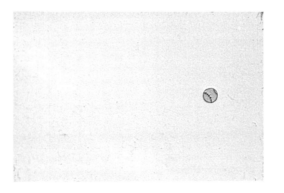

Directed by Charles M. Jones; Story by Tedd Pierce; Animation by Ben Washam, Ken Harris, Basil Davidovich, and Lloyd Vaughan; Layouts and Backgrounds by Robert Gribbroek and Earl Klein; Voice Characterization by Mel Blanc; Musical Direction by Carl W. Stalling. Released as a Bugs Bunny Special in the Merrie Melodies Series May 25, 1946.

One of Bugs' most oft-quoted lines is his speech as a manicurist to the monster in this picture: "My, I'll bet you *mahn*sters lead *inn*teresting lives. I said to my girlfriend just the other day, 'Gee, I'll bet mahnsters are *inn*teresting,' I said. The places you must go and the things you must see—*myyy* stars . . . !"

But taking this line out of context plunders it of most of its humor. It's not a one-line zinger, it's a brilliant bit of character development posing as satire. In *Hair-Raising Hare*, this line isn't just said, it's *whined*, in a nasal imitation of every small-talking shopgirl that still rings true forty years after its invention. It's Mel Blanc doing Bugs Bunny doing a manicurist, and, true to form, Bugs *is* a manicurist. And part of the comedy is his sudden decision to be a manicurist at just that instant: he's in a castle ten times more evil than Macbeth's, having just come so close to falling in a pit the depth of the Grand Canyon that he's chosen to pause in the midst of a furious chase to *pray* and give thanks for his deliverance, when, in mid-prayer, he backs into his pursuer, a growling, slobbering, hideously hairy horror, whose very existence implies bad judgment on the part of the Creator. *This* is the moment he picks to make the beast self-conscious over, of all things, his unsightly fingernails, prompting Bugs to materialize a manicurist's stand out of nowhere and provide, not just the manicure he seems so convinced this monster needs, but—as if it were one of the tools of the trade—the small talk to go with it. And aiding and abetting this unlikely strategem is the fact that it proves to be just the ticket, just bonkers enough to work, nothing this nightmare apparition has ever encountered before and so nothing he's prepared to handle, and he's flummoxed into submission like a doused firestorm.

The moment when he first meets the monster (later named "Gossamer") is another classic in personality and comic timing. Bugs has just come into this castle out of the night, bringing nothing with him, and heard the beast from behind a closed door. "Well, so long!" he replies, and proceeds to *pack* (an act which involves removing towels from a dresser and placing them in a suitcase, then putting a hat from a hatrack on his head and slinging a bag of golf clubs over his shoulder—all to the tune of "California, Here I Come," of course). "And don't think it hasn't been a little slice of Heaven," he declares for a parting shot, "'cause it hasn't!" Then suitcase, hat, and golf clubs fly in the air, as he makes a mad dash for the front door.

Hair-Raising Hare's director, Chuck Jones, has singled out this cartoon as something of a milestone, in his own career at least: "I no longer drew pictures of Bugs; I drew Bugs, I timed Bugs, I *knew* Bugs, because what Bugs aspired to, I aspired to. Aside from a few stumbles, Bugs and I were always at ease with one another."

It's the picture that Bugs opens by musing, "Did ya ever have the feeling you was bein' *watched*?" Turns out he's on television (in 1946, before *anybody* was on television, except Franklin Roosevelt). Being watched by Peter Lorre. And about to be lured to his Evil Scientist's castle (with a blinking neon sign to put all doubts to rest: "Evil Scientist"). By a wind-up sex goddess. Whom he follows crouched like Groucho.

The film's pattern is to switch from terror to amusement repeatedly, and most of the jokes become media references. Before he's through, Bugs begins to refer to himself as "Our Hero," after the manner of dime novels, and to give himself stage directions. He calls his monstrous opponent first "Frankenstein," then "Dracula," finally scaring him away by making him self-conscious a second time—pointing out the people in the audience looking right at him.

Then Bugs gets tamed himself, in a finale that has "Tedd Pierce" written all over it: another of those wind-up sex goddesses saunters by, and he's a goner. "So it's mechanical!" he exclaims, and shifts gears to follow her like a wind-up Bugs.

Though the surface subject of this cartoon is a monster in a mad scientist's lair, the hidden subject is play-acting—media figures and what they do to our heads. Its

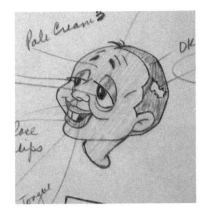

Above: *Animation drawing of Peter Lorre caricature who plays the film's mad scientist.* Opposite and left: *Frames from the completed film, showing Bugs making his first appearance on television, adopting the Groucho crouch, being pursued by the fearsome Beast through the evil labyrinthine castle, and turning a moment of sheer fright into one more chance to gain the upper hand.*

world is a make-believe circus, where Bugs Bunny becomes a manicurist, where a lamp does a soft-shoe routine, where a buffoon can become a hero, where rabbits become monsters and monsters grow timid as rabbits, where reality turns out to be one more illusion. Where we willingly follow graven images we know to be figures of cogwheels and paint.

Directed by I. Freleng; Story by
Tedd Pierce and Michael Maltese;
Animation by Manuel Perez, Ken
Champin, Virgil Ross, and Gerry
Chiniquy; Layouts and
Backgrounds by Hawley Pratt and
Terry Lind; Voice Characterization
by Mel Blanc; Musical Direction by
Carl W. Stalling. Released as a
Bugs Bunny Special in the Merrie
Melodies Series November 9, 1946.

When the great screenwriter and critic James Agee was
reviewing films for *The Nation*, it was rare for him to single out
a short subject for attention, but when he saw this cartoon he
enthused, ". . . The funniest thing I have seen since the decline
of sociological dancing is *Rhapsody Rabbit*. It is incredibly sim-
ple-minded: Bugs Bunny, interrupted by carrots and a mouse,
gives a cut yet definitive performance of the most familiar of
Liszt's Hungarian Rhapsodies (The Second) . . . The best of it
goes two ways: one, very observant parody of concert-pianistic
affectations, elegantly thought out and synchronized; the other,
brutality keyed into the spirit of the music to reach greater sub-
tlety than I have ever seen brutality reach before. I could hardly
illustrate without musical quotation; but there is a passage in
which the music goes up with an arrogant wrenching of slammed
chords—Ronk, *Ronk*, RONK (G-B-E)—then prisses down-
ward on a broken scale—which Bugs takes (a) with all four feet, charging madly,
scowling like a rockinghorse late for a date at stud, (b) friskily tiptoe, proudly smirk-
ing, like a dog toe-dancing through his own misdemeanor or the return of an I-Was-
There journalist, a man above fear or favor who knows precisely which sleeping dogs
to lie about. It killed me; and when they had the wonderful brass to repeat it exactly,
a few bars later, I knew what killed really meant . . . I usually loathe these hearty
burlesques of good ham art; chiefly because most of them are made in hatred of all
art, and in a total lack of understanding of the thing they are burlesquing. But a good
musician must have worked on this art. Barring Beatrice Lillie I have never seen
anything done from so deep inside the ham . . . I have always very much liked this
particular eruption of Liszt's, and though it made me laugh, the laughter was without
patronage, far less scorn. After seeing its guts torn out in this movie short I knew more
about it, and liked it better, than ever."

As Freleng remembers doing this film, "I started with Bugs Bunny and a piano.
I had Jakob Gimpel, the famous pianist, play 'The Hungarian Rhapsody' for me, but
I really wasn't sure what I was going to have Bugs do. To snap up my animation, I
had Gimpel play this at a speed that he had never dreamed of playing it in his life.
His fingers were bleeding by the time I got through with him. But he enjoyed doing
it very much.

"If there was a pause in the music, I had something happen there. I just kind
of built this, like a guy making a painting. He keeps adding, and he keeps touching
the blue here and a little green here, until he has a satisfactory painting. That's the
way I built a cartoon."

Terry Lind was painting the backgrounds for this production by April of 1946,
at which point the animation tests had wowed the rest of the department, and it was
already clear that a very special Bugs Bunny entry was on its way. The color spe-
cialists at the Technicolor laboratory would at this time work closely with the layout
people from the animation department to ensure that the colors coming up on the screen
were a good match for the colors coming off the brush. Everyone at Termite Terrace
was duly awed by the quality the lab was coming up with (and until you've seen one
of the original theatrical three-color Technicolor "imbibition" 35-millimeter prints of
one of these cartoons on a big screen, you haven't really experienced them in their
full majesty). But a logjam was being created by the amount of work that Technicolor
was being saddled with—far in excess of what they were equipped to handle—cou-
pled with drastic wartime restrictions on film stock, and it seemed to Warner Bros.
cartoon staffers in this immediate post-war period that scenes they had animated or
painted weren't coming up on the screen until a year or so later.

Tex Avery was a witness when the folks at Technicolor, evidently stressed out,
delivered one day's *Rhapsody Rabbit* footage by mistake to the MGM cartoon unit,
apparently confusing it with a disturbingly similar Tom & Jerry cartoon, on which Bill

Above and next five pages: *Animation drawings by Virgil Ross.*

140

Hanna and Joe Barbera were then pinning their Academy Award hopes for 1947. When Bugs Bunny came up on the MGM screen, it was Hanna and Barbera who were disturbed first: a project much like theirs was apparently closer to completion over at Termite Terrace, and it was clearly going to be an Oscar contender for 1946. The Tom & Jerry cartoon, finally titled *Cat Concerto*, was rushed through the studio's production process and put up for Academy consideration in the spring. (It was not theatri-

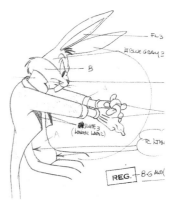

cally released until April of 1947.) That year's crop of animated short-subject Oscar contenders was screened for the Academy, and then it was Friz Freleng's turn to be disturbed.

"When they drew the rotation out of a hat," he remembers, "my cartoon was run after theirs, unfortunately for me. And the audience thought *I* stole from *them*. They got a nomination for it, and I didn't. But I felt that was one of the outstanding things I had done. I enjoyed doing it."

Hanna and Barbera got more than the nomination; they copped that year's animated-shorts Oscar. Friz had to content himself at the time with the personal congratulations of Jack Warner, relayed to him by Ed Selzer. But *Rhapsody Rabbit* is, in fact, generally recognized as one of the most enjoyable of all Bugs Bunnies and, in open defiance of the stuffiness of its setting, *savagely* funny.

"Rabbit Punch"

Directed by Charles M. Jones;
Story by Tedd Pierce and Michael
Maltese; Animation by Phil
Monroe, Ken Harris, Lloyd Vaughan
and Ben Washam; Layouts by
Robert Gribbroek; Backgrounds by
Peter Alvarado; Voice
Characterization by Mel Blanc;
Musical Direction by Carl Stalling.
Released as a Bugs Bunny Special
in the Merrie Melodies Series
April 10, 1948.

"Get your hot buttered popcorn, folks!" Bugs calls out in the middle of this cartoon. "Get it while it's hot! Get it while it's buttered!"

Thing is, he's not running a concession, he's ostensibly fighting a bout in the ring. But this is championship boxing, Bugs Bunny style, and no trick is too low, no charade too preposterous to pull off in full view of a thousand spectators and for the benefit of a radio audience. Before the 110 rounds of this match are over, "Bugsy" has feinted fainting, spilled the horseshoes out of his gloves, cracked a plank to convince the Champ he's cracked a leg, masqueraded as a doctor, slammed his opponent with a boulder in a slingshot, shot himself out of an archer's bow, and, finally, cut the motion picture film he's printed on. Much of this is not covered by the Marquis of Queensberry.

He's also pulled one of his cleverest bits of "stragedy": slammed to the mat, Bugs grabs the sportscaster's microphone and begins describing action that's not taking place—all of it so much in his favor that it wears down the Champ's resistance. "The Champ is confused," says Bugs, and his description is getting warmer. "Bugs lands a beauty to the solar plexus!" calls Bugs, and the Champ tries to ward it off, flinching from its impact at the very thought. "The Champ is groggy!" shouts Bugs, getting more feverish, making up so many "rabbit punches" the Champ can't figure out where they're all coming from, and finally, "The Champ is down!" and he is.

Apparently in an effort to save money, the artists have excluded the referee from all this, so no holds are barred in the Anything Goes rationale that is peculiarly Warner Bros. But Chuck Jones and his animators treat these low proceedings in high style, putting a sleek, classy polish on the down and dirty action. When the Champ decides to call Bugs' bluff, he hurls him in a Keatonesque straight line from his rabbit hole *through* the locker room—and apparently into the closest available pair of shorts—directly into the stool at the right corner of the ring, in four swift, stylishly angled, sharply perspective shots of his aerial progress. In the impudence of adding artistic style to low-down comedy, it's the dirtiest tricks that call for the cleanest action.

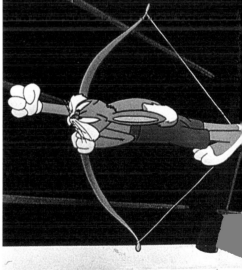

Frames from Rabbit Punch.
*Bugs tries to get into the spirit
of the thing, but the Champ is
somewhat more experienced.
Finally, using a few unconven-
tional methods, he manages to
stun the Champ and gain the
advantage over him.*

147

Featuring Yosemite Sam. Directed by I. Freleng; Story by Tedd Pierce and Michael Maltese; Animation by Ken Champin, Virgil Ross, Gerry Chiniquy, and Manuel Perez; Backgrounds by Paul Julian; Layouts by Hawley Pratt; Voice Characterization by Mel Blanc; Musical Direction by Carl Stalling. Released as a Bugs Bunny Special in the Merrie Melodies Series June 12, 1948.

The title derives from Jack Benny's feature *Buck Benny Rides Again*, but the action has nothing to do with Jack Benny, or the bumbling Easterner caught with his chaps down that Benny plays in his comedy. Bugs starts this cartoon tall in the saddle (whether he's actually on a horse is immaterial) and stays there till the end of its breathless but flawlessly timed seven minutes.

Yosemite Sam bursts into the Western saloon and throws out his imposing (and totally unnecessary) challenge, "Now, be there any livin' varmint as aims t' try t'tame me??? *Welllll, be there????*"

And Bugs answers with a long, laconic roll of a cigarette, a droopy-lidded glance, and a self-confident "*I* aims t'." The roll of the cigarette was one of Freleng's favorite stretches of personality animation, performed by Virgil Ross for *Hare Trigger*, adapted, with a new line of dialogue, for this one. "Bugs is really doing a Gary Cooper scene," says Friz. "Virgil Ross did that scene so well, I always remembered it."

Bugs soon gets the standard tenderfoot's challenge from Yosemite Sam—"Dance!" punctuated by gunshots to the tender feet (by 1948 a Western movie tradition that could boast, "I'm only forty-five-and-a-half years old")—and, in one of his funniest reversals, responds by *dancing*, antique-vaudeville style, all stops out, straw hat and cane at the ready, a burst of spirits so high that Sam is stunned, not sure whether his order has been complied with or defied.

Then Bugs shouts back a challenge of his own, the old entertainer's standard, "Take it, Sam!" and Sam, put on the spot, takes it—on the chin, finally, so whipped up by his own high spirits that he sends himself on a high-kickin' grand finale barnstormer exit, straight down a mine shaft.

In a way, this whole cartoon takes off around that one gag, a series of dances out of nowhere, rhythms foolishly surrendered to, then cold-bloodedly cut off in mid-beat, first countered, then counterpointed, then contrapunted, then drop-kicked into left field.

Bugs gets Sam to step over the edge of a cliff, then looks alarmed, *races* down the mountainside to reach ground level ahead of him, produces a mattress to cushion his fall. "You know," he confides—the offscreen slide whistle telling us Sam's still plummeting—"sometimes me conscience bodders me." Then he *removes* the mattress, remarking, "But not *dis* time!"—and Sam's a pancake.

Horses appear from behind rocks, and Bugs and Sam race back and forth across Western buttes like pinballs across the table, set against "The William Tell Overture" and the Turneresque orange and purple skies of Paul Julian. Without dismounting,

Below and below right: Virgil Ross does Bugs Bunny as Gary Cooper.

they appear *off* their horses, Sam chasing Bugs with a mallet, Sam's horse chasing Bugs' horse with another one, then back in the saddle again without skipping a beat.

Galloping down canyon roads, the unusual tracking shot following first The Rabbit through a tunnel, then The Bandit into it, total darkness for a second, a quick shot of Bugs laying bricks not quite preparing us for the EXPLOSIVE two frames of Sam's impact with a finished brick wall at tunnel's end. More time to take in his stunned, protracted fall, as Bugs admires his handiwork.

It's Freleng and Freleng's Bugs at their best, secure in their footing no matter how fancy their footwork.

This page: *Frames from the finished film: Bugs buffaloes Sam by going into his dance a little more vigorously than the badman had in mind, then coaxing him into one even better; by hastily erecting a brick wall at tunnel's end; and by getting him on the first train out of town—the Miami Special, full of bathing beauties.*

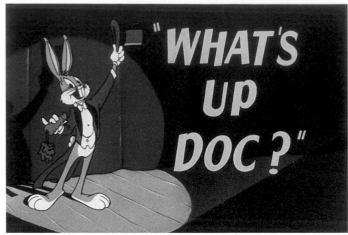

Elmer Fudd walks grandly through Central Park, ignoring Al Jolson, turning up his nose at Bing Crosby, waving Eddie Cantor on. But the next sight to greet his eyes brings the sparkle back to them. "Bugs Bunny!" he exclaims. "Why are you hangin' awound with *these* guys? They'll never amount to anything!"

Self-parody in 1950. Documentary reality on TV today—Jolson, Crosby, and Cantor a conglomerate nonentity to most of the audience; Bugs the only celebrity left in the scene.

Bugs and Elmer on a vaudeville stage, Bugs taking the brunt of Elmer's slapstick and corn-pone comedy. At the next whistle-stop, Bugs tries some unrehearsed variations in the act, stealing all the punchlines and saving the punches for Elmer. Fudd answers with a rifle, right there on stage. The Rabbit counters with "What's up, Doc?" Laughter and applause. "They *like* it," Bugs whispers.

Featuring Elmer Fudd. Directed by Robert McKimson; Story by Warren Foster; Animation by J.C. Melendez, Charles McKimson, Phil DeLara, and Wilson Burness; Layouts by Cornett Wood; Backgrounds by Richard H. Thomas; Voice Characterization by Mel Blanc; Musical Direction by Carl W. Stalling. Released as a Bugs Bunny Special in the Looney Tunes Series June 17, 1950.

But we *do* like it. "Gee, it floored 'em." All part of legend now, like "You ain't heard nothin' yet" and "Come up and see me sometime."

Bugs' theme song, "What's Up, Doc?" was written by Carl Stalling by November of 1944, and became the grand finale of this Robert McKimson cartoon in 1950. McKimson's best Bugs Bunny is also the best of The Rabbit's facetious "life stories."

At first glance, this cartoon has more than a little in common with *Singin' in the Rain*, the great MGM musical of two years later: the same struggle to the top, heard in terms of "dignity, always dignity," but seen as a series of camp indignities; the same air of cavalier mockery-as-tribute toward the last generation's favorite hokum; the same idiotically pat climaxes, no less lovable for being idiotic, and no less idiotic for having the ring of truth. Could it be that someone at MGM's Arthur Freed unit had a light bulb go on over his head when he saw this picture? Or was it just that, after a decade of *Alexander's Ragtime Band*, *Hollywood Cavalcade*, *The Al Jolson Story*, *Blue Skies*, and *Till the Clouds Roll By*, parody was the next logical step? When they won't accept the old corn anymore, give it a roast until it pops, and they'll eat it up. Get it while it's hot, get it while it's buttered.

In making *What's Up, Doc?*, the boys at Termite Terrace were reconciling two absolute truths of show business: you must love the thing you're lampooning, and all hokum must be played absolutely straight. Bugs' story, told in the musical-comedy format that had become Hollywood tradition, is just like everything else about Bugs. It becomes something to cherish by starting out as a spoof of something we *used* to cherish—Once Upon a Time.

Right*: Elmer waves on Eddie Cantor before discovering that he's in the celestial presence of Bugs Bunny. Far right: The "dignity" of Bugs' early days in vaudeville. Frames from the finished film.*

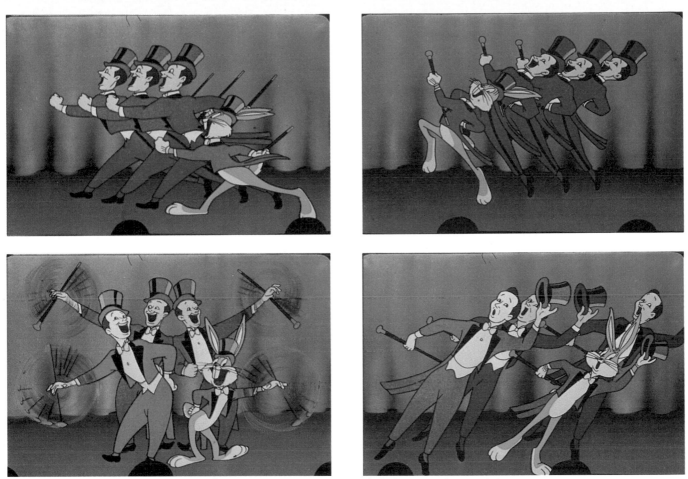

"Oh, we're the boys of the chorus!/We hope you like our show/We know you're rootin' for us/But now we have to go." Above: On the way up, Bugs is as enthusiastic as the next guy about performing these cookie-cutter gyrations. Below: Going through the motions on the way down, he manages to keep his enthusiasm well in check; note his scowl. More frames from the completed cartoon.

RABBITS

Left: *The soundstage where Bugs breaks into pictures, according to his slightly fictionalized biography; background painted by Richard H. Thomas from layout by Cornett Wood. Above: Frame from the "What's Up, Doc?" musical number that comprises his screen test. Top: Bugs the Vaudevillian—his model sheet.*

153

Featuring Elmer Fudd. Directed by Charles M. Jones; Story by Michael Maltese; Animation by Phil Monroe, Ben Washam, Lloyd Vaughan, Ken Harris, and Emery Hawkins; Layouts by Robert Gribbroek; Backgrounds by Philip DeGuard; Voice Characterization by Mel Blanc; Musical Direction by Carl W. Stalling. Released as a Bugs Bunny Special in the Looney Tunes Series December 16, 1950.

Opposite: *Frames from the cartoon, in which Bugs takes over the stage and the barber shop, and gives Elmer a scalp treatment of his own—culminating, naturally and inevitably, in marriage.*

When is a comedy not a comedy? When it becomes a classic.

Lovers of film comedy everywhere find *Rabbit of Seville* something to get excited about, something worth keeping a copy of, worth savoring, worth sharing, worth learning from. We wish they wouldn't cut it for television, and we hope the original negative is kept in good condition so that it will be around for our children, and for our children's children.

Animation historian Greg Ford has already amplified his admiration for a single moment from this masterwork in the magazine *Film Comment*, saying, "There was surprisingly little levity ever levelled at Fudd's bald pate, but the baldness was as permanent a fixture in the weakling image of Elmer as was the timorous *r*'s-and-*l*'s-to-*w*'s ailment in the milksop speech of Fudd, and it must have been predestined that a note on Elmer's hairlessness crop up amid the sundry madcap haircut-shampoo-barber jokes of 1950's *Rabbit of Seville* . . . Among several dozen merry pranks that he plays on his barber-chaired victim, Bugs Bunny, to breezy orchestration, sprinkles Figaro Fertilizer on Elmer's scalp instead of any more orthodox restorative lotion stimulant, and Elmer's noggin, ever so briefly, seems to sprout real hair. Fudd lights up at this, of course, and only then do red wildflowers bloom on the fertilized hair-like stems, to the victim's shocked dismay. What's telltale, though, are those six or seven microseconds of sheer elation on Elmer's face, when he believes that he's grown actual hair. It's this brief uplift that makes his final letdown funny, and furthermore gives the tipoff that the baldness may have been bothering Elmer for lo, these many years."

Students of animation have discovered that, in defiance of cartoon tradition, Bugs sprouts a fifth digit for the closeup of his scalp massage (to stay in step with the music). They have analyzed the musical and comic precision of the film's final sequence, in which Bugs and Elmer pursue each other back and forth across the stage, one producing a new and more frightening weapon at the conclusion of each bar, turning the tide of battle in his favor only till they reach the other side of the stage and the escalation continues—a meat axe just prompts a fire axe, a pistol inspires a rifle, which inspires a cannon, which necessitates a bigger cannon, until Bugs, impressed by the size of Fudd's cannon, proposes marriage, produces the ring, and the ceremony is performed right there on stage, Bugs taking Elmer off for their honeymoon to a little flat high in the fly gallery, where he carries him over the threshold and drops him about 1,001 stories into a cake decorated with "MARRIAGE OF FIGARO."

Like everything else in the development of cartoon comedy, what killed them last season is good only for a nostalgic smile this year, and, in the Jerry Colonna phrase that became a Bob Clampett byword, "Something new has been added!" to make the gag of an animated character doing arias good for a laugh in the movie houses of 1950. Parody lyrics have been provided, elaborate sight gags have been engineered, and a superb harmony has been created between the visual dynamics of a Fudd-and-Rabbit sortie and the lilting spirit of Rossini's music.

Rabbit of Seville is another spoof of something we used to cherish, but it's also a spoof of something we used to *laugh* at. A comedy that is also a classic has to reconcile opposites all the way down the line, and if we make the mistake of approaching it with reverence, we threaten to destroy the *irreverence* that was at the heart of its inception. In a way, Jones, Maltese, and company are collaborators with Rossini, keeping alive the marvelous comic spirit he captured in his music and making it fresh for millions of people who don't know the language and would never have paid to see a real production of the original. Maybe this is the only real way of preserving a comic masterpiece, to send it up anew every decade or so, just to keep the crust from forming on its surface.

But when they try to send up the comedy in *Rabbit of Seville*, they'll have their work cut out for them.

Directed by Charles M. Jones;
Story by Michael Maltese;
Animation by Ben Washam, Lloyd
Vaughan, and Ken Harris; Layouts
by Maurice Noble; Backgrounds by
Philip DeGuard; Voice
Characterization by Mel Blanc;
Musical Direction by Carl W.
Stalling. Released as a Bugs
Bunny Special in the Looney Tunes
Series August 8, 1953.

Below: *"Stop steamin' up my
tail! What're ya tryin' to do,
wrinkle it?"* protests Bugs in the
confrontation that sets off the
battle royal. Frame from final
film.

Chuck Jones has described the challenges of an animation director in the studio system this way: "We didn't do experimental pictures. We did all our experimenting in the arena. All of us must eventually do what the matador does: Go out and face not only the bull but the crowd. It does the matador little good to make beautiful passes alone in a moonlit pasture. And it doesn't do any good to tell the Plight of Man in a theater that only shows it to people who know it already. Every film director, actor, cutter, or anything else that has ever been great, has eventually had to face the large audience. And I think that's where all the fun is, to accept the idea that you've got certain problems, but never to let those diminish you, in the sense of keeping you down."

It's apparent that, for Jones, the arena was the making of crowd-pleasing cartoons at the Warner Bros. studio, and the chief problem was its problem chief, Ed Selzer. When Selzer happened to see a sketch of a bull on Jones' sketchpad, his chance remark was "I don't want any bullfights—bullfights aren't funny."

Mike Maltese commented, "If Eddie hates it, there's got to be something funny there."

"So I made *Bully for Bugs*," as Chuck puts it, "not because I was interested in bullfighting, particularly, but just because he said *not* to. *Bully for Bugs* was easy to write, to gag and to direct, because, unlike other stories where we suffered hideous tortures of uncertainty, we *knew* it would be a success before we saw it—and it was one of the best Bugs Bunny's to come out of our unit."

The cartoon that emerged is one that Jones considers "the most satisfying structurally" of Bugs' confrontations with an outsized opponent. Warner cartoon historian Steve Schneider calls it a "finely realized . . . classically correct" film. Its conflict centers on the situation of the man in the arena, becoming a graphically ritualized, formalized look at Bugs' customary ability to face his opponent with aplomb, savoir faire, and total assurance. "Bugs I meant to move with about the same kind of grace that a matador does," says Jones, "and of course a matador must be able to move very gracefully, because his life depends on it. I learned to my horror that these men learn to hold that straight stance by wearing splints on their knees when they're practicing. And they make their passes with the calves, with their legs splinted, so they can't bend their knees. Even with a calf after you, there's no way to get away! The result is, however, these men move with extraordinary grace, and that's what I tried to get in Bugs' attitude."

But if the arena threw the weight of the attention on style and grace under pressure, the bull, as Jones remembers, threw his weight in another direction—toward the threat of annihilation expressed through graphics:

"I want Bugs Bunny's—or anybody else's—menace to have true menace in it. Bugs obviously had to win, but there wasn't any reason why he couldn't get batted around a little bit in the process. And this guy's big and strong, and the noise he makes is the kind of noise that a bull *really* makes. So the anatomy of this guy is pretty accurate. He scared me, I know.

"Just one of the many things that you have to learn as an animator is how to make anything heavy. Many people think, for instance, that heavy creatures tend to move very sloppily; they don't. A giraffe probably moves in a much more spastic and loose-limbed way than an elephant does. Fat people *have* to be precise; they can't make the same mistakes other people make. Stan Laurel can fall down and get up, but if Hardy falls down it's a real problem to get back up again.

"One of the things I got that from is watching fat people ice skate. It's beautiful to watch: They don't move from side to side or up and down at all. They won't stay fat if they use too much action.

Left: *Bugs' opponent in Chuck Jones' model sheet for the character, demonstrating how he wants his animators to draw and to move this immoveable object.* Above: *Michael Maltese (left) goes over his storyboard for this cartoon with Jones (right), trying to figure out what it is that makes a bullfight so funny that Selzer couldn't stand the thought of it.* Top: *The Arena, as visualised in one of Philip DeGuard's background paintings, from Maurice Noble's layout.*

157

"Fat and skill, and a lot of things, tend to limit action rather than to broaden it. When a child or a puppy goes around a corner, he will either clear it by six feet or run into it. A great hurdler is the guy who comes the closest to the hurdle, not the guy who goes the highest over it. The basic thing with the bull, then, was to keep him heavy on the ground, and to keep his feet *under* him, except when he moved. And when he moved, he moved *laterally* to the ground; there's not a lot of up and down movement to it."

Bully for Bugs, with its ritual, its style, its ominous threat, and the sureness of its technique, becomes an elaborate visualization of the concept that to function successfully in the arena, a man is compelled to go before a huge crowd, and face a lot of bull.

Below: *The bull warms up for the next round in this Chuck Jones layout drawing.*

Below, left, and opposite: *Bugs assumes the poise of a real matador, and exhibits grace under pressure in an exuberant victory dance.*

Left: *The bull, after Bugs gets through with him.*

159

There was a time when *What's Opera, Doc?* was a cartoon fan's discovery, when you came across it unprepared for spectacle, and the sheer wonderfulness of the thing, the visual wit running through every frame, could catch you by surprise and gently roll you in the aisles.

By this point, saying that *What's Opera, Doc?* is a great cartoon is a little like saying that *Citizen Kane* is a good movie, or that your family likes to watch *The Wizard of Oz*, or that *North by Northwest* is still fun the second time.

What is said less often is that *What's Opera, Doc?* is a great cartoon not because it's an extravagant exercise in grand production, as could be said of so many Disney cartoons, but a uniquely single-visioned and at the same time multileveled effort that takes off in all directions at once from a basically simple premise: imagining the story of *A Wild Hare* as Wagner might have scored it and the UPA studio might have designed it if they were in a mood to trash Disney. In other words, running the old Bugs-and-Elmer mythology through the sprocket holes again, to see if it can support the grand Wagnerian treatment—and, if not, to see if it can get laughs by pretending it can.

Again Elmer entreats us to "be vewy quiet," since he's "hunting wabbits." Again he explains his plans to Bugs, failing to notice that he's "a wabbit." Bugs masquerades as a woman again (Brunhilda this time—a gag from Freleng's *Herr Meets Hare*, which Maltese wrote). Elmer, furious when he finds out, kills Bugs, then repents. And Bugs has the last word at the finale.

Producing a series of films can achieve many things beyond the sharpening of a character. This film is the product of a superbly well-functioning unit of talents —not only Jones, Noble, and Maltese (whose song, "Return My Love," is set to the "Pilgrim's Chorus" from Wagner's *Tannhauser*), but everyone else as well, from Ken Harris and his wonderful animation of Bugs and Elmer's ballet, to cameraman Ken Moore, who came up with the idea of cutting holes in sheets of theatrical gel to create the "spotlight" effect during their duet.

But producing a series tends to create uniformity rather than unique undertakings like *What's Opera, Doc?* Though the official production cost of the film is listed as $35,510, unusually high for Warner Bros. in 1957, it's difficult to tell whether or not this figure reflects the fact that Jones and Noble had learned to cheat in their budget allotments, to make special projects like this one possible by stealing precious time and art supplies from more routine pictures on the schedule.

The comic sophistication in the end result is apparent at virtually every stage of the animation process. When the majestic "Night on Bald Mountain" figure that opens the film, commanding thunder to roll and the Heavens to part, turns out to be the shadow of puny little Elmer Fudd, pulling his standard line to Wagner's accompaniment, his pretense to such power is ludicrous, but his actually carrying it all off is captivating, and ennobling. When the beautiful Brunhilda turns out to be funny little Bugs Bunny, Elmer's fury turns the sky a brimstone blue and his entire face, body, costume, everything a deep crimson. The extremity of this mood change is hilarious in its intensity, but at the same time his cry of "I'll kill the *wabbit*!", in as good an approximation of anger as his quivering voice is capable, blows that intensity altogether, sends the mood madly spinning in another uproarious direction. Everywhere the film equates elegance with deceit, with a fancy icing on a fallen cake.

The ironic twists of the mountains themselves posit a wry, tolerant universe. Maurice Noble's production design is beautiful, inventive, surprising—but at the same time it communicates, through its rocks, trees, Doric columns, and especially that overstuffed horse that Bugs-as-Brunhilda is mounting, that it's all too much, that it *knows* it's too much, and that it loves it! *What's Opera, Doc?* sends you away with the notion that there's something funny about everything grand, and something grand about everything funny.

Featuring Elmer Fudd. Directed by Chuck Jones; Story by Michael Maltese; Animation by Ken Harris, Richard Thompson, and Abe Levitow; Effects Animation by Harry Love; Layouts by Maurice Noble; Backgrounds by Philip DeGuard; Film Editor: Treg Brown; Voice Characterization by Mel Blanc; Musical Direction by Milt Franklyn; Song "Return My Love," Lyrics by Michael Maltese. Released as a Bugs Bunny Special in the Merrie Melodies Series July 6, 1957.

Below: Elmer casts a giant shadow in Chuck Jones' layout drawing. It's standard film lore that this short cartoon contains 106 cuts, that it boils the entire four operas of Richard Wagner's The Ring of the Nibelung *(or* Der Rin des Nibelungen*) down to six minutes, that Warner Bros. library footage of Tatiana Riabouchinska and David Lichine of the Ballets Russes de Monte Carlo was studied by the animators to get the dance movements right.*

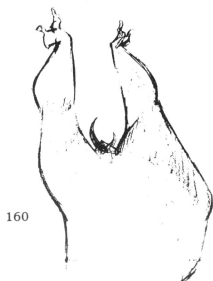

Left: "Magic Helmet!" says Elmer. " . . . magic helmet . . . " says Bugs. Below and bottom: Bugs and Elmer join in a chorus of "Return My Love," highlighted by Ken Moore's "spotlight" effect. In the scene in the lower right corner, Bugs waves, either at Elmer or the camera, from high in the bower. Following pages: The Masquerader revealed and the honeymoon over: cel and background from the pivotal moment, where Bugs loses his own "magic helmet" and his wig.

Hell hath no fury like a Fudd bamboozled. Above: Frames from the completed film. Right: Elmer's rage, in Maurice Noble's original design painting. Noble: "They thought I was bats when I put that bright red on Elmer with those purple skies . . . I had the Ink and Paint Department come in and say, 'You really mean you want that magenta red on that?' Yet they thought it was great when they finally saw it on the screen."

Featuring Daffy Duck. Directed by
Friz Freleng; Story by Warren
Foster; Animation by Gerry
Chiniquy, Art Davis, and Virgil
Ross; Layouts by Hawley Pratt;
Backgrounds by Boris Gorelick;
Film Editor: Treg Brown; Voice
Characterization by Mel Blanc;
Musical Direction by Milt Franklyn.
Released as a Bugs Bunny Special
in the Looney Tunes Series
November 2, 1957.

This cartoon, one of the most famous of the Bugs-Daffy
confrontations, has a long pedigree. It reworks the Bugs-as-
celebrity in-joke exploited so well in *What's Up, Doc?* combines
it with the Daffy-as-Iago touch originally explored in *You Ought
to Be in Pictures*, and even manages to borrow two major gags
wholesale from a 1949 Freleng cartoon, *Curtain Razor*.

For many people, the Bugs-Daffy relationship pivots on
this specific film, which became the inspiration for the framing
sequences on television's *Bugs Bunny Show* of three years later.
It's even been used, by writer Richard Corliss, as a paradigm
for its director's entire career:

"Like a vaudeville entertainer who traveled with the same
act from town to town and always knew where the laughs were,
Show Biz Friz kept putting his cartoon stars onstage for another
softshoe turn, pie in the face, or Dr. Krankheit routine. Bugs,
Daffy, Porky, and the rest may have been funny animals to some viewers, and seven-
minute stars to others, but to Freleng they were the third act on the bill struggling
toward top-banana status or sliding down past the singing parakeets."

All of which is just another way of saying that the routines employed by Freleng
in this cartoon were time-tested and reliable, and gave him the assurance to use them
with utter deftness to create an onstage conflict that is not only funny the first time
around, but indefinitely memorable thereafter. Whatever Bugs does brings down the
house, and whatever Daffy does, he's received by the sound of the same house empty,
invaded by crickets.

By 1957 Bugs' perennial popularity had become as much a bewilderment as a
source of pride. The theatrical short-subject market had gone through a series of drastic

Below, right, and opposite
bottom: *Bugs and Daffy are on!
Frames from the completed film.*
Opposite top: *The front of the
theater on the big night, in Boris
Gorelick's background, from
Hawley Pratt's layout.*

Above and below: Frames from the completed film. Daffy yells, "I'm not cut in half! Stop applauding!" after Bugs tries his prestidigitational skills on him.
Right: Animation drawing.

168

changes, Bugs' contemporaries from the early '40s had largely faded from the scene, even Disney had phased out the one-reel cartoon, and television was posing new threats every year. Didn't matter. Bugs went on being Champ, no matter what. This is the implicit joke in scenes like the one in which Bugs simply sticks his head out in view of the audience and gets a rousing ovation (and Treg Brown's sound cutting adds to the gag here—the applause doesn't segue up in any kind of natural effect, it simply slams in at crescendo level and settles there).

But, while *What's Up, Doc?*, *You Ought to Be in Pictures*, and *Curtain Razor* are fine cartoons, the elements come together in *Show Biz Bugs* in a way that seems very sophisticated and, at the same time, extremely basic, in the manner of the very best cartoons, animated, single-panel, or political. Any one of the scenes in this film could make a prize-winning political cartoon, in fact, with Bugs labeled "Success" or "Television" or "Elvis," and Daffy tagged "Greed" or "McCarthy" or "Edsel," in a *reductio ad comedium* of not one, but a variety of similar conflicts we're all intimately familiar with, in or out of show biz.

Possibly, in accordance with Jones' remark, it would most make sense to caption Bugs "Aspiration" and Daffy "Recognition," rendering this picture the updated equivalent of those older cartoons with the little angel character on one shoulder and the little devil on the other. *Show Biz Bugs* is hipper than that simplistic conflict, but no less graphic or elemental. It uses characters we've shown our affection for, to act out a drama we're readily familiar with, from both sides—sometimes simultaneously. Any one of us could probably drape the cape of "Good Hope" on Bugs and hang the shroud of "Black Moods" on Daffy.

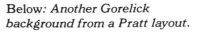

Below: *Another Gorelick background from a Pratt layout.*

Featuring Yosemite Sam. Directed by Friz Freleng; Story by Warren Foster; Animation by Virgil Ross, Gerry Chiniquy, and Art Davis; Layouts by Hawley Pratt; Backgrounds by Tom O'Laughlin; Film Editor: Treg Brown; Voice Characterization by Mel Blanc; Musical Direction by Milt Franklyn. Released as a Bugs Bunny Special in the Looney Tunes Series August 23, 1958. Winner of Academy Award for Best Animated Short Subject of 1958.

Below: *Bugs and the Singing Sword in an original cel from this production.*

When Mary Pickford established the Academy Award in the late '20s with the goal of recognizing cinematic excellence, she failed to see one Achille's heel in her game plan: that if you take a panoply of varying types of films, actors, actresses, and creators, and send them clamoring yearly for a *single* award in each category, you're going to bypass some of the most consistently excellent careers in Hollywood, for the sake of rewarding the trendy, the flashy, the obvious, and the different. It would seem that the Oscar was designed specifically to honor a creation like Bugs Bunny, yet year after year his very reliability lost him the trophy to the surprise value of a film that has since faded from the scene. (It's worth pointing out that the venerable Mickey never did get the Academy nod.)

But the Oscar's importance, whether as authentic gold star or as winning lottery ticket, perseveres as mightily as our Heckling Hare, no doubt the reason for the lingering affection for this, the one cartoon to snare for Bugs the industry's brass ring—in spite of numerous complaints, both published and voiced, that it's really just one more Bugs Bunny cartoon. Where was *A Hare Grows in Manhattan* when Oscars were given out? *High Diving Hare*? *Racketeer Rabbit*? *Long-Haired Hare*? *Rabbit Seasoning*? Virtually any of the other cartoons in this section?

But *Knighty-Knight Bugs*, taking place in a time of legend and involving the search for a Grail, is virtually *about* the situation of Bugs finally acquiring a trophy for which he seems destined, a talisman designed only for him.

The authentic hero of any culture is a reluctant hero, according to Joseph Campbell, who made a lifetime study of world myths and legends. They don't come any more reluctant than Bugs, the Court Jester, when the quest for the precious Singing Sword is proposed in this cartoon: he breaks down in tears. It's never been any clearer that Bugs Bunny is Foole and Hero at once.

He takes up the Quest, and, it seems, seconds later, is holding the Singing Sword, having rescued it from Yosemite Sam as The Black Knight, and from the locked strongbox in which it had been moldering, just as easily as Arthur had rescued Excalibur from its formidable prison of stone. Once in his hands, the mute object bursts into song, arousing The Black Knight and his slumbering, lumbering dragon, and setting off the series of skirmishes that constitute the main action of the cartoon—the skirmishes whose outcome, Bugs being Bugs, is preordained.

When Daffy Duck tries to be the Scarlet Pumpernickel, it's funny because it's so apparent that he's not. When Bugs tries *not* to be the Hero of the Singing Sword, it's funny because it's so clear that that's who he was all along. Warren Foster, whether writing for McKimson, for Clampett, or for Freleng, clearly finds it endlessly funny that Bugs can do no wrong.

The battle that Bugs fought so hard to ward off is, once he's engaged in it, nearly effortless for him, and nearly impossible for the Black Knight, who is incapable even of keeping his idiot dragon from sneezing and incinerating him. Just as the Singing Sword sings only in Bugs' hands, its possession seems clearly intended only for him.

These echoes of Arthurian and other legends would seem to butt up against misplaced anachronism in the film's final gags, when the Black Knight's dragon sneezes for the final time in a gunpowder arsenal, turning a medieval tower, turret and all, into a premature missile, blasting off on a crash course for the moon, while the old faithful Singing Sword launches into a refrain of "Aloha Oe." But, twenty years before the *Star Wars* trilogy made hay out of Arthurian reverberations, this ending demonstrates that myths and legends, like time-tested gags and long-lived cartoon characters, hang around for a reason—that mixing elements of the new and strange with traditional patterns that make us feel grounded and secure is one way of reaching goals that had seemed so elusive.

Bugs: foole, before finding out he's being sent on Mission: Impossible.

Frames from completed film. Right: Bugs tiptoes past the dozing Black Knight (Yosemite Sam, miles from Yosemite) and risks the wrath of the Sneezing Dragon (Below) to rescue the Singing Sword. Eventually, Bugs takes over the castle and leaves Sam on the outside (Opposite center). "Open that drawbridge! Open it, I say!" screams Sam, then instantly recants: "Close it! Close it up again!" Opposite bottom: Bugs observes castle-as-spaceship, while holding sword-as-jukebox. Opposite top: Gerry, the sneezing dragon, as sketched out in his model sheet.

"Baton Bunny"

Directed by Chuck Jones and Abe Levitow; Story by Michael Maltese; Animation by Ken Harris, Richard Thompson, and Ben Washam; Layouts by Maurice Noble; Backgrounds by Tom O'Loughlin; Film Editor: Treg Brown; Voice Characterization by Mel Blanc; Orchestrations by Milt Franklyn. The Warner Bros. Symphony Orchestra Performing "Morning, Noon and Night in Vienna," by Franz Von Suppe. Released as a Bugs Bunny Special in the Looney Tunes Series January 10, 1959.

Above: *Background by Tom O'Loughlin from layout by Maurice Noble*. Below: *frame from the finished film.*

This concert situation turns into a solo outing for Bugs, in which an audience and an orchestra are presumably present, but—except for a bothersome fly, who is ultimately dispatched—no one besides The Rabbit is ever shown. Instruments glisten in the light, bows are seen in closeup poised over strings, an audience responds. But only Bugs Bunny appears in person. Jones and his animators can then concentrate their increasingly limited resources on creating a tour-de-force performance for their inveterate performer.

The Masquerader undertakes the conducting of a symphony orchestra, so must *become* a conductor, which he does with a gusto that out-conducts all previous conductors, then must *become* all the imaginary characters in the dramatic music he's bringing to life. Jones credits Abe Levitow with the animation of some of Bugs' funniest flourishes in this cartoon, and Levitow earned his co-direction credit by overseeing the completion of the film when its director grew busy with other work.

By now this kind of classical music cartoon was turning into a genre all its own, with a developing classicism that defined its parameters. As far back as Mickey Mouse's *The Band Concert*, right up through *Corny Concerto* and *Rhapsody Rabbit*, the inherent gag in framing your star cartoon character with symphonic music was to poke a little fun at highbrow pretentions, to jab the self-absorption of serious musicians, and, by extension, all self-important *artistes*, in the ribs a little. But in *Rabbit of Seville* and *What's Opera, Doc?* Bugs' actions seemed directed toward blending into the spirit of the proceedings, in characteristic all-character style, less in counterpoint and more in harmony with the mood of the music he was getting involved in. In *Baton Bunny*, without the elaborate production and mythic resonances of *Seville* or *What's Opera* behind him, without a conflict or story of any kind except the completion of the composition on the stand, it's his entering full-bloodedly into the spirit of the music, into the spirit of the musician, into the throes of the passion he's illustrating, that inspires the comedy. He *embodies* the music, the way he *embodies* the various characterizations of his other performances. In this cartoon, more than in any of the previous maestro-pieces, the ridicule and the impersonation become inseparable, the love and the lampoon are fused, the celebration and the satire merge into a statement of pure joy.

Exhausted by the exertion of all this, Bugs arranges himself for his bow and is caught up short by an unearthly silence, then the sound that greeted Daffy in *Show Biz Bugs*: crickets. The house is empty. The lot of many an artist: his solo performance a little more solo than he had in mind.

But, in the booming cavern of the Hollywood Bowl, the sound of one tiny pair of hands clapping finally emerges. It's the fly he had squashed just a half-moment before. With all the dignity possible, our Hero bows to his one admirer.

So a rabbit named Bugs finds himself between the insects, taking his bows wherever he can. He's an older, wiser bunny than the one who allowed himself to be flummoxed by a tortoise or sent into a tailspin by a gremlin. But he's still the self-mocking personality who doesn't ask questions; he just has fun.

Bugs, the great Winner, had shown us that Winning and Losing are no different from Kipling's view of Success and Failure—two imposters to treat both the same. He hadn't said it; he had demonstrated it. He hadn't just acted it out; he had *embodied* it.

And by doing that, the Heckling Hare had triumphed again.

174

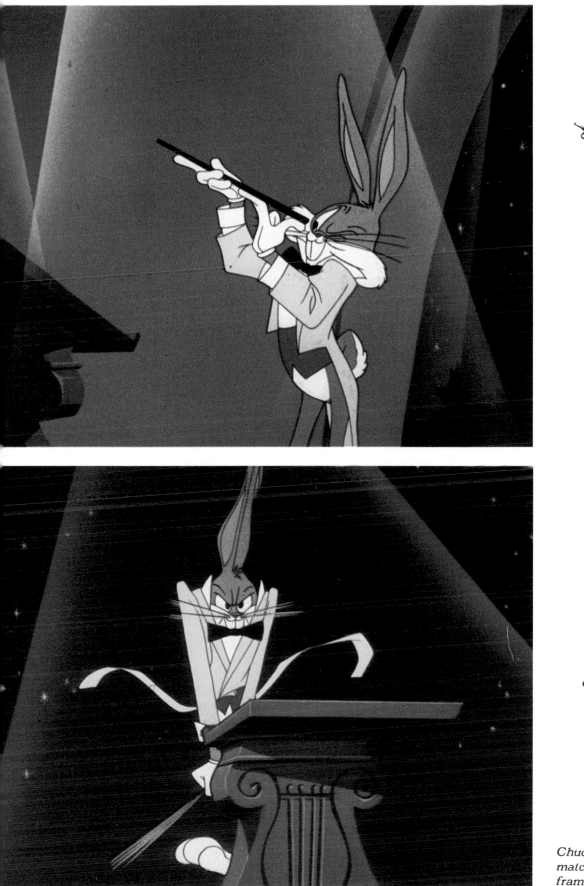

Chuck Jones' layout sketches, as matched by the animators in frames from the final film.

Filmography

This list is based on the information compiled and the synopses written by Jerry Beck and Will Friedwald for their landmark book, *Looney Tunes and Merrie Melodies*, with minor alterations where necessary. The availability of theatrical cartoons and recent compilations in specials on videocassettes in *current* release at press time, by either Warner Bros. or MGM/UA Home Video, has been added

PART I: THE BUGS BUNNY THEATRICAL CARTOONS, 1940-1964

1940

A WILD HARE

Elmer Fudd; July 27; MM; Supervision by Fred Avery; Story by Rich Hogan; Animation by Virgil Ross; Musical Supervision by Carl W. Stalling.
Elmer goes hunting Bugs. He lives to know better. See pages 54-55. Video: *Bugs Bunny: Superstar*, MGM/UA

1941

ELMER'S PET RABBIT

Elmer Fudd; Jan 4; MM; Supervision by Charles M. Jones; Story by Rich Hogan; Animation by Rudolf Larriva; Musical Direction by Carl W. Stalling
Elmer sees Bugs in a pet shop window and takes him home, but gets heckled by him all evening. (This early in Bugs' life, he complains about having to eat carrots.)

TORTOISE BEATS HARE

Cecil Turtle; Mar 15; MM; Supervision by Fred Avery; Story by Dave Monahan; Animation by Charles McKimson; Musical Direction by Carl W. Stalling.
Bugs races Cecil, who posts spitting-image relatives all along the course. When Bugs himself reads the title card, mispronouncing the credits, and discovers the name and outcome of the picture, he screams, "The big bunch of joiks."

HIAWATHA'S RABBIT HUNT

June 7; MM; Supervision by I. Freleng; Story by Michael Maltese; Animation by Gil Turner; Musical Direction by Carl W. Stalling.
Bugs reads "Little Hiawatha" and realizes that the "mighty hunter" is going to hunt him. For most of the picture, he stays one step ahead of the little guy.

THE HECKLING HARE

July 5; MM; Supervision by Fred Avery; Story by Michael Maltese; Animation by Bob McKimson; Musical Direction by Carl W. Stalling.
For no stated purpose other than to fulfill his destiny as a hunting dog, Willoughby goes hunting Bugs in the woods. Video: *Bugs Bunny Classics*, MGM/UA

ALL THIS AND RABBIT STEW

Sept 13; MM; Supervision by Fred Avery (uncredited); Story by Dave Monahan; Animation by Virgil Ross; Musical Direction by Carl Stalling.
An unfortunate blackface caricature spoils a succession of awfully funny and well-timed gags, as one more hunter tests his wits against the wily rabbit and comes out second.

WABBIT TWOUBLE

Elmer Fudd; Dec 20; MM; Supervision by Wobert Cwampett; Story by Dave Monahan; Animation by Sid Suthewand; Musical Direction, Carl W. Stawwing.
Elmer looks forward to "peace and wewaxation" during his vacation at Jellostone National Park. But what he encounters is Bugs Bunny and a very unpeaceful bear.

1942

WABBIT WHO CAME TO SUPPER

Elmer Fudd; Mar 28; MM; Supervision by I. Freleng; Story by Michael Maltese; Animation by Richard Bickenbach; Musical Direction by Carl Stalling.
Elmer is hunting Bugs when news comes that his Uncle Louie will leave him three million dollars on condition that he doesn't harm any animals, especially rabbits. Bugs takes this as his cue to move in on Fudd. Video: *Elmer!* MGM/UA

THE WACKY WABBIT

Elmer Fudd; May 2; MM; Supervision by Robert Clampett; Story by Warren Foster; Animation by Sid Sutherland; Musical Direction by Carl W. Stalling.
Elmer is prospecting for gold in the desert when Bugs descends upon him, finally driving him to pull his own gold tooth. Video: *Elmer!* MGM/UA

HOLD THE LION, PLEASE

June 13; MM; Supervision by Charles M. Jones; Story by Ted Pierce; Animation by Ken Harris; Musical Direction by Carl W. Stalling.
The goofy lion, trying to hold onto his "King of the Jungle" title, goes out to hunt a rabbit to prove he's not washed up. Unfortunately, he chooses the wrong rabbit and proves nothing.

BUGS BUNNY GETS THE BOID

Beaky Buzzard; July 11; MM; Supervision by Robert Clampett; Story by Warren Foster; Animation by Rod Scribner; Musical Direction by Carl W. Stalling.
Mama Buzzard instructs her children to bring back some meat for dinner. Beaky, the bashful one, is reluctant to go, but is kicked out of the nest and told to try for at least a rabbit. But he tries for Bugs Bunny. Video: *Bugs!* MGM/UA

FRESH HARE

Elmer Fudd; Aug 22; MM; Supervision by I. Freleng; Story by Michael Maltese; Animation by Manuel Perez; Musical Direction by Carl W. Stalling.
Elmer Fudd is a Mountie pursuing our Heckling Hare through the snowy Canadian North Woods. Bugs is wanted dead or alive, and resists arrest with a variety of tricks.

THE HARE-BRAINED HYPNOTIST

Elmer Fudd; Oct. 31; MM; Supervision by I. Freleng; Story by Michael Maltese; Animation by Philip Monroe; Musical Direction by Carl W. Stalling.
Elmer tries stalking Bugs with hypnotism, but it only confuses the hunter-prey relationship, and sets off a pattern of role reversal that is hound the hunter for years. Video: *Elmer!* MGM/UA

CASE OF THE MISSING HARE

Dec 12; MM; Supervision by Charles M. Jones; Story by Ted Pierce; Animation by Ken Harris; Musical Direction by Carl W. Stalling.
Bugs, irritated at the pompous magician Ala Bama for sticking posters of his show over his hollow tree home, heckles throughout his stage act.

1943

TORTOISE WINS BY A HARE

Cecil Turtle; Feb 20; MM; Supervision by Robert Clampett; Story by Warren Foster; Animation by Robert McKimson; Musical Direction by Carl W. Stalling.
Bugs challenges Cecil Turtle to another race--constructing, on his suggestion, an airflow chassis like the turtle's. But this makes him look like a turtle, and the gambling ring has bet everything on the "the rabbit" to win. Video: *Bugs!* MGM/UA.

SUPER RABBIT

Apr 3; MM; Supervision by Charles M. Jones; Story by Tedd Pierce; Animation by Ken Harris; Musical Direction by Carl W. Stalling.
In this spoof of the Superman character and the Fleischer's popular Superman animated cartoons, Bugs is given super carrots in the lab of Prof. Canafrazz and goes off to fight that notorious Texas rabbit hater, Cottontail Smith. Video: *Bugs and Daffy: The Wartime Cartoons*, MGM/UA

JACK-WABBIT AND THE BEANSTALK

June 12; MM; Supervision by I. Freleng; Animation by Jack Bradbury; Story by Michael Maltese; Musical Direction by Carl W. Stalling.
Bugs proves that even a Giant is no match for him, as he duels it out with this dodo in Giantland. See pages 124-127.

WACKIKI WABBIT

July 3; MM; Supervision by Charles M. Jones; Story by Tedd Pierce; Animation by Ken Harris; Musical Direction by Carl W. Stalling.
Bugs, as a native rabbit on a tropical island, tangles with a pair of castaways who see him as a potential meal, in a situation apparently based on Jones' real-life shipwreck experience.

A CORNY CONCERTO

Elmer Fudd; Sept 18; MM; Supervision by Robert Clampett; Story by Frank Tashlin; Animation by Robert McKimson; Musical Direction by Carl W. Stalling.
In a parody of *Fantasia*, Elmer introduces "A Tale of the Vienna Woods," in which Bugs, Porky, and Porky's dog enact a hunting charade in ballet form to the "Stwauss" music. See pages 128-129. Video: *Bugs Bunny Superstar*, MGM/UA

FALLING HARE

Oct 30; MM; Supervision by Robert Clampett; Story by Warren Foster; Animation by Rod Scribner; Musical Direction by Carl W. Stalling.

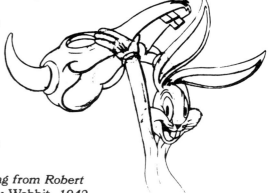

Animation drawing from Robert Clampett's Wacky Wabbit, *1942*

Bugs laughs at the notion that gremlins are sabotaging American planes in the skies, but encounters one on an airfield and is soon doing battle with him in a flying plane. Video: *Bugs and Daffy: The Wartime Cartoons*, MGM/UA.

1944

LITTLE RED RIDING RABBIT
Jan 4; MM; Supervision by I. Freleng; Story by Michael Maltese; Animation by Manuel Perez; Voice Characterizations by Mel Blanc; Musical Direction by Carl Stalling.
Bugs, the Wolf, and a teen-aged bobby-soxer Red Ridinghood chase each other around Grandma's house, while Grandma is busy on the swing shift at Lockheed. See pages 130-131. Video: *Bugs and Daffy: The Wartime Cartoons*, MGM/UA.

WHAT'S COOKIN' DOC?
Jan 8; MM; Supervision by Robert Clampett; Animation by Bob McKimson; Story by Michael Sasanoff; Musical Direction by Carl W. Stalling.
Bugs is furious when he loses the Oscar for Best Actor to James Cagney, and runs a clip from Hiawatha's Rabbit Hunt to encourage a recount. Video: *Bugs Bunny Superstar*

BUGS BUNNY AND THE THREE BEARS
The Three Bears; Feb 26; MM; Supervision by Charles M. Jones; Animation by Robert Cannon; Story by Tedd Pierce; Voice Characterization by Mel Blanc; Musical Direction by Carl W. Stalling.
Jones' great Three Bears characters try to lure Goldilocks with carrot soup and end up with Bugs Bunny. Bugs escapes Mama Bear's clutches by romancing her, but she falls for him and he can't get rid of her. Video: *Bugs!* MGM/UA

BUGS BUNNY NIPS THE NIPS
Apr 22; MM; Supervision by I. Freleng; Story by Tedd Pierce; Animation by Gerry Chiniquy; Musical Direction by Carl Stalling.
Strictly wartime stuff, as Bugs battles it out with Japanese stereotypes on a South Pacific island.

HARE RIBBIN'
June 24; MM; Directed by Robert Clampett; Story by Lou Lilly; Animation by Robert McKimson; Voice Characterizations by Mel Blanc; Musical Direction by Carl W. Stalling.
A red-haired Russian dialect dog chases Bugs to a lake, and the rest of the cartoon takes place underwater. Video: *Bugs!* MGM/UA

HARE FORCE
Feb 22; MM; Directed by I. Freleng; Story by Tedd Pierce; Animation by Manuel Perez; Voice Characterization by Mel Blanc; Musical Direction by Carl Stalling.
Granny brings a frozen Bugs out of a cold, snowy night to thaw by the fireplace and instructs her dog Sylvester to take care of the bunny. But while she goes to bed, the two take turns throwing each other out. Video: *Starring Bugs Bunny!* MGM/UA.

BUCKAROO BUGS
Aug 26; LT; Directed by Robert Clampett; Story by Lou Lilly; Animation by M. Gould; Voice Characterization by Mel Blanc; Musical Direction by Carl W. Stalling.
Bugs is a carrot thief known as The Masked Marauder, whom Red Hot Ryder, Brooklyn's finest cowboy, rides to bring to justice. Bugs is ruthless against the little twerp.

THE OLD GREY HARE
Elmer Fudd; Oct 28; MM; Direction by Robert Clampett; Animation by Robert McKimson; Story by Michael Sasanoff; Voice Characterization by Mel Blanc; Musical Direction by Carl W. Stalling.
The voice of God (Mel Blanc) takes Elmer far into the future--past 1990!--to see his pursuit of Bugs Bunny reach a successful conclusion. But Bugs reminisces about their first meeting, as babies, and finally has the last laugh. See pages 132-133. Video: *Bugs Bunny Superstar*, MGM/UA

STAGE DOOR CARTOON
Elmer Fudd; Dec 30; MM; Directed by I. Freleng; Story by Michael Maltese; Animation by Jack Bradbury; Voice Characterization by Mel Blanc; Musical Direction by Carl W. Stalling.
Elmer chases Bugs from the woods into the city and the backstage of a vaudeville theater, which only means that his humiliation at The Rabbit's hands now has an audience.

1945

HERR MEETS HARE
Jan 13; MM; Directed by I. Freleng; Story by Michael Maltese; Animation by Gerry Chiniquy; Musical Direction by Carl W. Stalling.
Bugs tangles with Nazi Hermann Goering in Germany's Black Forest, disguising himself as the Fuehrer, as a blonde-wigged Brunhilde, and as Josef Stalin. Video: *Bugs and Daffy: The Wartime Cartoons*, MGM/UA

THE UNRULY HARE
Elmer Fudd, Feb 10; MM; Directed by Frank Tashlin; Story by Melvin Millar; Animation by Cal Dalton; Voice Characterization by Mel Blanc; Musical Direction by Carl W. Stalling.
Elmer Fudd is a surveyor for the railroad, disturbing Bugs Bunny's peace, so Bugs retaliates by confusing his survey.

HARE TRIGGER
Yosemite Sam; May 5; MM; Directed by I. Freleng; Story by Michael Maltese; Animation Gerry Chiniquy, Manuel Perez, Ken Champin, Virgil Ross, and Gerry Chiniquy; Layouts and Backgrounds by Paul Julian and Hawley Pratt; Musical Directed by Carl W. Stalling.
In the first of many encounters with Yosemite Sam, Bugs foils Sam's holdup of the Superchief as the train barrels through the West. Video: *Bugs Bunny Classics*, MGM/UA.

HARE CONDITIONED
Aug 11; LT; Direction by Charles M. Jones; Story by Tedd Pierce; Animation by Ken Harris, Ben Washam, Basil Davidovich and Lloyd Vaughan; Musical Direction by Carl Stalling.
Bugs is part of a department store display window depicting a woodland scene when a store official (a caricature of radio's Throckmorton P. Gildersleeve) tries stuffing him for a transfer to the Taxidermy Department, setting off a chase around the store. Video: *Starring Bugs Bunny!* MGM/UA.

HARE TONIC
Elmer Fudd; Nov 10; LT; Directed by Charles M. Jones; Story by Tedd Pierce; Animation by Ben Washam, Lloyd Vaughan and Ken Harris; Layouts and Backgrounds by Earl Klein and Robert Gribbroek; Voice Characterization by Mel Blanc; Musical Direction by Carl Stalling.

Elmer Fudd heads home with a captive Bugs Bunny from the market, singing "Mammy's little baby loves rabbit stew." But Bugs saves his own life by convincing Elmer he's got that dread disease, Rabbititus. Video: *Starring Bugs Bunny!* MGM/UA

1946

BASEBALL BUGS
Feb 2; LT; Directed by I. Freleng; Story by Michael Maltese; Animation by Manuel Perez, Ken Champin, Virgil Ross, and Gerry Chiniquy; Layouts and Backgrounds by Hawley Pratt and Paul Julian; Voice Characterization by Mel Blanc; Musical Direction by Carl Stalling.
A series of gags around the baseball diamond, with Bugs playing all positions against the gruesome Gas-House Gorillas (a tough group of "Brooklyn Bums"). See pages 134-137. Video: *Bugs!* MGM/UA.

HARE REMOVER
Elmer Fudd; Mar 23; MM; Directed by Frank Tashlin; Story by Warren Foster; Animation by Richard Bickenbach, Art Davis, Cal Dalton, and I. Ellis; Backgrounds by Richard H. Thomas; Voice Characterizations by Mel Blanc; Effects Animation by A.C. Gamer; Musical Direction by Carl W. Stalling.
Elmer "traps" Bugs to use as a guinea pig for his experiments, but this plan backfires: Elmer becomes the guinea pig as he, Bugs, and a stray bear play out a series of mistaken identity situations.

HAIR-RAISING HARE
Bugs Bunny; May 25; MM; Directed by Charles M. Jones; Story by Tedd Pierce; Animation by Ben Washam, Ken Harris, Basil Davidovich, and Lloyd Vaughan; Layouts and Backgrounds by Robert Gribbroek and Earl Klein; Voice Characterization by Mel Blanc; Musical Direction by Carl W. Stalling.
Bugs is pursued by a hairy, orange, sneaker-wearing monster through the castle of evil scientist Peter Lorre. See pages 138-139. Video: *Bugs Bunny Superstar*, MGM/UA.

ACROBATTY BUNNY
June 29; LT; Directed by Robert McKimson; Story by Warren Foster; Animation by Arthur Davis, Cal Dalton, and Richard Bickenbach; Layouts and Backgrounds by Cornett Wood and Richard H. Thomas; Voice Characterization by Mel Blanc; Musical Direction by Carl W. Stalling.
The circus comes to town, and the lion's cage is put directly atop Bugs' rabbit hole, leading to a battle that proceeds into the Big Top and onto the flying trapeze. Video: *Bugs Bunny Classics*, MGM/UA.

RACKETEER RABBIT
Sept 14; LT; Directed by I. Freleng; Story by Michael Maltese; Animation by Gerry Chiniquy, Manny Perez, Ken Champin and Virgil Ross; Layouts and Backgrounds by Hawley Pratt and Paul Julian; Voice Characterization by Mel Blanc; Musical Direction by Carl W. Stalling.
Bugs makes himself at home in an abandoned house that turns out to be the hideout of Edward G. Robinson and Peter Lorre. Bugs has soon eliminated Lorre and driven Robinson to give himself up to the police. Video: *Bugs Bunny Classics*, MGM/UA.

Staff—including Friz Freleng, Bob Clampett, and Eddie Selzer—at storyboard meeting for Freleng's A Hare Grows in Manhattan, *1947. Michael Maltese acts out the story for them. The man with the dual-purpose pointer is Tedd Pierce, Termite Terrace's Don Juan.*

THE BIG SNOOZE

Elmer Fudd; Oct 5; LT; Directed by Robert Clampett; Animation by Rod Scribner, I. Ellis, Manny Gould, and J.C. Melendez; Layouts and Backgrounds by Thomas McKimson, Philip DeGuard; Voice Characterization by Mel Blanc; Musical Direction by Carl W. Stalling.

When Elmer stomps out of a typical Bugs-and-Elmer cartoon, Bugs retaliates by disturbing his sleep with "Nightmare Paint," creating a surreal fantasy. Video: *Cartoons For Big Kids*, Turner Home Video

RHAPSODY RABBIT

Bug Bunny; Nov 9; MM; Directed by I. Freleng; Story by Tedd Pierce and Michael Maltese; Animation by Gerry Chiniquy, Manuel Perez, Ken Champin, Virgil Ross, and Gerry Chiniquy; Layouts and Backgrounds by Hawley Pratt and Terry Lind; Voice Characterization by Mel Blanc; Musical Direction by Carl W. Stalling.

Bugs takes to the stage to perform Liszt's Second Hungarian Rhapsody, but is foiled by a little mouse. See pages 140–145. Video: *Bugs Bunny Superstar*, MGM/UA.

1947

RABBIT TRANSIT

May 10; MM; Directed by I. Freleng; Story by Michael Maltese and Tedd Pierce; Animation by Manuel Perez, Ken Champin, Virgil Ross, and Gerry Chiniquy; Layouts by Hawley Pratt; Backgrounds by Philip DeGuard; Effects Animation by A.C. Gamer; Voice Characterization by Mel Blanc; Musical Direction by Carl W. Stalling.

The third race between Bugs Bunny and Cecil Turtle involves a rocket-powered tortoise shell and extends as far as Chicago. Video: *BUGS!*, MGM/UA

A HARE GROWS IN MANHATTAN

May 22; MM; Directed by I. Freleng; Story by Michael Maltese, and Tedd Pierce; Animation by Virgil Ross, Gerry Chiniquy, Manuel Perez, and Ken Champin; Layouts by Hawley Pratt; Backgrounds by Philip DeGuard; Voice Characterization by Mel Blanc; Musical Direction by Carl Stalling.

What begins as Bugs' life story, rattled off for gossip columnist Lola Beverly, becomes the story of his street fight with a gang of tough dogs. Video: *Starring Bugs Bunny!* MGM/UA.

EASTER YEGGS

Elmer Fudd; June 28; LT; Directed by Robert McKimson; Story by Warren Foster; Animation by Charles McKimson, Richard Bickenbach, and I. Ellis; Layouts by Cornett Wood; Backgrounds by Richard H. Thomas; Voice Characterization by Mel Blanc; Musical Direction by Carl W. Stalling.

Bugs promises the Easter Bunny, "I'll deliver the Technicolor hen fruit for ya!" but encounters a mean little kid and his whole family, and an angry Elmer Fudd. Video: *Starring Bugs Bunny!* MGM/UA.

SLICK HARE

Elmer Fudd; Nov 1; MM; Directed by I. Freleng; Story by Tedd Pierce, and Michael Maltese; Animation by Virgil Ross, Gerry Chiniquy, Manuel Perez, and Ken Champin; Layouts by Hawley Pratt; Backgrounds by Paul Julian; Voice Characterization by Mel Blanc; Musical Direction by Carl W. Stalling.

At the Mocrumbo restaurant, Humphrey Bogart orders fried rabbit from waiter Elmer Fudd and gives him twenty minutes to serve it. Elmer finds Bugs Bunny and chases him around the club.

1948

GORILLA MY DREAMS
Jan 3; LT; Directed by Robert McKimson; Story by Warren Foster; Animation by Charles McKimson, Manny Gould, and John Carey; Layouts by Cornett Wood; Backgrounds by Richard H. Thomas; Voice Characterization by Mel Blanc; Musical Direction by Carl W. Stalling.
Bugs is plucked out of a barrel by Mrs. Gorilla, who wants to adopt him. But Mr. Gorilla chases the rabbit all over the jungle to the tune of Raymond Scott's "Dinner Music for a Pack of Hungry Cannibals." Video: *Bugs! MGM/UA*

A FEATHER IN HIS HARE
Bugs Bunny; Feb 7; LT; Directed by Charles M. Jones; Story by Michael Maltese and Tedd Pierce; Animation by Ken Harris, Phil Monroe, and Lloyd Vaughan; Layouts by Robert Gribbroek; Backgrounds by Peter Alvarado; Voice Characterization by Mel Blanc. Musical Direction by Carl Stalling.
A dopey Indian goes hunting for Bugs Bunny. Video: *Starring Bugs Bunny! MGM/UA.*

RABBIT PUNCH
Apr 10; MM; Directed by Charles M. Jones; Story by Tedd Pierce and Michael Maltese; Animation by Phil Monroe, Ken Harris, Lloyd Vaughan and Ben Washam; Layouts by Robert Gribbroek; Backgrounds by Peter Alvarado; Voice Characterization by Mel Blanc; Musical Direction by Carl W. Stalling.
At the World Championship fight, spectator Bugs Bunny heckles the Champ, and the Champ takes him on. See pages 146-147. Video: *Bugs Bunny Classics, MGM/UA.*

BUCCANEER BUNNY
Yosemite Sam; May 8; LT; Directed by I. Freleng; Story by Michael Maltese and Tedd Pierce; Animation by Manuel Perez, Ken Champin, Virgil Ross, and Gerry Chiniquy; Layouts by Hawley Pratt; Backgrounds by Paul Julian; Voice Characterization by Mel Blanc; Musical Direction by Carl W. Stalling.
Bugs knows where Pirate Sam has buried his treasure chest, so Sam chases Bugs all over the ship. Video: *Starring Bugs Bunny! MGM/UA.*

BUGS BUNNY RIDES AGAIN
Yosemite Sam; June 12; MM; Directed by I. Freleng; Story by Tedd Pierce and Michael Maltese; Animation by Ken Champin, Virgil Ross, Gerry Chiniquy, and Manuel Perez; Backgrounds by Paul Julian; Layouts by Hawley Pratt; Voice Characterization by Mel Blanc; Musical Direction by Carl W. Stalling.
Into a rough Western town stomps Yosemite Sam, looking for any varmint who dares to tame him. He finds Bugs Bunny up to the task. See pages 148-149. Video: *Bugs Bunny Classics, MGM/UA.*

HAREDEVIL HARE
Marvin Martian; July 24; LT; Directed by Charles M. Jones; Story by Michael Maltese; Animation by Ben Washam, Lloyd Vaughan, Ken Harris, and Phil Monroe; Layouts by Robert Gribbroek; Backgrounds by Peter Alvarado; Effects Animation by A.C. Gamer; Voice Characterization: Mel Blanc; Musical Direction by Carl W. Stalling.
Bugs is the first test rabbit to be blasted into space. Crash landing on the moon, he

encounters Marvin Martian (known in this film as Commander X-2) preparing to blow up the Earth. Video: *Bugs Bunny Classics, MGM/UA.*

HOT CROSS BUNNY
Aug 21; MM; Directed by Robert McKimson; Story by Warren Foster; Animation by Manny Gould, Charles McKimson, and Phil DeLara; Layouts by Cornett Wood; Backgrounds by Richard H. Thomas; Voice Characterization by Mel Blanc; Musical Direction by Carl W. Stalling.
Inside the Eureka Experimental Hosptial, Paul Revere Foundation ("Hardly a Man Is Still Alive!") a doctor plans to put the brains of a chicken into experimental rabbit No. 46, a.k.a. Bugs Bunny. A chase ensues. Bugs finally declares the doctor "a victim of fowl play."

HARE SPLITTER
Sept 25; MM; Directed by I. Freleng; Story by Tedd Pierce; Animation by Gerry Chiniquy, Manuel Perez, Ken Champin, and Virgil Ross; Backgrounds by Paul Julian; Layouts by Hawley Pratt; Voice Characterization by Mel Blanc; Musical Direction by Carl W. Stalling.
Bugs is sprucing up for a date with his girl Daisy Lou, but finds she has gone shopping. This gives him a chance to dress up in her clothes and fool his rival, Casbah.

A-LAD-IN HIS LAMP
Oct 23; LT; Directed by Robert McKimson; Story by Warren Foster; Animation by Phil DeLara, Manny Gould, John Carey, and Charles McKimson; Layouts by Cornett Wood; Backgrounds by Richard H. Thomas; Effects Animation by A.C. Gamer; Voice Characterization by Mel Blanc; Musical Direction by Carl W. Stalling.
Bugs finds Aladdin's lamp. He shines it up, and out pops an arm-flailing genie, nicknamed Smokey (voiced by Jim Backus). Bugs decides to go with the genie to Baghdad. Video: *Bugs Bunny's Hare-Raising Tales, WB.*

MY BUNNY LIES OVER THE SEA
Dec 14; MM; Directed by Charles M. Jones; Story by Michael Maltese; Animation by Ken Harris, Phil Monroe, Ben Washam, and Lloyd Vaughan; Layouts by Robert Gribbroek; Backgrounds by Peter Alvarado; Voice Characterization by Mel Blanc; Musical Direction by Carl W. Stalling.
Bugs finds himself in Scotland and comes to the rescue of an old lady being attached by a monster--which turns out to be a Scotsman in kilts playing a bagpipe. He challenges Bugs to a game of golf, leading to a round of golf gags.

1949

HARE DO
Jan 15; MM; Directed by I. Freleng; Story by Tedd Pierce; Animation by Ken Champin, Virgil Ross, Gerry Chiniquy, and Manuel Perez; Backgrounds by Paul Julian; Layouts by Hawley Pratt; Voice Characterization by Mel Blanc; Musical Direction by Carl W. Stalling.
As in *Stage Door Cartoon,* Elmer Fudd chases Bugs from the woods into the city and into a theater, where a series of theater gags ensue. Video: *Bugs Bunny's Wacky Adventures, WB.*

Cel from Haredevil Hare, *1948.*

MISSISSIPPI HARE
Feb 26; LT; Directed by Charles M. Jones; Story by Michael Maltese; Animation by Ben Washam, Lloyd Vaughan, Ken Harris, and Phil Monroe; Layouts by Robert Gribbroek; Backgrounds by Peter Alvarado; Effects Animation by A.C. Gamer; Voice Characterization by Mel Blanc; Musical Direction by Carl W. Stalling.
Cotton pickers accidentally pick cotton-tailed Bugs out of the field and throw him in with the cotton being shipped via riverboat. Bugs disguises himself as a Southern gentleman and spars with Colonel Shuffle, a hot-tempered river gambler.

REBEL RABBIT
Apr 9; MM; Directed by Robert McKimson; Story by Warren Foster; Animation by Charles McKimson, Phil DeLara, Manny Gould, and John Carey; Layouts by Cornett Wood; Backgrounds by Richard H. Thomas; Voice Characterization by Mel Blanc; Musical Direction by Carl W. Stalling.
Bugs notices the bounty signs for his fellow woodland creatures: $50 for a fox, $75 for a bear, and only 2 cents for a rabbit. Insulted, he becomes determined to prove a rabbit can be more obnoxious than anybody.

HIGH DIVING HARE
Yosemite Sam; Apr 30; LT; Directed by I. Freleng; Story by Tedd Pierce; Animation by Gery Chiniquy. Manuel Perez, Ken Champin, Virgil Ross, and Pete Burness; Backgrounds by Paul Julian; Layouts by Hawley Pratt; Voice Characterization by Mel Blanc; Musical Direction by Carl W. Stalling.
Bugs is a carnival barker, and one of the acts in a sideshow, Fearless Freep the high diver, can't make it. An angry Yosemite Sam tries to force Bugs at gunpoint to perform the high-diving act, but the bunny repeatedly tricks Sam into jumping. Video: *Salute to Friz Freleng, WB*

Drawing by Robert McKimson for
A Windblown Hare, *1949*

BOWERY BUGS

June 4; MM; Directed by Arthur Davis; Story by William Scott, Lloyd Turner; Animation by Emery Hawkins, Basil Davidovich, J.C. Melendez, and Don Williams; Layouts by Don Smith; Backgrounds by Philip DeGuard; Voice Characterization by Mel Blanc; Musical Direction by Carl W. Stalling.

Bugs tells an old-timer the story of Steve Brodie, the man who jumped off the Brooklyn Bridge in 1886. Brodie needed a rabbit's foot and tried to get one of Bugs', forcing The Rabbit to adopt a series of transparent masquerades.

LONG-HAIRED HARE

June 25; LT; Directed by Charles M. Jones; Story by Michael Maltese; Animation by Phil Monroe, Ben Washam, Lloyd Vaughan, and Ken Harris; Layouts by Robert Gribbroek; Backgrounds by Peter Alvarado; Voice Characterization by Mel Blanc; Musical Direction by Carl W. Stalling.

When the opera singer Giovanni Jones smashes Bugs' banjo, harp, and tuba, The Rabbit declares war and disrupts the singer's solo performance at the Hollywood Bowl. Video: *Bugs Bunny's Wacky Adventures,* WB

KNIGHTS MUST FALL

July 16; MM; Directed by I. Freleng; Story by Tedd Pierce; Animation by Ken Champin, Virgil Ross, Manuel Perez, and Gerry Chiniquy; Layouts by Hawley Pratt; Backgrounds by Paul Julian; Voice Characterization by Mel Blanc; Musical Direction by Carl W. Stalling.

In medieval times, for the horrendous act of tossing a half-eaten carrot into a suit of armor, Bugs is challenged to a duel by Sir Pantsalot of Drop Seat Manor. What follows is a series of jousting tournament gags.

THE GREY HOUNDED HARE

Aug. 6; LT; Directed by Robert McKimson; Story by Warren Foster; Animation by John Carey, Charles McKimson, Phil DeLara, and Manny Gould; Layouts by Cornett Wood; Backgrounds by Richard Thomas; Voice Characterization by Mel Blanc; Musical Direction by Carl W. Stalling.

Bugs falls in love with the mechanical bunny at the dog track and lures all the dogs but No. 7 off the track to rescue her. No. 7 requires more time, but Bugs eventually kisses his "dreamboat," and gets an electric shock. Video: *Bugs Bunny's Wacky Adventures,* WB

THE WINDBLOWN HARE

Aug 27; LT; Directed by Robert McKimson; Story by Warren Foster; Animation by Charles McKimson, Phil DeLara, Manny Gould, and John Carey; Layouts by Cornett Wood; Backgrounds by Richard H. Thomas; Voice Characterization by Mel Blanc; Musical Direction by Carl W. Stalling.

Three little pigs, fearful of the wolf, sell their houses of straw and sticks to Bugs. When the wolf blows them both down, Bugs gives him the works. Then Bugs and the wolf team up and get even with the pigs. Video: *Bugs Bunny's Hare-Raising Tales,* WB

FRIGID HARE

Oct 7; MM; Directed by Charles M. Jones; Story by Michael Maltese; Animation by Phil Monroe, Ben Washam, Lloyd Vaughan, and Ken Harris; Layouts by Robert Gribbroek; Backgrounds by Peter Alvarado; Voice Characterization by Mel Blanc; Musical Direction by Carl W. Stalling.

Bugs rescues a penguin from an Eskimo at the South Pole.

WHICH IS WITCH?

Dec 3; LT; Directed by I. Freleng; Story by Tedd Pierce; Animation by Ken Champin, Virgil Ross, Arthur Davis, and Gerry Chiniquy; Layouts by Hawley Pratt; Backgrounds by Paul Julian; Effects Animation by A.C. Gamer; Voice Characterization by Mel Blanc; Musical Direction by Carl W. Stalling.

An African witch doctor, Dr. I.C. Spots, is preparing a potion and needs a rabbit to complete it. When Spots sees Bugs strolling through the jungle, the chase is on.

RABBIT HOOD

Dec 24; MM; Directed by Charles M. Jones; Story by Michael Maltese; Animation by Ken Harris, Phil Monroe, Ben Washam, and Lloyd Vaughan; Layouts by Robert Gribbroek; Backgrounds by Peter Alvarado; Voice Characterization by Mel Blanc; Musical Direction by Carl W. Stalling.

Sherwood Forest is studded with "No Poaching" signs, "Not even an egg!" Bugs tries to swipe a carrot from the King's carrot patch, but is caught crimson-fisted by the Sheriff of Nottingham.

1950

HURDY GURDY HARE

Jan 21; MM; Directed by Robert McKimson; Story by Warren Foster; Animation by J.C. Melendez, Emery Hawkins, Charles McKimson, John Carey, and Phil DeLara; Layouts by Cornett Wood; Backgrounds by Phil DeGuard; Voice Characterization by Mel Blanc; Musical Direction by Carl W. Stalling.

Bugs goes into the hurdy gurdy business, but his monkey "pockets" the take in his cap, leaving Bugs to can him. The little monkey sics a pal on Bugs, a gruesome gorilla from the Central Park Zoo.

MUTINY ON THE BUNNY

Yosemite Sam; Feb 11; LT; Directed by I. Freleng; Story by Tedd Pierce; Animation by Gerry Chiniquy, Ken Champin, Virgil Ross, and Arthur Davis; Backgrounds by Paul Julian; Layouts by Hawley Pratt; Voice Characterization by Mel Blanc; Musical Direction by Carl W. Stalling.

Shanghai Sam, the cruel captain of "The Sad Sack" (formerly "The Bounty"), needs to recruit a new crew. Bugs takes him up on his offer, but causes trouble when he wises up to conditions aboard ship.

HOMELESS HARE

Mar 11; MM; Directed by Charles M. Jones; Story by Michael Maltese; Animation by Ken Harris, Phil Monroe, Ben Washam, and Lloyd Vaughan; Layouts by Robert Gribbroek; Backgrounds by Peter Alvarado; Voice Characterizations by Mel Blanc; Musical Direction by Carl W. Stalling.

A roughneck construction worker upearths Bugs' rabbit hole with a steam shovel, ignoring Bugs' plea to restore it--setting off a *contretemps* all over the construction site.

BIG HOUSE BUNNY

Yosemite Sam; Apr 22; LT; Directed by I. Freleng; Story by Tedd Pierce; Animation by Virgil Ross, Arthur Davis, Gerry Chiniquy, and Ken Champin; Layouts by Hawley Pratt; Backgrounds by Phil DeGuard; Voice Characterization by Mel Blanc; Musical Direction by Carl W. Stalling.

Bugs hops in a rabbit hole and comes up in Sing Song Prison. Mistaken for a convict by the prison guard (Yosemite) Sam Shultz, he spends the rest of the film trying to get out of the pen.

WHAT'S UP, DOC?

Elmer Fudd; June 17; LT; Directed by Robert McKimson; Story by Warren Foster; Animation by J.C. Melendez, Charles McKimson, Phil DeLara, and Wilson Burness; Layouts by Cornett Wood; Backgrounds by Richard H. Thomas; Voice Characterization by Mel Blanc; Musical Direction Carl W. Stalling.

Bugs' career in flashback, from piano-playing as a baby to stardom at Warner Bros. Bugs and Elmer perform the song, "What's Up Doc?" See pages 150-153. Video: *Elmer Fudd's Comedy Capers,* WB

8 BALL BUNNY

July 8; LT; Directed by Charles M. Jones; Story by Michael Maltese; Animation by Phil Monroe, Ben Washam, Lloyd Vaughan, Ken Harris, and Emery Hawkins; Layouts and Backgrounds by Peter Alvarado; Voice Characterization by Mel Blanc; Musical Direction by Carl W. Stalling.

Bugs again befriends the penguin from *Frigid Hare,* consenting this time to take him home. The expedition covers New Orleans, Martinique, the Panama Canal, and finally the South Pole, before the penguin reveals that he's actually from Hoboken.

HILLBILLY HARE

Aug 12; MM; Directed by Robert McKimson; Story by Tedd Pierce; Animation by Rod Scribner, Phil DeLara, John Carey, Emery Hawkins, and Charles McKimson; Layouts by Cornett Wood; Backgrounds by Richard H. Thomas; Voice Characterization by Mel Blanc; Musical Direction by Carl W. Stalling.

Bugs, vacationing in the Ozarks, encounters Curt Martin and his brother Pumpkinhead. Climaxes in a very funny square dance.

BUNKER HILL BUNNY

Yosemite Sam; Sept 23; MM; Directed by I. Freleng; Story by Tedd Pierce; Animation by Gerry Chiniquy, Ken Champin, Virgil Ross, and Arthur Davis; Layouts by Hawley Pratt; Backgrounds by Paul Julian; Voice Characterization by Mel Blanc; Musical Direction by Carl W. Stalling.

The historic Revolutionary War Battle of Bagel Heights is fought when Bugs Bunny defends his fort against (Yosemite) Sam Von Schamm, the Hessian, turning him into "a Hessian with no agression." Video: *Salute to Friz Freleng*, WB.

BUSHY HARE

Nov 11; LT; Directed by Robert McKimson; Story by Warren Foster; Animation by Phil DeLara, J.C. Melendez, Charles McKimson, Rod Scribner, and John Carey; Layouts by Cornett Wood; Backgrounds by Richard H. Thomas; Voice Characterization by Mel Blanc; Musical Direction by Carl W. Stalling.
Bugs Bunny arrives in the Australian outback through a series of accidents and tangles with a maternal marsupial and an abrasive aborigine.

RABBIT OF SEVILLE

Elmer Fudd; Dec 16; LT; Directed by Charles M. Jones; Story by Michael Maltese; Animation by Phil Monroe, Ben Washam, Lloyd Vaughan, Ken Harris, and Emery Hawkins; Layouts by Robert Gribbroek; Backgrounds by Philip DeGuard; Voice Characterization by Mel Blanc; Musical Direction by Carl W. Stalling.
Bugs and Elmer invade a performance of *The Barber of Seville* and provide their own lyrics for Rossini's music. See pages 154-55.
Videos: *Elmer Fudd's Comedy Capers, A Salute to Mel Blanc*, WB

1951

HARE WE GO

Jan 6; MM; Directed by Robert McKimson; Story by Warren Foster; Animation by Phil DeLara, Charles McKimson, John Carey, Rod Scribner, and J.C. Melendez; Layouts by Cornett Wood; Backgrounds by Richard H. Thomas; Voice Characterization by Mel Blanc; Musical Direction by Carl W. Stalling.
Bugs, as mascot, accompanies Christopher Columbus and his crew to America in 1492, but Columbus gets all the credit for discovering the continent.

RABBIT EVERY MONDAY

Yosemite Sam; Feb 10; LT; Directed by I. Freleng; Animation by Manuel Perez, Ken Champin, Virgil Ross, and Arthur Davis; Layouts by Hawley Pratt; Backgrounds by Paul Julian; Voice Characterization by Mel Blanc; Musical Direction by Carl W. Stalling.
Yosemite Sam stalks Bugs, who takes refuge in Sam's rifle, then messes up the works and the owner with bubblegum. Hunt picture climaxes with party scene inside Sam's oven.

BUNNY HUGGED

Bunny Hugged; Mar 10; MM; Directed by Charles M. Jones; Story by Michael Maltese; Animation by Ken Harris, Phil Monroe, Ben Washam, and Lloyd Vaughan; Layouts by Peter Alvarado; Backgrounds by Philip DeGuard; Voice Characterization by Mel Blanc; Musical Direction by Carl W. Stalling.
Rabbit Punch had Jones, Maltese, and Bugs taking on boxing; this slightly lesser followup has then trying to out-cartoon the ludicrousness of real-life wrestling, with its slurry announcers and good guy/bad guy theatrics.
Video: *Bugs Bunny's Wacky Adventures*, WB

THE FAIR HAIRED HARE

Yosemite Sam; Apr 14; LT; Directed by I. Freleng; Story by Warren Foster; Animation by Ken Champin, Virgil Ross, Arthur Davis, Manuel Perez, and John Carey; Layouts by Hawley Pratt; Backgrounds by Paul Julian; Voice Characterization by Mel Blanc; Musical Direction by Carl W. Stalling.
Bugs and Sam battle over property rights to the land above Bugs' rabbit hole, finally trying to obey a judge's ruling that they "share" the property.

RABBIT FIRE

Daffy Duck, Elmer Fudd; May 19; LT; Directed by Charles M. Jones; Story by Michael Maltese; Animation by Lloyd Vaughan, Ken Harris, Phil Monroe, and Ben Washam; Layouts by Robert Gribbroek; Backgrounds by Philip DeGuard; Voice Characterization by Mel Blanc; Musical Direction by Carl W. Stalling.
The first entry of a trilogy in which Bugs and Daffy try to use hunting regulations to induce Elmer to shoot the other, arguing endlessly whether it's really rabbit season or duck season. Video: *Daffy Duck: The Nuttiness Continues...* WB

FRENCH RAREBIT

June 30; MM; Directed by Robert McKimson; Story by Tedd Pierce; Animation by Rod Scribner, Phil DeLara, Charles McKimson, and Emery Hawkins; Layouts by Cornett Wood; Backgrounds by Richard H. Thomas; Voice Characterization by Mel Blanc. Musical Direction by Eugene Poddany; Orchestrations by Milt Franklyn.
Two Parisian chefs, Francois and Louie, who have restaurants on opposite sides of the street on which Bugs is strolling, insist on having thees rabbit for ze dinner menu. Bugs plays the two against each other.

HIS HARE RAISING TALE

Aug 11; LT; Directed by I. Freleng; Story by Warren Foster; Animation by Virgil Ross, Manuel Perez, Ken Champin, and Arthur Davis; Layouts by Paul Julian; Backgrounds by Hawley Pratt; Voice Characterization by Mel Blanc; Musical Direction by Carl W. Stalling.
Bugs tells tales to his nephew, Clyde Rabbit, illustrated by clips from *Baseball Bugs, Stage Door Cartoon, Rabbit Punch, Falling Hare*, and *Haredevil Hare*.

BALLOT BOX BUNNY

Yosemite Sam; Oct 6; MM; Directed by I. Freleng; Story by Warren Foster; Animation by Ken Champin, Virgil Ross, Arthur Davis, and Manuel Perez; Layouts by Hawley Pratt; Backgrounds by Paul Julian; Voice Characterization by Mel Blanc; Musical Direction by Carl W. Stalling.
Bugs hears candidate Sam campaigning on a platform that includes rabbit genocide. He fights fire with fire by running against Sam himself. Video: *Salute to Mel Blanc*, WB

BIG TOP BUNNY

Dec 12; MM; Directed by Robert McKimson; Story by Tedd Pierce; Animation by Charles KcKimson, Rod Scribner, Phil DeLara, and Bob Wickersham; Layouts by Peter Alvarado; Backgrounds by Richard H. Thomas; Voice Characterization by Mel Blanc; Musical Direction by Carl W. Stalling.
Bugs vies with Bruno, an egotistical Russian acrobat bear, jealous of The Rabbit's coveted spot as star of Kolonel Korney's World Famous Circus.

1952

OPERATION: RABBIT

Wile E. Coyote; Jan 19; LT; Directed by Charles M. Jones; Story by Michael Maltese; Animation by Lloyd Vaughan, Ben Washam,

Background study by Peter Alvarado for Bunny Hugged, *1951*

Ken Harris, and Phil Monroe; Layouts by Robert Gribbroek; Backgrounds by Philip DeGuard; Voice Characterization by Mel Blanc; Musical Direction by Carl W. Stalling.
Wile E. Coyote, from Jones' Roadrunner cartoons, makes the first of several attempts to use Bugs to satisfy both his craving for food and his mental craving for the thrill of capturing some helpless desert animal with an elaborate scientific contraption. Video: *Roadrunner Vs. Wile E. Coyote: The Classic Chase.*

14 CARROT RABBIT
Yosemite Sam; Feb 16; LT; Directed by I. Freleng; Story by Warren Foster; Animation by Manuel Perez, Ken Champin, Virgil Ross, and Arthur Davis; Layouts by Hawley Pratt; Backgrounds by Irv Wyner; Voice Characterization by Mel Blanc; Musical Direction by Carl W. Stalling.
In the Klondike, prospectors are terrified of claim-jumping Chillicothe (Yosemite) Sam, who tries to go into partnership with Bugs when he realized a "funny feeling" comes over The Rabbit whenever he's near gold.

FOXY BY PROXY
Feb 23; MM; Directed by I. Freleng; Story by Warren Foster; Animation by Virgil Ross, Arthur Davis, Manuel Perez, and Ken Champin; Layouts by Hawley Pratt; Backgrounds by Irv Wyner; Voice Characterization by Mel Blanc; Musical Direction by Carl W. Stalling.
This is Tex Avery's *Of Fox and Hounds* refitted for Bugs. To liven up what he was afraid would be a dull day, Bugs uses last year's Halloween costume to masquerade as a fox and confuse the hunting dogs.

WATER, WATER EVERY HARE
Apr 19; LT; Directed by Charles M. Jones; Story by Michael Maltese; Animation by Ben Washam, Ken Harris, Phil Monroe, and Lloyd Vaughan; Layouts by Robert Gribbroek; Backgrounds by Philip DeGuard; Effects Animation by Harry Love; Voice Characterization by Mel Blanc; Musical Direction by Carl W. Stalling.
Jones' surreal extension of *Hair-Raising Hare* has fewer big gags and more of a mesmerizing quality. Again Bugs is pursued through the castle of an evil scientist by the hairy orange hump-headed humanoid in sneakers.

THE HASTY HARE
Marvin Martian; June 7; LT; Directed by Charles M. Jones; Story by Michael Maltese; Animation by Ken Harris, Lloyd Vaughan, and Ben Washam; Layouts by Robert Gribbroek; Backgrounds by Philip DeGuard; Voice Characterization by Mel Blanc; Musical Direction by Carl W. Stalling.
Marvin Martian lands on Earth, with the assignment "to bring back one (1) Earth creature" and makes the mistake of choosing Bugs Bunny.

OILY HARE
July 26; MM; Directed by Robert McKimson; Story by Tedd Pierce; Animation by Rod Scribner, Phil DeLara, Charles McKimson, and Herman Cohen; Layouts by Peter Alvarado; Backgrounds by Richard H. Thomas; Voice Characterization by Mel Blanc; Musical Direction by Carl W. Stalling.
Bugs battles with a millionaire Texas oilman (sort of Yosemite Sam with a haircut and more of an accent) and his sidekick Maverick over squatting rights to his rabbit hole.

RABBIT SEASONING
Daffy Duck, Elmer Fudd; Sept 20; MM; Directed by Charles M. Jones; Story by Michael Maltese; Animation by Ben Washam, Lloyd Vaughan, and Ken Harris; Layouts by Maurice Noble; Backgrounds by Philip DeGuard; Voice Characterization by Mel Blanc; Musical Direction by Carl W. Stalling.
"Pronoun trouble:" The hunting routine from *Rabbit Fire* gets extended to extremes here to emphasize verbal one-upsmanship, which translates directly into shots in the head, inevitably directed at Daffy. Videos: *Elmer Fudd's Comedy Capers, Salute to Chuck Jones,* WB

RABBIT'S KIN
Nov 15; MM; Directed by Robert McKimson; Story by Tedd Pierce; Animation by Charles McKimson, Herman Cohen, Rod Scribner, and Phil DeLara; Layouts by Robert Givens; Backgrounds by Richard H. Thomas; Voice Characterization by Mel Blanc; Musical Direction by Carl W. Stalling.
Bugs saves a smaller bunny from the hungry slob Pete Puma and shows him a few pointers in the fine art of cartoon heckling.

HARE LIFT
Yosemite Sam; Dec 20; LT; Directed by I. Freleng; Story by Warren Foster; Animation by Manuel Perez, Ken Champin, Virgil Ross, and Arthur Davis; Layouts by Hawley Pratt; Backgrounds by Irv Wyner; Voice Characterization by Mel Blanc; Musical Direction by Carl W. Stalling.
Bugs is calmly inspecting the world's largest airplane when bankrobber Sam, making a getaway, forces him at gunpoint to fly the thing.

1953

FORWARD MARCH HARE
Feb 4; LT; Directed by Charles M. Jones; Story by Michael Maltese; Animation by Ben Washam, Lloyd Vaughan, and Ken Harris; Layouts by Maurice Noble; Backgrounds by Philip DeGuard; Voice Characterization by Mel Blanc; Musical Direction by Carl W. Stalling; Orchestrations by Milt Franklyn.
Bugs gets a draft notice intended for his neighbor. Most of the laughs come from the reaction of a straitlaced military types to the presence of a cartoon animal in this man's army.

UPSWEPT HARE
Elmer Fudd; Mar 14; MM; Directed by Robert McKimson; Story by Tedd Pierce; Animation by Charles McKimson, Herman Cohen, Rod Scribner, and Phil DeLara; Layouts by Robert Givens; Backgrounds by Richard H. Thomas; Voice Characterization by Mel Blanc; Musical Direction by Carl W. Stalling.
When Elmer brings hom a rare plant specimen, he unwittingly brings Bugs home with it. The Rabbit suggests, "If you can prove you're better than me, I'll leave," leading to a series of contests.

SOUTHERN FRIED RABBIT
Yosemite Sam; May 2; MM; Directed by I. Freleng; Story by Warren Foster; Animation by Art Davis, Manuel Perez, Ken Champin, and Virgil Ross; Layouts by Hawley Pratt; Backgrounds by Irv Wyner; Voice Characterization by Mel Blanc; Musical Direction by Carl W. Stalling.
News of a record carrot crop in Alabama sends Bugs south, but he finds the Mason-

Dixon line defended by Colonel Sam of the Confederate Army, who has been ordered by General Lee not to let any Yankee cross it.

HARE TRIMMED
Yosemite Sam; June 20; MM; Directed by I. Freleng; Story by Warren Foster; Animation by Manuel Perez, Ken Champin, Virgil Ross, and Arthur Davis; Layouts by Hawley Pratt; Backgrounds by Irv Wyner; Voice Characterization by Mel Blanc; Musical Direction by Carl W. Stalling.
Bugs and Sam are fighting each other over Granny. Bugs is a self-declared boy scout, anxious to protect Granny from snake-in-the-grass Sam, who has heard that she has inherited 50 million dollars.

BULLY FOR BUGS
Aug 8; LT; Directed by Charles M. Jones; Story by Michael Maltese; Animation by Ben Washam, Lloyd Vaughan, and Ken Harris; Layouts by Maurice Noble; Backgrounds by Philip DeGuard; Voice Characterization by Mel Blanc; Musical Direction by Carl W. Stalling.
Bugs tunnels into the middle of a bullfight arena just as the bull makes short work of the matador, and takes on the beast himself. See pages 156-159. Video: *Bugs Bunny's Hare-Raising Tales,* WB

DUCK! RABBIT, DUCK!
Daffy Duck, Elmer Fudd; Oct 3; MM; Directed by Charles M. Jones; Story by Michael Maltese; Animation by Ken Harris, Ben Washam, Lloyd Vaughan, Richard Thompson, and Abe Levitow; Layouts by Maurice Noble; Backgrounds by Philip DeGuard; Voice Characterization by Mel Blanc; Musical Direction by Carl W. Stalling.
Follow-up to *Rabbit Fire* and *Rabbit Seasoning,* taking place in the snow and featuring the greatest number of "seasons" on record: skunk, pigeon, mongoose, baseball. Video: *Bugs Bunny's Wacky Adventures,* WB

ROBOT RABBIT
Elmer Fudd; Dec 12; LT; Directed by I. Freleng; Story by Warren Foster; Animation by Virgil Ross, Arthur Davis, Manuel Perez, and Ken Champin; Layouts by Hawley Pratt; Backgrounds by Irv Wyner; Voice Characterization by Mel Blanc; Musical Direction by Carl W. Stalling.
Farmer Fudd, peeved at carrot-thief Bugs, phones the ACME Pest Control service for their "ewectwonic pest contwoller with a wobot bwain."

1954

CAPTAIN HAREBLOWER
Yosemite Sam; Feb 16; LT; Directed by I. Freleng; Story by Warren Foster; Animation by Manuel Perez, Ken Champin, Virgil Ross, and Art Davis; Layouts by Hawley Pratt; Backgrounds by Irv Wyner; Voice Characterization by Mel Blanc; Musical Direction by Carl W. Stalling.
Pirate Sam, terror of the Main, has reputation enough to frighten the entire crew of an "unprotected" ship, save Bugs Bunny. We're talking *lots* of explosions in the face here, in rapid-fire succession.

BUGS AND THUGS
Rocky and Mugsy; Mar 2; LT; Directed by I. Freleng; Story by Warren Foster; Animation by Manuel Perez, Ken Champin, Virgil Ross and Art Davis; Layouts by Hawley Pratt; Backgrounds by Irv Wyner; Voice Characteri-

zation by Mel Blanc; Musical Direction by Milt Franklin.

Sophisticated urbanite Bugs calls a cab that he doesn't realize is actually the getaway vehicle for bank robbers Rocky and Mugsy. They take him for a ride because he "knows too much" (among other things that Carson City is the capital of Nevada).

NO PARKING HARE
May 1; LT; Directed by Robert McKimson; Story by Sid Marcus; Animation by Herman Cohen, Rod Scribner, Phil DeLara, and Charles McKimson; Layouts by Robert Givens; Backgrounds by Richard H. Thomas; Voice Characterization by Mel Blanc; Musical Direction by Carl W. Stalling.

The Bugs versus construction worker theme of *Homeless Hare* is revived, with the big cruel lummox trying to blast Bugs out of his rabbit hole so that he can build a freeway.

DEVIL MAY HARE
Tasmanian Devil; June 19; LT; Directed by Robert McKimson; Story by Sid Marcus; Animation by Herman Cohen, Rod Scribner, Phil DeLara, and Charles McKimson; Layouts by Robert Givens; Backgrounds by Richard H. Thomas; Voice Characterization by Mel Blanc; Musical Direction by Carl W. Stalling.

In Bugs' first confrontation with the Tasmanian Devil, he looks up the beast in his encyclopedia as it enters his home and makes ready to devour him.

BEWITCHED BUNNY
Witch Hazel; July 24; LT; Directed by Charles M. Jones; Story by Michael Maltese; Animation by Lloyd Vaughan, Ken Harris, and Ben Washam; Layouts by Maurice Noble; Backgrounds by Philip DeGuard; Voice Characterization by Mel Blanc; Musical Direction by Carl W. Stalling.

Bugs rescues Teutonic toddlers Gretel and Hansel from wicked Witch Hazel (June Foray) by disguising himself as a bespectacled truant officer.

YANKEE DOODLE BUGS
Aug 28; LT; Directed by I. Freleng; Story by Warren Foster; Animation by Art Davis, Manuel Perez, and Virgil Ross; Layouts by Hawley Pratt; Backgrounds by Irv Wyner; Voice Characterization by Mel Blanc; Musical Direction by Milt Franklin.

Bugs gives his little nephew Clyde pointers on early Americana, writing himself into about half the events.

LUMBER JACK-RABBIT
Nov 13; LT; Directed by Charles M. Jones; Story by Michael Maltese; Animation by Ben Washam, Lloyd Vaughan, Richard Thompson, Abe Levitow, and Ken Harris; Layouts by Maurice Noble; Backgrounds by Philip DeGuard; Voice Characterization by Mel Blanc; Musical Direction by Carl W. Stalling.

Bugs wanders into Paul Bunyan country and does battle with Paul 124-foot, 4,600-ton puppy Smidgen. Warner's only cartoon produced in 3-D.

Cel and matching background from Lumber Jack-Rabbit, *1954*

BABY BUGGY BUNNY
Dec 18; MM; Directed by Charles M. Jones; Story by Michael Maltese; Animation by Abe Levitow, Lloyd Vaughan, Ken Harris, and Ben Washam; Layouts by Ernest Nordli; Backgrounds by Philip DeGuard; Voice Characterization by Mel Blanc; Musical Direction by Milt Franklin.

The midget gangster Baby-Faced Finster pulls a bank job, then disguise himself as a baby in a buggy. When the carriage, with the loot, rolls down Bugs' rabbit hole, Finster tries to rescue his booty. Probable inspiration for Baby Herman in *Who Framed Roger Rabbit.*

1955

BEANSTALK BUNNY
Daffy Duck, Elmer Fudd; Feb 12; MM; Directed by Charles M. Jones; Story by Michael Maltese; Animation by Ken Harris, Richard Thompson, Abe Levitow, and Keith Darling. Layouts by Robert Givens; Backgrounds by Richard H. Thomas; Voice Characterization by Mel Blanc; Musical Direction by Carl Stalling.

Daffy, as Jack, climbs the beanstalk eagerly when it sprouts of of a rabbit hole. Bugs gets involved because his bed has been carried upwards by the beanstalk. Elmer, as the Giant, enjoys a rare opportunity to play a genuine threat. Video: *Daffy Duck: The Nuttiness Continues...* WB

SAHARA HARE
Bugs Bunny, Yosemite Sam; Daffy Duck Cameo; Mar 26; LT; Directed by I. Freleng; Story by Warren Foster; Animation by Gerry Chiniquy, Ted Bonnicksen, and Arthur Davis; Layouts by Hawley Pratt. Backgrounds by Irv Wyner; Voice Characterization by Mel Blanc; Music by Milt Franklin.

By getting footprints all over the Sahara Desert, Bugs rouses the ire of Riff Raff Sam, bedsheeted bandit (riding on an un-whoable bump-backed camel), who chases Bugs into a nearby Foreign Legion outpost.

HARE BRUSH
May 7; LT; Directed by I. Freleng; Story by Warren Foster; Animation by Ted Bonnicksen, Art Davis and Gerry Chiniquy; Layouts by Hawley Pratt; Backgrounds by Irv Wyner; Voice Characterization by Mel Blanc; Music by Milt Franklin.

Tycoon Elmer thinks he's a rabbit, which worries his corporate board. They send him to a sanitarium, where he get to indulge his delusion further. Bugs, not knowing what's going on, agrees to trade places with Elmer. Video: *Elmer Fudd's Comedy Capers,* WB

RABBIT RAMPAGE
Elmer Fudd Cameo; June 11; LT; Directed by Charles M. Jones; Story by Michael Maltese. Animation by Ben Washam; Layouts by Ernest Nordli; Backgrounds by Philip DeGuard; Voice Characterization by Mel Blanc; Music by Milt Franklin.

Bugs, who has definite ideas as to how he should be drawn, clashes with the cartoonist who creates him in his version of Daffy's classic *Duck Amuck.*

THIS IS A LIFE?

Daffy Duck, Elmer Fudd, Yosemite Sam; July 9; MM; Directed by I. Freleng; Story by Warren Foster; Animation by Ted Bonnicksen and Arthur Davis; Layouts by Hawley Pratt; Backgrounds by Mel Blanc; Music by Milt Franklyn.

Bugs has been unexpectedly put at the center of "America's most talked-about program" by the show's emcee, Elmer; he also has to worry about Daffy, who is convinced that he was meant to be the guest on the show.

HYDE AND HARE

Bugs Bunny: Aug 27; LT; Directed by I. Freleng; Story by Warren Foster; Animation by Gerry Chiniquy, Virgil Ross, Art Davis and Ted Bonnicksen; Layouts by Hawley Pratt; Backgrounds by Irv Wyner; Voice Characterization by Mel Blanc; Music by Carl Stalling.

Bugs is adopted as a pet by Dr. Jekyll, who gives in to the temptation to drink his evil potion.

KNIGHT-MARE HARE

Oct 1; MM; Directed by Chuck Jones; Story by Tedd Pierce; Animation by Ken Harris, Ben Washam, Abe Levitow, and Richard Thompson; Layouts by Ernie Nordli; Backgrounds by Philip DeGuard; Voice Characterization by Mel Blanc; Music by Milt Franklyn.

Bugs's episodic treatment of *A Connecticut Yankee in King Arthur's Court*, both the Twain original and the Bing Crosby version. He battles an angry knight, extinguishes a fire-breathing dragon, and parries with Merlin the sorcerer. Video: *Bugs Bunny's Hare-Raising Tales*, WB.

ROMAN LEGION HARE

Yosemite Sam; Nov 12; LT; Directed by Friz Freleng; Story by Warren Foster; Animation by Virgil Ross, Art Davis, and Gerry Chiniquy; Layouts by Hawley Pratt; Backgrounds by Irv Wyner; Voice Characterization by Mel Blanc; Music by Milt Franklyn.

When in Rome, in 54 A.D., Sam must do as the Romans do and find a victim to throw to the lions. He ends up chasing Bugs Bunny in and out of the lions' cages. Video: *Bugs Bunny's Wacky Adventures*, WB.

1956

BUGS' BONNETS

Elmer Fudd; Jan 14; MM; Directed by Chuck Jones; Story by Tedd Pierce; Animation by Ben Washam, Abe Levitow, Richard Thompson and Ken Harris. Layouts by Robert Gribbroek; Backgrounds by Richard H. Thomas; Voice Characterization by Mel Blanc; Music by Milt Franklyn.

This UPA-style cartoon purports to be an examination of the psychological effects on Bugs' and Elmers' behavior of a constant switching of headgear. Video: *Elmer Fudd's Comedy Capers*

BROOM-STICK BUNNY

Witch Hazel; Feb 25, LT; Directed by Chuck Jones; Story by Tedd Pierce; Animation by Richard Thompson, Ken Harris, Ben Washam and Abe Levitow; Layouts by Ernie Nordli. Film Editor: Treg Brown; Backgrounds by Philip DeGuard; Voice Characterization by Mel Blanc; Music by Milt Franklyn.

Witch Hazel is afraid her claim to the title of "the ugliest one of all" is threatened by a creepy halloween witch who comes to the door. When she realizes it's Bugs trick-or-treating, she sees him as just the rabbit to provide a clavicle for her brew.

RABBITSON CRUSOE

Yosemite Sam; Apr 28; LT; Directed by Friz Freleng; Story by Warren Foster; Aninmation by Gerry Chiniquy, Virgil Ross, and Art Davis; Layouts by Hawley Pratt; Backgrounds by Irv Wyner; Voice Characterization by Mel Blanc; Music by Milt Franklyn.

Yosemite Sam as Crusoe, sustaining himself with coconuts for 20 years, is delighted to find Bugs washed ashore on his island. But between Bugs' tricks and a man-eating shark, he finds neither sustenance nor relief. Video: *Bugs Bunny's Hare-Raising Tales*, WB.

NAPOLEON BUNNY-PART

June 16; MM; Directed by Friz Freleng; Story by Warren Foster; Animation by Gerry Chiniquy, Virgil Ross, and Art Davis; Layouts by Hawley Pratt; Backgrounds by Irv Wyner; Voice Characterization by Mel Blanc; Musical Direction by Milt Franklyn.

Bugs tunnels into the "headquarters du Napoleon" (apparently wrong turns "off the Hollywood freeway" mislead him through time as well as geography) and annoys Napoleon.

BARBARY COAST BUNNY

July 21; LT; Directed by Chuck Jones; Story by Tedd Pierce; Animation by Abe Levitow, Richard Thompson, and Ken Harris; Layouts by Robert Gribbroek; Film Editor: Treg Brown; Backgrounds by Philip DeGuard; Musical Direction by Carl Stalling.

Bugs, swindled out a solid gold boulder by Nasty Canasta, comes back to Canasta's Casino six months later and cleans the place out.

HALF FARE HARE

Aug 18; MM; Directed by Robert McKimson; Story by Tedd Pierce; Animation by George Grandpre, Russ Dyson, Keith Darling, and Ted Bonnicksen; Layouts by Robert Gribbroek; Backgrounds by Richard H. Thomas; Voice Characterization by Mel Blanc; Musical Direction by Carl W. Stalling.

One of the lost episodes of *The Honeymooners*. Bugs hops the Chattanooga Choo Choo and finds Ralph Cramden and Ed Norton, who take one look at him and yell, "Food!"

A STAR IS BORED

Daffy Duck, Elmer Fudd, Yosemite Sam; Sept 15; LT; Directed by Friz Freleng; Story by Warren Foster; Animation by Arthur Davis, Gerry Chiniquy, and Virgil Ross; Layouts by Hawley Pratt; Backgrounds by Irv Wyner; Film Editor: Treg Brown; Voice Characterization by Mel Blanc; Musical Direction by Milt Franklyn.

At the movie studio where Bugs is a star, Daffy gets stuck as Bugs' double in all the stock Warner Bros. slapstick considered too hazardous for him. Video: *Daffy Duck: The Nuttiness Continues...* WB.

WIDEO WABBIT

Elmer Fudd; Oct 27; MM; Directed by Robert McKimson; Story by Tedd Pierce; Animation by George Grandpre, Ted Bonnicksen, Keith Darling, and Russ Dyson; Layouts by Robert Gribbroek; Backgrounds by Richard H. Thomas; Film Editor: Irvin Jay; Voice Characterization by Mel Blanc; Musical Direction by Carl W. Stalling.

Bugs bows out of his intended role as victim of Elmer Fudd's shotgun on "The Sportsman's Hour," and leads Fudd instead on a merry chase through every other TV show in the studio.

Color chart from A Star Is Bored, 1956

TO HARE IS HUMAN

Wile E. Coyote; Dec 15; MM; Directed by Chuck Jones; Story by Michael Maltese; Animation by Ken Harris, Abe Levitow, Richard Thompson, and Ben Washam; Layouts by Maurice Noble; Backgrounds by Philip DeGuard; Film Editor: Treg Brown; Voice Characterization by Mel Blanc; Musical Direction by Milt Franklyn.

The Coyote relies even more heavily on complicated technology here than he did in *Operation: Rabbit*, consulting a "Univac Electronic Brain (Do It Yourself)" for most of the screen time.

Frame enlargement from Bugsy and Mugsy, *1957*

1957

ALI BABA BUNNY

Daffy Duck; Feb 9; MM; Directed by Chuck Jones; Story by Michael Maltese; Animation by Richard Thompson, Ken Harris, Abe Levitow, and Ben Washam; Effects Animation by Harry Love; Layouts by Maurice Noble; Backgrounds by Philip DeGuard; Film Editor: Treg Brown; Voice Characterization by Mel Blanc; Musical Direction by Carl Stalling and Milt Franklyn.

Practically a morality play, with Daffy playing Greed and Bugs Moderation, as they tunnel to ancient Baghdad and try to deal with a Sultan's ransom and its bloodthirsty guard Hassan. Video: *Bugs Bunny's Wacky Adventures*, WB.

BEDEVILLED RABBIT

Tasmanian Devil; Apr 13; MM; Directed by Robert McKimson; Story by Tedd Pierce; Animation by George Grandpre, Ted Bonnicksen, and Keith Darling; Layouts by Robert Gribbroek; Backgrounds by Richard H. Thomas; Film Editor: Treg Brown; Voice Characterization by Mel Blanc; Musical Direction by Milt Franklyn.

Bugs is parachuted into Tasmania by mistake, giving "Taz Boy: the home court advantage. Video: *Salute to Mel Blanc*, WB.

PIKER'S PEAK

Yosemite Sam; May 25; LT; Directed by Friz Freleng; Story by Warren Foster; Animation by Gerry Chiniquy, Art Davis, and Virgil Ross; Layouts by Hawley Pratt; Film Editor: Treg Brown; Voice Characterization by Mel Blanc; Musical Direction by Carl W. Stalling and Milt Franklyn.

"Vas ist der Uppenzie, Herr Doktor?" asks Bugs of Sam as they encounter each other on an Alp. "50,000 Cronkites for the one who dares to climb the Schmatterhorn. . .and I dares!" Sam answers. Bugs becomes his only challenger.

WHAT'S OPERA, DOC?

Elmer Fudd; July 6; MM; Directed by Chuck Jones; Story by Michael Maltese; Animation by Ken Harris, Richard Thompson, and Abe Levitow; Effects Animation by Harry Love; Layouts by Maurice Noble; Backgrounds by Philip DeGuard; Film Editor: Treg Brown; Voice Characterization by Mel Blanc; Musical Direction by Milt Franklyn. Song "Return My Love" Lyrics by Michael Maltese.

Matching and mis-matching of Wagner to Warners. Elmer is the hunter as the demigod Siegried, Bugs in drag and blonde wig as the Valkyric Brunhilde atop an obese horse. See pages 160-165. Video: *Elmer Fudd!*, *Salute to Chuck Jones*, WB

BUGSY AND MUGSY

Rocky and Mugsy; Aug 31; LT; Directed by Friz Freleng; Story by Warren Foster; Animation by Virgil Ross. Gerry Chiniquy, and Art Davis; Layouts by Hawley Pratt; Backgrounds by Boris Gorelick; Film Editor: Treg Brown; Voice Characterizations by Mel Blanc; Musical Direction by Carl Stalling and Milt Franklyn.

Bugs finds himself in the hideout of Rocky and Mugsy and feels that "Someone oughta show them that crime doesn't pay." He stirs up trouble between the two pals so that they practically kill each other.

SHOW BIZ BUGS

Daffy Duck; Nov 2; LT; Directed by Friz Freleng; Story by Warren Foster; Animation by Gerry Chiniquy, Art, Davis, and Virgil Ross; Layouts by Hawley Pratt; Backgrounds by Boris Gorelick; Film Editor: Treg Brown; Voice Characterizations by Mel Blanc; Musical Direction by Milt Franklyn.

As vaudevillians, Bugs and Daffy vie for the audience's approval. But Bugs' basic charisma charms them no matter what he does, while Daffy's despicableness turns viewers off. See pages 166-169. Video: *Salute to Friz Freleng*, WB.

RABBIT ROMEO

Elmer Fudd; Dec 14; MM; Directed by Robert McKimson; Story by Michael Maltese; Animation by Ted Bonnicksen and George Granpre; Layouts by Robert Gribbroek; Backgrounds by Bill Butler; Film Editor: Treg Brown; Voice Characterizations by Mel Blanc; Musical Direction by Milt Franklyn.

Bugs tries to evade the advance of a two-ton lovesick Slobovian rabbit donated to Elmer by his Uncle Judd.

1958

HARE-LESS WOLF

Feb 1; MM; Directed by Friz Freleng; Story by Warren Foster; Animation by Gerry Chiniquy, Art Davis, and Virgil Ross; Layouts by Hawley Pratt; Backgrounds by Boris Gorelick; Film Editor: Treg Brown; Voice Characterizations by Mel Blanc; (Uncredited: June Foray) Musical Direction by Milt Franklyn

An absent-minded wolf tries to catch Bugs for dinner, but keeps forgetting who it is he's after and why he was trying to catch him.

HARE-WAY TO THE STARS

Marvin Martian; Mar 29; LT; Directed by Chuck Jones; Story by Michael Maltese; Animation by Richard Thompson, Ken Harris, and Abe Levitow; Layouts by Maurice Noble; Backgrounds by Philip DeGuard; Effects Animation by Harry Love; Film Editor: Treg Brown; Voice Characterizations by Mel Blanc; Musical Direction by Milt Franklyn

Bugs finds himself in a rocket as it takes off and propels him to a city suspended in space where he encounters Marvin the Martian and saves the Earth from destruction at his hands.

NOW HARE THIS

May 31; LT; Directed by Robert McKimson; Story by Tedd Pierce; Animation by Tom Ray, George Granpre, Ted Bonnicksen, and Warren Batchelder; Layouts by Robert Gribbroek; Backgrounds by Bill Butler; Film Editor: Treg Brown; Voice Characterizations by Mel Blanc; Musical Direction by Milt Franklyn

Big Bad Wolf and his nephew think they're going to trap Bugs, but he sees through all their plans in advance and just goes along with the gags to test the Wolf's mettle.

KNIGHTY KNIGHT BUGS

Yosemite Sam; LT; Directed by Friz Freleng; Story by Warren Foster; Animation by Virgil Ross; Gerry Chiniquy, and Art, Davis; Layouts by Hawley Pratt; Backgrounds by Tom O'Loughlin; Film Editor: Treg Brown; Voice Characterizations by Mel Blanc; Musical Direction by Milt Franklyn

Bugs as the court jester jokes that "Only a fool would go after the Singing Sword," and so is sent after it and must face the treacherous Black Knight (Sam) and his hideous sneezing dragon. See pages 170-173. Video: *Salute to Friz Freleng*, WB

PRE-HYSTERICAL HARE

Elmer Fudd; Nov 1; LT; Directed by Robert McKimson; Story by Tedd Pierce; Animation by Ted Bonnicksen, Warren Batchelder, Tom Ray, and George Grandpre; Layouts by Robert Gribbroek; Backgrounds by William Butler; Film Editor: Treg Brown; Voice Characterizations by Mel Blanc; Musical Direction by John Seely

Bugs discovers "A Micronesian Film Documentary in Cromagnonscope," detailing life in 10,000 BC, with Elmer Fuddstone pursuing the saber-toothed rabbit. Voted by exhibitors one of the Top Ten Shorts of the year in *Boxoffice*.

1959

BATON BUNNY

Jan 10; LT; Directed by Chuck Jones and Abe Levitow; Story by Michael Maltese; Animation by Ken Harris, Richard Thompson, and Ben Washam; Layouts by Maurice Noble; Backgrounds by Tom O'Loughlin; Film Editor: Treg Brown; Voice Characterizations by Mel Blanc; Orchestrations by Milt Franklyn

Bugs conducts the Warner Bros. Symphony Orchestra in Franz Von Suppe's "Morning, Noon, and Night in Vienna," contending all the while with an annoying fly and a pair of traveling cuffs. See pages 174-175.

HARE-ABIAN NIGHTS

Yosemite Sam; Feb 28; MM; Directed by Ken Harris; Story by Michael Maltese; Animation by Ben Washam and Ken Harris; Layouts by Samuel Armstrong; Backgrounds by Philip

DeGuard; Film Editor: Treg Brown; Voice Characterizations by Mel Blanc; Musical Direction by Milt Franklyn

Bugs finds himself having an audience with the Sultan, and attempts to entertain with tales of *Bully for Bugs*, *Sahara Hare*, and *Water, Water Every Hare*.

APES OF WRATH

Apr 18; MM; Directed by Friz Freleng; Story by Warren Foster; Animation by Art Davis, Virgil Ross, and Gerry Chiniquy; Layouts by Hawley Pratt; Backgrounds by Tom O'Loughlin; Treg Brown; Voice Characterizations by Mel Blanc; Musical Direction by Milt Franklyn

The stork, missing a baby ape from his bundle, knocks out Bugs and delivers him to Mr. and Mrs. Elvis Ape on a jungle island.

BACKWOODS BUNNY

June 13; MM; Directed by Robert McKimson; Story by Tedd Pierce; Animation by Warren Batchelder, Tom Ray, George Grandpre, and Ted Bonnicksen; Layouts by Robert Gribbroek; Backgrounds by William Butler; Film Editor: Treg Brown; Voice Characterizations by Mel Blanc; Musical Direction by Milt Franklyn

Bugs tries vacationing in the Ozarks, where a couple of zany buzzards set out to catch him for their stew.

WILD AND WOOLY HARE

Yosemite Sam; Aug 1; Directed by Friz Freleng; Story by Warren Foster; Animation by Virgil Ross, Gerry Chiniquy, and Art Davis; Layouts by Hawley Pratt; Backgrounds by Tom O'Loughlin; Film Editor: Treg Brown; Voice Characterizations by Mel Blanc; Musical Direction by Milt Franklyn

A "Gunfight at the U.P.A. Corral," with very attractive stylized settings and some of the old Bugs-Sam vinegar. Ends on a duel with trains.

BONANZA BUNNY

Sept 5; MM; Directed by Robert McKimson; Story by Tedd Pierce; Animation by Tom Ray, George Grandpre, Ted Bonnicksen, and Warren Batchelder; Layouts by Robert Gribbroek; Backgrounds by William Butler; Film Editor: Treg Brown; Voice Characterizations by Mel Blanc; Musical Direction by Milt Franklyn

Dawson City in the Klondike, the middle of the Gold Rush, is the setting for a struggle between Bugs and Blacque Jacque Shellaque over a sack of "little yellow rocks."

A WITCH'S TANGLED HARE

Witch Hazel; Oct 31; LT; Directed by Abe Levitow; Story by Michael Maltese; Animation by Richard Thompson, Ken Harris, Ben Washam, and Keith Darling; Layouts by Owen Fitzgerald; Backgrounds by Bob Singer; Film Editor: Treg Brown; Voice Characterizations by Mel Blanc; Musical Direction by Milt Franklyn

William Shakespeare searches for inspiration amid Bugs and Witch Hazel's wacky dialogue as they battle it out in the castle of Macbeth. But Willy the Shake turns out in reality to be mild-manners Sam Krubish.

Video: *Bugs Bunny's Hare-Raising Tales*, WB

PEOPLE ARE BUNNY

Daffy Duck; Dec 19; MM; Directed by Robert McKimson; Story by Tedd Pierce; Animation by Ted Bonnicksen, Warren Batchelder, Tom Ray, and George Grandpre; Layouts by Robert Gribbroek; Backgrounds by William Butler; Film Editor: Treg Brown; Voice Characterizations by Mel Blanc; Musical Direction by Milt Franklyn

Daffy lures Bugs to a TV studio to collect a thousand-dollar bounty on him, then gets distracted by his own greed, while Bugs becomes the real prizewinner.

1960

HORSE HARE

Yosemite Sam; Feb 13; LT; Directed by Friz Freleng; Story by Michael Maltese; Animation by Gerry Chiniquy, Virgil Ross, and Art Davis; Layouts by Hawley Pratt; Backgrounds by Tom O'Loughlin; Film Editor: Treg Brown; Voice Characterizations by Mel Blanc; Musical Direction by Milt Franklyn

In 1886, cavalry soldier Bugs Bunny is ordered to guard Fort Lariat while the troops are away. Taking advantage, Yosemite Sam leads his outlaw Indians in an attack on the fort.

PERSON TO BUNNY

Daffy Duck, Elmer Fudd; Apr 1; MM; Directed by Friz Freleng; Story by Michael Maltese; Animation by Art Davis, Gerry Chiniquy, and Virgil Ross; Layouts by Hawley Pratt; Backgrounds by Tom O'Loughlin; Film Editor: Treg Brown; Voice Characterizations by Mel Blanc; Musical Direction by Milt Franklyn

The TV program *People to People* is interviewing Bugs Bunny in his Hollywood home when Daffy Duck and Elmer interrupt the proceedings.

RABBIT'S FEAT

Wile E. Coyote; June 4; LT; Directed by Chuck Jones; Animation by Ken Harris and Richard Thompson; Layouts and Backgrounds by Philip DeGuard; Film Editor: Treg Brown; Voice Characterizations by Mel Blanc; Musical Direction by Milt Franklyn

Another confrontation between Bugs and The Coyote, probably the least elaborate in terms of gizmos and the wackiest in terms of humor.

FROM HARE TO HEIR

Yosemite Sam; Sept 3; MM; Directed by Friz Freleng; Story by Friz Freleng; Animation by Art Davis, Gerry Chiniquy, and Virgil Ross; Layouts by Hawley Pratt; Backgrounds by Tom O'Loughlin; Film Editor: Treg Brown; Voice Characterizations by Mel Blanc; Musical Direction by Milt Franklyn

In a sort of replay of the *Wabbit Who Come to Supper* situation, Sam, the Duke of Yosemite in the 18th century, is told by Bugs that he will inherit one million pounds if he can control his temper.

LIGHTER THAN HARE

Yosemite Sam; Dec 17; MM; Directed by Friz Freleng; Story by Friz Freleng; Animation by Virgil Ross, Art Davis, and Gerry Chiniquy;

Layouts by Hawley Pratt; Backgrounds by Tom O'Loughlin; Film Editor: Treg Brown; Voice Characterizations by Mel Blanc; Musical Direction by Milt Franklyn

Yosemite Sam of Outer Space tries to capture a typical earth creature and somehow decides that Bugs Bunny qualifies.

1961

THE ABOMINABLE SNOW RABBIT

Daffy Duck; May 20; LT; Directed by Chuck Jones; Co-Directed by Maurice Noble; Story by Tedd Pierce; Animation by Ken Harris, Richard Thompson, Bob Bransford, and Tom Ray; Backgrounds by Philip DeGuard; Film Editor: Treg Brown; Voice Characterizations by Mel Blanc; Musical Direction by Milt Franklyn

Bugs and Daffy inadvertantly find themselves in the Himalayan Mountains, where they encounter The Abominable Snowman.

COMPRESSED HARE

Wile E. Coyote; July 29; MM; Directed by Chuck Jones; Co-Director: Maurice Noble; Story by Dave Detiege; Animation by Ken Harris, Richard Thompson, Bob Bransford, and Tom Ray; Assistant Layout: Corny Cole; Backgrounds by Philip DeGuard and William Butler; Effects Animation by Harry Love; Film Editor: Treg Brown; Voice Characterizations by Mel Blanc; Musical Direction by Milt Franklyn

Bugs tangles again with The Coyote in Great American Southwest desert. Climaxes with a 10,000,000,000-volt electric magnet that attracts everything from street lamps to satellites in orbit.

PRINCE VIOLENT

Yosemite Sam; Sept 2; LT; Directed by Friz Freleng; Co-Director: Hawley Pratt; Story by Dave Detiege; Animation by Gerry Chiniquy, Art Davis, and Bob Matz; Layouts by Wille Ito; Backgrounds by Tom O'Loughlin; Film Editor: Treg Brown; Voice Characterizations by Mel Blanc; Musical Direction by Milt Franklyn; Retitled Prince Varmint for network TV broadcast.

Yosemite Sam is the villain in Viking clothing who is terrorizing a little Norse village, until Bugs steps into the picture and kicks him out of the castle. Sam uses a goofy Viking elephant to try breaking back in.

1962

WET HARE

Jan 20; LT; Directed by Robert McKimson; Story by Dave Detiege; Animation by George Grandpre, Ted Bonnicksen, Warren Batchelder, and Keith Darling; Layouts and Backgrounds by Robert Gribbroek; Film Editor: Treg Brown; Voice Characterizations by Mel Blanc; Musical Direction by Milt Franklyn

Bugs battles Black Jacque Shellacque again, this time over water rights, when Jacque dams up the river to keep all the water for himself and to charge everybody else for its use.

BILL OF HARE

Tasmanian Devil; June 9; MM; Directed by Robert McKimson; Story by John Dunn; Animation by Keith Darling, Ted Bonnicksen, Warren Batchelder, and George Grandpre; Layouts and Backgrounds by Robert Gribbroek; Film Editor: Treg Brown; Voice Characterizations by Mel Blanc; Musical Direction by Milt Franklyn

Cel from *Wild and Wooly Hare*, 1959

The Tasmanian Devil breaks loose on a pier and encounters Bugs cooking dinner under the boardwalk, giving rise to a succession of food gags and several new concotions of cookery.

SHISHKABUGS
Yosemite Sam; Dec 8; LT; Directed by Friz Freleng; Story by John Dunn; Animation by Gerry Chiniquy, Virgil Ross, Bob Matz, Lee Halpern, and Art Leonardi; Layouts by Hawley Pratt; Backgrounds by Tom O'Loughlin; Film Editor: Treg Brown; Voice Characterizations by Mel Blanc; Musical Direction by Bill Lava
When royal chef Sam needs a rabbbit for "Hassenpheffer" he alights on Bugs as a logical choice.

1963
DEVIL'S FEUD CAKE
Yosemite Sam; Feb 9; MM; Directed by Friz Freleng; Story by Friz Freleng and Warren Foster; Animation by Gerry Chiniquy, Virgil Ross, Box Matz, Art Leonardi, and Lee Halpern; Layouts by Hawley Pratt; Backgrounds by Tom O'Loughlin and Irv Wyner; Film Editor: Treg Brown; Voice Characterizations by Mel Blanc; Musical Direction by Milt Franklyn
Sam has three chances in Hell to bring Bugs to the Devil and gain his freedom: a wrap-around concept for re-using footage from *Hare Lift*, *Roman Legion Hare*, and *Sahara Hare*.

THE MILLION HARE
Daffy Duck; Apr 6; LT; Directed by Robert McKimson; Story by Dave Detiege; Animation by Ted Bonnicksen, Warren Ratchelder, Georghe Grandpre, and Keith Darling; Layouts and Backgrounds by Robert Gribbroek; Effects Animation by Harry Love; Film Editor: Treg Brown; Voice Characterizations by Mel Blanc; Musical Direction by Bill Lava.
Bugs and Daffy race each other to a TV studio to claim the prize on *Beat Your Buddy*.

HARE-BREADTH HURRY
Wile E. Coyote; June 8; LT; Directed by Chuck Jones; Co-Director: Maurice Noble; Story by John Dunn; Animation by Tom Ray, Ken Harris, Richard Thompson, and Bob Bransford; Backgrounds by William Butler; Effects Animation by Harry Love; Film Editor: Treg Brown; Voice Characterizations by Mel Blanc; Musical Direction by Bill Lava
Bugs substitutes for the Roadrunner in a Roadrunner cartoon, which throws the Coyote for a double loop, since the rules for Bugs Bunny pictures get mixed up with the rules for Roadrunner cartoons.

THE UNMENTIONABLES
Rocky and Mugsy; Sept 7; MM; Directed by Friz Freleng; Story by John Dunn; Animation by Gerry Chiniquy, Virgil Ross, Bob Matz, Art Leonardi, and Lee Halpern; Layouts by Hawley Pratt; Backgrounds by Tom O'Loughlin; Film Editor: Treg Brown; Voice Characterizations by Mel Blanc;, Ralph James Musical Direction by Bill Lava
A spoof of the TV series, *The Untouchables*, with Bugs in the role of agent "Elegant Mess" in the Prohibition era. Rocky and Mugsy chase Bugs through the ACME cereal factory.

MAD AS MARS HARE
Marvin Martian; Oct 19; MM; Directed by Chuck Jones; Co-Director Maurice Noble; Story by John Dunn; Animation by Ken Har-
ris, Richard Thompson, Bob Bransford, and Tom Ray; Backgrounds by Bob Singer; Effects Animation by Harry Love; Film Editor: Treg Brown; Voice Characterizations by Mel Blanc; Musical Direction by Bill Lava
"There's absolutely no evidence of any intelligence on the Earth," claims Marvin from a small planet where Bugs is rocketed. When the Heckling Hare tries to claim the place in the name of Earth, the fireworks begin.

TRANSYLVANIA 6-5000
Nov 30; MM; Directed by Chuck Jones; Co-Director: Maurice Noble; Story by John Dunn; Animation by Bob Bransford, Tom Ray, Ken Harris, and Richard Thompson; Layouts by Bob Givens; Backgrounds by Philip DeGuard; Film Editor: Treg Brown; Voice Characterizations by Mel Blanc, Ben Frommer, and Julie Bennett; Musical Direction by Bill Lava
Bugs finds himself at the castle of Count Bloodcount in Transylvania, where he is offered a room for the night. Thanks to a series of serendipitously-discovered magic words, he lives to see daybreak.

1964
DUMB PATROL
Yosemite Sam, Porky Pig; Jan 18; Directed by Gerry Chiniquy; Story by John Dunn; Animation by Virgil Ross, Bob Matz, Lee Halpern and Art Leonardi; Layouts by Bob Givens; Backgrounds by Tom O'Loughlin; Film Editor: Treg Brown; Voice Characterizations by Mel Blanc; Musical Direction by Bill Lava
Bugs takes it upon himself to rid the skies of Baron (Yosemite) Sam Von Shamm, and they battle in biplanes over France during World War I.

DR. DEVIL AND MR. HARE
Tasmanian Devil; Mar 28; MM; Directed by Robert McKimson; Story by John Dunn; Animation by Ted Bonnicksen, Warren Batchelder, and George Grandpre; Layouts and Backgrounds by Robert Gribbroek; Film Editor: Treg Brown; Voice Characterizations by Mel Blanc; Musical Direction by Bill Lava.
This scramble takes Bugs and Taz into a doctor's ofice, where medical gags occupy the bulk of the footage.

THE ICEMAN DUCKETH
Daffy Duck; May 16; LT; Directed by Phil Munroe; Co-Directed by Maurice Noble; Story by John Dunn; Animation by Bob Bransford, Tom Ray, Ken Harris, Richard Thompson, Bob Matz, and Alex Inatiev; Layouts by Bob Givens; Backgrounds by William Butler; Effects Animation by Harry Love; Film Editor: Treg Brown; Voice Characterizations by Mel Blanc; Musical Direction by Bill Lava
At a trading post in the Klondike, Daffy overhears that they are paying big bucks for furs and heads north to relieve Bugs of his pelt.

FALSE HARE
Foghorn Leghorn Cameo; July 16; LT; Directed by Robert McKimson; Story by John Dunn; Animation by Warren Batchelder, George Grandpre, and Ted Bonnicksen; Layouts by Bob Givens; Backgrounds by Robert Gribbroek; Film Editor: Treg Brown; Voice Characterizations by Mel Blanc; Musical Direction by Bill Lava
Big Bad Wolf and his nephew make another attempt to catch Bugs, their major ploy this time being the Club del Conejo, a private club for rabbits.

PART II: CAMEOS, COMPILATIONS, AND SPECIAL APPEARANCES, 1942-1990
Because the list of compilations, reissues, repackagings, TV Specials, and video compilations is practically endless, entries in this list have been restricted to those items featuring at least some new animation of Bugs Bunny. Unless otherwise specified, all entries are in color.

1942
ANY BONDS TODAY?
Porky Pig, Elmer Fudd; Directed by Robert Clampett; Animation by Virgil Ross, Bob McKimson, and Rod Scribner; Song "Any Bonds Today?" by Irving Berlin.
Bugs, dressed as Uncle Sam, appears before a patriotic backdrop entreating the audience to buy War Bonds in this three-minute government-sponsored film.

CRAZY CRUISE
Mar 14; MM; Supervision uncredited, begun by Fred Avery, completed by Robert Clampett; Story by Michael Maltese; Animation by Rod Scribner; Musical Direction by Carl Stalling
Bugs appears in literally the last shot of this travelogue spoof of Avery's, as one of a cluster of little grey rabbits about to be attacked by a vulture, who respond with anti-aircraft artillery.

1943
PORKY PIG'S FEET
Porky Pig, Daffy Duck; July 17; LT; Supervision by Frank Tashlin; Story by Melvin Millar; Animation by Phil Munroe; Musical Direction by Carl W. Stalling; Black and white.
After numerous attempts to escape from their hotel room without paying the bill, Porky and Daffy are trapped for the winter, calling Bugs in hope of an alternate plan. Again Bugs appears in only the very last shot: He turns out to be trapped in the room next door.

1944
JASPER GOES HUNTING
Jasper, Scarecrow; Jul 28; Puppetoon; Produced and Directed by George Pal; Released by Paramount; Bugs Bunny Animated by Robert McKimson; Voice Characterizations by Mel Blanc
Bugs pops out of a rabbit hole in the middle of the jungle before he realized that he's in the wrong picture.

GAS
Private Snafu; May; Directed by Chuck Jones; Probably animated by Ken Harris, Ben Washam, Robert Cannon, and others in Jones unit; Black and white.
Bugs makes a cameo appearance in this Armed Forces training film, in which Private Snafu is attacked by an anthropomorphic gas cloud.

THE THREE BROTHERS
Private Snafu; Sept; Directed by I. Freleng; Probably Animated by Ken Champin, Manuel Perez, Virgil Ross, and Richard Bickenbach. Black and white.
Another surprise appearance for the boys in uniform in this episode showing Technical Fairy First Class in a demonstration of why Snafu's menial shoe-sorting is important to the war effort.

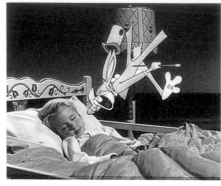

Above: *Frames from Bugs'
cameo appearance in the feature
film* My Dream Is Yours, *1949.*

1945
ODOR-ABLE KITTY
*Pepe LePew; Jan 6; LT; Directed by Chuck
Jones; Story by Tedd Pierce; Animation by
Robert Cannon; Musical Direction by Carl
Stalling*
A tomcat, to escape Pepe's amorous
advances, disguises himself as Bugs just long
enough to get in a "What's up, Doc?"

1947
THE GOOFY GOPHERS
*Goofy Gophers; Jan 25; LT; Directed by
Arthur Davis; Animation by Don Williams,
Manny Gould, J.C. Melendez, and Cal Dalton.*
The gophers spend the entire picture getting
rid of the watchdog who stands between
them and a vegetable patch, then rejoice,
"Now we have the garden all to ourselves!"
But a pan over to Bugs munching on a carrot
and declaring, "Well, I wouldn't say that!"
dispels that notion.

1948
TWO GUYS FROM TEXAS
*Sept 4; Warner Bros. Feature Starring Jack
Carson, Dennis Morgan, Dorothy Malone;
Aug; Produced by Alex Gottleib; Directed by
David Butler; Screenplay by I.A.L. Diamond
and Allen Boretz, Based on the play by Rob-
ert Sloane and Louis Pelletier; Actually a
Remake of Warners' 1938 Feature A Cowboy
from Brooklyn, starring Dick Powell and Pat
O'Brien; Animation Sequence Directed by I.
(Friz) Freleng. Black and white.*
Bugs has no more than a single line in an
extended animation sequence intended to
represent Carson's recurring dream involving
his fear of animals.

1949
MY DREAM IS YOURS
*Apr 16; Warner Bros. Feature Starring Jack
Carson, Doris Day; Mar; Produced and
Directed by Michael Curtiz; Screenplay by
Harry Kurnitz and Dane Lussier, from Adap-
tation by Allen Rivkin and Laura Kerr;
Remake of Warners' 1934 Feature Twenty
Million Sweethearts, Starring Dick Powell,
Ginger Rogers, and Pat O'Brien; Bugs
Bunny sequence directed by I. (Friz) Fre-
leng; Probably Animated by Virgil Ross, Ken
Champin, Gerry Chiniquy, and/or Manuel
Perez; Voice Characterization by Mel Blanc*
Bugs stars in a wonderful three-minute
sequence here, with a cameo by Tweety Pie.
The animation is fuller than was normal for a
short cartoon, and Bugs' personality comes
across beautifully as he sings "Freddy Get
Ready" to the tune of that old standard,
Liszt's Second Hungarian Rhapsody.

1953
DUCK AMUCK
*Daffy Duck; Feb 28; MM; Directed by Chuck
Jones; Story by Michael Maltese; Animation
by Ben Washam, Ken Harris, and Lloyd
Vaughan; Layouts by Maurice Noble; Backgrounds by Philip DeGuard; Voice Characterizations by Mel Blanc; Musical Direction by
Carl Stalling*
Though Bugs' appearance at the tail end of
this exceptional Daffy Duck cartoon amounts
to no more than a cameo in terms of screen
time, it is in story terms the revelation of the
identity of the Unseen Animator who is, in
effect, Daffy's only co-star throughout the
picture. Video: *Daffy Duck: The Nuttiness
Continues...* WB

1960-62
THE BUGS BUNNY SHOW
*ABC TV Network; 52 Episodes; Tuesdays,
7:30-8:00 pm.*
Bugs and practically all of the rest of the
Looney Tunes gang appeared in framing
sequences written and produced by Chuck
Jones and Friz Freleng, directed by Jones,
Freleng, and McKimson; co-directed by
Maurice Noble, Robert Tronson, Hawley
Pratt, Tom Ray, and Ken Harris; with ani-
mation by their regular crews. The theme
song, "This Is It," was written by Jay Liv-
ingston and Mack David.

1974
A POLITICAL CARTOON
*Independently Produced Non-theatrical Short
Film; Odradek Prod; Written, Produced, and
Directed by Jim Morrow and Joe Adamson;
Bugs Bunny Animated by Mark Kausler;
Voice by Mel Blanc*

Bugs appears twice this 22-minute comedy
combining animation and live action: once in
a public service announcement for "Suffering
Succotash, Washington, D.C." and once in a
quick news interview.

1976
CARNIVAL OF THE ANIMALS
*Daffy Duck; Nov 22; CBS Special; Produced,
Written, and Directed by Chuck Jones; Master
Animators: Phil Munroe, Ben Washam, Manny
Perez, Tom Ray; Special Animation: Lloyd
Vaughan; Production Design by Herbert
Klynn; Musical Supervision by Dean Elliot.*
All new animation combined with live action,
as Bugs and Daffy accompany Michael Til-
son Thomas in a 25-minute performance
based on the music of Camille Saint-Saens
and the poetry of Ogden Nash. Video: As
Bugs and Daffy's Carnival of the Animals,
WB.

1977
THE BUGS BUNNY EASTER SPECIAL
*Granny, Daffy Duck; Apr 7; CBS Special;
Executive Director: Hal Geer; Supervising
Director: Friz Freleng; Directed by Robert
McKimson and Gerry Chiniquy; Story by Friz
Freleng and David Detiege; Music by Doug
Goodwin*
Bugs is recruited to help deliver the Easter
Bunny's eggs in this framing story for
Knighty Knight Bugs, Sahara Hare, and oth-
ers. New title: *Bugs Bunny's Easter Funnies.*

1978
A CONNECTICUT RABBIT IN KING ARTHUR'S COURT
*Daffy Duck, Porky Pig, Elmer Fudd, Yosemite
Sam; Feb 23; CBS Special; Produced,
Directed, and "Plagerized" by Chuck Jones;
Master Animators: Ben Washam, Virgil Ross,
Phil Monroe, Lloyd Vaughan; Music by Dean
Elliot.*
Following Twain's story, Bugs finds himself
in Arthurian England and attains special sta-
tus by pretending to engineer an eclipse
of the sun in this 25-minute special. Video:
As *Bugs Bunny in King Arthur's Court,* WB

BUGS BUNNY'S HOWL-OWEEN SPECIAL
*Oct 26; CBS Special; Producer: Hal Geer;
Directed by David Detiege, Abe Levitow, and
Maurice Noble; Story by Cliff Roberts; Music
by Harper McKay*
Bugs appears in framing footage introducing
Broomstick Bunny, Transylvania 6-5000, and
others.

1979
BUGS BUNNY'S VALENTINE
*Feb 14; CBS Special; Executive Producer:
Hal Geer; Animation Director: Jim Davis*
Elmer is the Cupid who zaps Bugs in fram-
ing footage for *Hare Trimmed, The Grey
Hounded Hare, Hare Splitter,* and others.

THE BUGS BUNNY MOTHER'S DAY SPECIAL
*May 12; CBS Special; Executive Producer:
Hal Geer; Directed by Jim Davis; Story by
Hal Geer; Music by Harper McKay*
Bugs has to deal again with a pixillated stork
in the bridging sequence for *Apes of Wrath,
Bushy Hare,* and others.

THE BUGS BUNNY/ROADRUNNER MOVIE
*Sept 30; Warner Bros. Feature Compilation;
Produced and Directed by Chuck Jones; Writ-
ten by Michael Maltese and Chuck Jones;
Production Designed by Maurice Noble;*

Animated by Phil Monroe; Ben Washam, Ken Harris, Abe Levitow, Dick Thompson, Lloyd Vaughan, Virgil Ross, Manny Perez, and Irv Anderson; Music by Carl Stalling, Milt Franklyn, and Dean Elliot

Bugs gives us a tour of his mansion, introduces his various creators, reminisces about his career and discusses the origins of humor and the chase. Video: Warner Bros.

BUGS BUNNY'S THANKSGIVING DIET

Nov 15; CBS; Executive Producer: Hal Geer; Directed by David Detiege; Story by Jack Envart and Hal Geer; Music by Harper McKay

Bugs is the diet doctor who prescribes *Bedevilled Rabbit, Rabbit Every Monday,* and clips from others

BUGS BUNNY'S LOONEY CHRISTMAS TALES

Nov 27; CBS; Executive Producer: Hal Geer; Bugs Bunny Sequences Produced and Directed by Friz Freleng; Written by Friz Freleng, John Dunn and Tony Benedict; Sequence Directors: Tony Benedict, Bill Perez, David Detiege, and Art Vitello; Voices by Mel Blanc and June Foray; Music by Doug Goodwin

Two new shorts feature Bugs in Christmas themes: *Bugs Bunny's Christmas Carol* has him teaching Yosemite Sam (as Scrooge) the meaning of Christmas, with Porky Pig as Cratchet; *Fright Before Christmas* sets him against the Tasmanian Devil as a perverse Santa Claus in the house where he is reading "The Night Before Christmas" to his nephew Clyde.

1980

BUGS BUNNY'S BUSTING OUT ALL OVER

May 21; CBS Special; Written, Produced, and Directed by Chuck Jones; Co-Director: Phil Monroe; Music by Dean Elliot

Bugs appears in two new shorts: *Portrait of the Artist as a Young Bunny* flashes back to Bugs and Elmer's youth a la *The Old Grey Hare*; *Spaced Out Bunny* pits him against both Marvin the Martian and Hugo, the Abominable Snowman, on the planet Mars.

1981

BUGS BUNNY: ALL-AMERICAN HERO

May 21; CBS Special; Executive Producer: Hal Geer; Producer/Director: Friz Freleng; Co-Director: David Detiege; Story by Friz Freleng and John Dunn; Music Composer: Rob West

Bugs relates his own version of our nation's past to his nephew Clyde in an expanded version of *Yankee Doodle Bugs,* introducing footage from *Bunker Hill Bunny, Dumb Patrol, Ballot Box Bunny, Southern Fried Rabbit,* and *Yankee Doodle Bugs.*

FRIZ FRELENG'S LOONEY LOONEY LOONEY BUGS BUNNY MOVIE

Nov 20; Warner Bros. Compilation Feature; Produced and Directed by Friz Freleng; Screenplay by John Dunn, David Detiege and Friz Freleng; Sequence Directors: David Detiege, Phil Monroe, and Gerry Chinquy; Animated by Warren Batchelder, Charles Downs, Marcia Fertig, Bob Matz, Manuel Perez, Virgil Ross, and Lloyd Vaughan; Production Design by Cornelius Cole; Layouts by Peter Alvarado, Robert Givens, and Michael Mitchell; Backgrounds by Richard H. Thomas; Voices by Mel Blanc, June Foray,

Frank Nelson, Frank Welker, Stan Freberg, and Ralph James; Music by Rob Walsh, Don McGinnis, Milt Franklym, Bill Lava, Shorty Rogers, and Carl Stalling.

Yosemite Sam makes deals with the Devil, Bugs outwits Rocky and Mugsy, and a parody of Hollywood award programs is staged, with Bugs as host, in framing footage for *Knighty Knight Bugs, Sahara Hare, Roman Legion Hare, High Diving Hare, Hare Trimmed, Wild and Wooly Hare, The Unmentionables, Show Biz Bugs,* and others. Video: WB.

1982

BUGS BUNNY'S 3RD MOVIE: 1001 RABBIT TALES

Nov 19; Warner Bros.; Produced by Friz Freleng; Sequence Directors: David Detiege and Friz Freleng; Animation by Warren Batchelder, Bob Bransford, Marcia Fertig, Terrence Lennon, Bob Matz, Norm McCabe, Tom Ray, and Virgil Ross; Backgrounds by Richard H. Thomas; Voices by Mel Blanc, Shep Menken, and Lennie Weinrib; Music by Rob Walsh, Bill Lava, Milt Franklym, and Carl Stalling.

Bugs, Daffy's rival as rival book salesman for Rambling House Publishers, travels to the Arabian desert and meets Sultan (Yosemite) Sam, who forces him to read stories to his son Prince Abadaba. His stories include *Ali Baba Bunny, Apes of Wrath, Bewithed Bunny.* Video: As *Bug's Bunny's 1001 Rabbit Tales,* WB

1983

DAFFY DUCK'S MOVIE: FANTASTIC ISLAND

Aug 5; Warner Bros. Compilation Feature; Produced and Directed by Friz Freleng; Screenplay by John Dunn, David Detiege, and Friz Freleng; Sequence Directors: David Detiege, Friz Freleng, and Phil Monroe; Production Design and Layout by Bob Givens and Michael Mitchell; Animation by Brenda Banks, Warren Batchelder, Bob Bransford, Brad Case, Terrence Lennon, Bob Matz, Norm McCabe, Sam Nicholson, Jerry Ray, and Richard Thompson; Voices by Mel Blanc, June Foray, and Les Tremayne.

Bugs appears briefly on Daffy's island to introduce footage from *Mutiny of the Bunny.* Video: As *Daffy Duck's Fantastic Island,* WB

1986

BUGS BUNNY/LOONEY TUNES 50TH ANNIVERSARY SPECIAL

Jan 14; CBS Special; Executive Produce: Lorne Michaels; Produce by Mary Salter; Director by Gary Weis; Written by Tom Gammil, Max Pross, and Greg Ford; New Animation Directed by Chuck Jones; Animated by Phil Monroe

Bugs appears in new introductory footage with Daffy, then in the previously unseen pencil test for the dance in *Mississippi Hare,* as well as clips from his early, pre-*Wild Hare* days, and clips from *High Diving Hare, Rabbit of Seville, Long-Haired Hare, My Bunny Lies Over the Sea,* and other cartoons. New Title: *Bug's Bunny's All-Star 50th Anniversary Special.*

1987

THE 59TH ANNUAL ACADEMY AWARD

Mar 30; ABC Broadcast

Bugs, appearing with Tom Hanks, presented the Oscar for Best Animated Short for that year, to Nicole Van Goethem's *A Greek Tragedy.*

1988

WHO FRAMED ROGER RABBIT

June 22; Amblin Entertainment/Touchstone Pictures Feature; Released by Buena Vista; Executive Producers: Steven Spielberg and Kathleen Kennedy; Produced by Robert Watts and Frank Marshall; Directed by Robert Zemeckis; Screenplay by Jeffrey Price and Peter Seaman; Based on the Book Who Censored Roger Rabbit? by Gary K. Wolfe.

Bugs Bunny and Mickey Mouse, wearing unopened parachutes, float to Earth with Bob Hoskins, wearing none, in this brief but effective cameo. When Hoskins asks if they have a spare, Bugs lends him what turns out to be an ACME spare tire. Video: Touchstone

DAFFY DUCK'S QUACKBUSTERS

Sept 24; Warner Bros. Compilation Feature; Produced by Steven S. Greene and Kathleen Helppie-Shipley; Story and Direction by Greg Ford and Terry Lennon; Animation by Brenda Banks, Norm McCabe, Rebecca Rees, Mark Kausler, Nancy Beiman, Daniel Haskett, Darrel Van Citters, and Frans Vischer; Production Design and Layout by Robert Givens; Backgrounds by Richard H. Thomas and Alan Bodner; Voices by Mel Blanc, Roy Firestone and B. J. Ward; Music Coordinated by Hal Willner; Classical Music by Carl Stalling, Milt Franklyn, and Bill Lava.

Bugs assists Daffy in his ghost-busting service and helps to introduce footage from *Water, Water Every Hare, The Abominable Snow Rabbit, Transylvania 6-5000,* and others. Video: WB

BUGS VS. DAFFY: BATTLE OF THE MUSIC VIDEO STARS

Oct 21; CBS Special; Produced by Steven S. Greene and Kathleen Helppie-Shipley; Story and Direction by Greg Ford and Terry Lennon

Bugs, as video disc jockey on music channel W.A.B.B.I.T. introduces song sequences from old Warner cartoons, as does his rival Daffy at station K.P.U.T.

1989

BUGS BUNNY'S WILD WORLD OF SPORTS

Feb. 15; CBS Special; Produced by Steven S. Greene

Bugs and Daffy spar again, in bridging footage for clips with Warner characters in sporting activities, including *Bunny Hugged, High Diving Hare,* and *My Bunny Lies Over the Sea.*

FIFTY YEARS OF BUGS BUNNY IN 3½ MINUTES

Dec. 1; Short Theatrical Compilation; Produced and Directed by Chuck Workman; Calliope Films; Released by Warner Bros.

1990

THE 62ND ANNUAL ACADEMY AWARDS

Mar. 26; ABC Broadcast.

Once again, Bugs presented the Oscar for Best Animated Short Subject.

BOX OFFICE BUNNY

Daffy Duck, Elmer Fudd; Summer; Warner Bros. Theatrical Short; Produced by Kathleen Helppie-Shipley; Written and Directed by Darrell Van Citters.

When a mammoth cinema complex is built over Bugs' rabbit hole, he investigates and is confronted by usher Elmer and patron Daffy.

NOTES AND BIBLIOGRAPHY

NOTES

Unless otherwise indicated, all quotations throughout text from Peter Alvarado, Robert Givens, Chuck Jones, Walter Lantz, Michael Maltese, Maurice Noble, and Steve Schneider are from Author's interviews, as listed in the Bibliography, and all quotations from Friz Freleng are from Author's interviews of 1968-69 (*Oral History of Friz Freleng*) or 1989. All quotations from Tex Avery are from Author's Interviews of 1969 and 1971; in some instances, wording differs from the edited versions appearing in Adamson, *Tex Avery*. Likewise, unless otherwise indicated, all quotations from Mel Blanc are from Blanc and Bashe, *That's Not All, Folks!*, 1988; all quotations from Bob Clampett are from Barrier and Gray, "Bob Clampett: An Interview with a Master Cartoon Maker and Puppeteer," *Funnyworld*, 1970; all quotations from Robert McKimson are from David Butler's interview of 1977; and all quotations from Paul Julian, Phil Monroe, and Virgil Ross are from Charles Solomon's interviews for *Enchanted Drawings* in 1985-89. See Bibliography for further details.

BUGS

The Rabbit

Bugs Bunny's Number One Rating in the *Motion Picture Herald* poll from Schneider, *That's All Folks!*, confirmed by *Motion Picture Herald* issues of their supplement *Fame: The Annual Audit of the Creative Personalities of Screen and Radio* for 1946 to 1961. Robert Klein's remark on *Late Night With David Letterman*, NBC, 10/19/89; Charles Young from "Oryctolagus Cuniculus—a.k.a. Bugs Bunny," see Bibliography; *People* Annual Poll: Unsigned, "Just the Facts, Ma'am," *People Weekly*, Vol. 23 No. 17, 4/29/85. Results of C.A. Walker Poll, June, 1989, printed in *The Appeal of Warner Bros. Cartoon Characters*, brochure distributed by Licensing Corporation of America, which also quoted *The Los Angeles Times* (hereafter *LAT*), 7/13/89, with similar results in a Marketing Evaluations, Inc., study. A. Lincoln cited in Shales, "Bugs, Abe Score as TV Pitchmen." • Contest winners from Barrier and Gray, "Bob Clampett." Scott story from Jones, "132 Takes/Th-Th-That's All Folks." Leonard Maltin's comment on Bugs and Daffy being "real" comes from a 1986 broadcast of *Entertainment This Week*, from undated cassette at Warner Bros. Animation in Burbank, Calif. Foster quote in caption from "What's Cookin', Doc?", *Warner Club News* (hereafter *WCN*), 3/47. • Portions of Freleng on Bugs existing from Michaels, *Bugs Bunny/Looney Tunes 50th Anniversary Special*, 1986; and Young, "A New 'Golden Era' of Animation?", *LAT*, 11/28/81. Jones on character taking over from *Chuck Amuck*. • Bugs' Star: Charles Solomon, "What's Up, Doc? Bugs Gets His Star," *LAT*, 12/21/85. Accounts of the ceremony from "Teleclips," Luce Press Clippings: Television News Transcripts of the Channel 7 Eyewitness News coverage of the event, KABC Channel 7, Los Angeles, 12/21/85; and "Bugs Bunny's Star," videotape covering the entire ceremony at Warner Bros. Animation, Burbank. • Story of Blanc's accident from Blanc and Bashe, *That's Not All Folks!*, buttressed by accounts from Smith, "Mel Blanc: 50 Years of Magical Voices," and Bob Thomas, "Mel Blanc, Nearing Recovery, Grateful for Crash, Survival," *Los Angeles Mirror* (Associated Press Story), 11/15/61. Dr. Conway quote from Ralph Edwards Productions, *This Is Your Life, Mel Blanc*.

The Real Bugs

Jones quote partially from Michaels, *Bugs Bunny/Looney Tunes 50th Anniversary Special*. • Model sheet referred to is the 1942-1943 standard model of Bugs, the 1943 version of which appears in Schneider, *That's All Folks!* Fire prevention: Unsigned, "Lovable 'Wabbit' Starstruck on Hollywood Walk of Fame," *Los Angeles Daily News*, 12/20/85; Earthquake safety: Chris Woodyard, "Bugs Bunny on Quake Safety," *LAT*, 10/6/76. The "aggressive child" from John Needham, Patrons Interview, 1979. Shawles from *Entertainment Tonight*, NBC, 9/11/85. Rosemont from "Bugs Bunny." McKimson quote from Bullis, McKimson Interview. Trade periodical piece from Unsigned, "Leading Short Subjects." •Poll quotes from Walker, *Popularity of Warner Bros. Cartoon Characters*. Jones' comment on Bugs and Daffy being "individuals" partially from Francesconci, "What's Happening." • Bullis quoted p. 22 from *Thematic Study*. Bugs' quote p. 29 is authentic, though the publicist is unnamed. The article, entitled "Backstage with Bugs Bunny," is part of "Warner Bros. Cartoon Publicity Brochure," and was meant to be run in local newspapers as an interview with The Rabbit. Starting in natural environment is in many sources, including Adamson, Jones Interviews; CNN, Jones Interview, 8/19/84; and Ford and Thompson, "Chuck Jones Interview." Jones on Bugs' motivation partially from CNN, Jones Interview, and Jones, *Chuck Amuck*. Karl Von Clausewitz' basic theory has been expressed in several different ways, including "War is…nothing but the continuation of state policy with other means," from *On War*, and "War is nothing but a continuation of political intercourse with an admixture of other means," from *Arming the Nation*. The wording here is probably Jones', but the meaning is the same. Jones on Bugs as a male Dorothy Parker, late quips, from Francesconi, "What's Happening." Weale's term from his book *Canned Good as Caviar*, Chicago: The University of Chicago Press, 1985.

BIRTH O' DE BUGS

The Big Bang

Various birthdays: from Unsigned, "Irrepressible Bugs Bunny 5 Years Old"; Hubbell, "What's Up, Doc?", *WCN*, 12/61; Christon, "Bugs' Follies: What's Up, Doc?"; "New Animated Feature Celebrates Bugs Bunny's 40th Anniversary," Warner Bros. Publicity Release, 1979. • Clampett quote from Chapman College Address, 1974. The creation of Bugs Bunny is a much-debated issue, but evidence for Avery's primacy in the matter comes from Adamson, Avery Interviews, 1969; Adamson, Maltese Interview, 1971; and Jones, "Confessions of a Cel Washer," *Take One*, Sept., 1978, reprinted in Jones, *Chuck Amuck*. • Roy Bean material chiefly from Sonnichsen, *Roy Bean*, and from Adamson, Heck Allen Interview, 1971. Avery's genealogical link to Bean established by Allen and confirmed by Avery, already published in Adamson, *Tex Avery*, which states that Bean was descended from Daniel Boone. Further research, however, reveals that this was probably one more legend, created by Bean himself to advance his reputation. • Avery at Lantz from Adamson, Walter Lantz Interviews, 1981; Leo Salkin Interview, 1981; Avery Interviews, 1969 and 1971. Some of this material appeared in Adamson, *Tex Avery* and *The Walter Lantz Story*.

The Looney Tunes Bin

Jones quote in photo caption from Musilli, *The Boys from Termite Terrace*. • Bugs' quote is again from "Backstage With Bugs Bunny," Warner Bros. Cartoon Publicity Brochure. Hubbell quote from "What's Up, Doc?", *WCN*, 5/57. • "Atmosphere": Jones quote from Alex Ward, "Chuck Jones, Animated Man"; Schlesinger speech from Adamson, Maltese Interview, 1971; the Maltese quote, "Of course, we had exaggerated Friz," is from Brasch, *Cartoon Monickers*. Maltese is also the source for the German World War I aviator gag, and the fact that it was a favorite request of Blanc's, which was backed up by Adamson, Jones Interview, 1989. • Laguna Beach gambit, Pierce as con artist, "Theater Day," bottles in drawers, all from Adamson, Alvarado and Givens Interview, 1989. Details on the literal Termite Terrace courtesy of Butler, McKimson Interview, 1977. Pierce's Fiat from Adamson, Freleng Interview, 1989. • Pennies: Avery story from Adamson, *Tex Avery*; Jones gags from Hubbell and Schilt, "What's Up Doc?" *WCN*, 7/56; Pierce and Washam Story from Hubbell, "What's Up, Doc?" *WCN*, 1/59. • Warning System and Cal Howard's lunch counter from Jones, *Chuck Amuck*, as is "Sour persimmons," Howard on Schlesinger's slurp, Jones on Pierce, and Pierce's logic for adding the extra "d" to this name. "A-go-ny!" from Barrier and Gray, "Clampett Interview." Corliss quote from "Warnervana." • Schlesinger: Some Clampett quotes from Onosko, "Bob Clampett—Cartoonist"; and Musilli, *The Boys from Termite Terrace*. Jones quote partially from *Chuck Amuck*. Julian from Solomon, *Enchanted Drawings*. • Stalling: Jones quote partially from Ford and Thompson, "Chuck Jones Interview." Scott info from Schneider, *That's All Folks!* Songs listed by title: Telegrams from Herman Starr in Warner Bros.' New York office giving OK for cartoon use to Leo Forbstein or Nina Sampson in Burbank, dated 2/28/45, 3/6/45, 3/14/45, 4/27/45; now in Warner Bros. Archive at the University of Southern California, Los Angeles. Freleng in Photo Caption from conversation with author, 10/19/89. Brown: Musical pedigree and other biographical details from Jones, *Chuck Amuck*; Foster, "What's Cookin', Doc?", *WCN*, 2/45; and Maltese, "What's Up, Doc?", *WCN*, 11/46. Details on sound effects from examination of Brown's Sound Effect File at The Burbank Studios. • Blanc: Confirmation that Pierce, Howard, and Avery, as well as various voice actors, did voices for the cartoons, from Blanc and Bashe, *That's Not All Folks!* Blanc's exclusive credit from Adamson, Maltese Interview, confirmed by Stamelman, "A Chat with Mel Blanc." • Tashlin on Pierce from Barrier, "Interview" in Johnston and Willeman, *Frank Tashlin*. Other Pierce details from Maltese, "What's Cookin', Doc?" *WCN*, 12/44; Foster, "What's Cookin', Doc?", *WCN*, 3/47; Blanchard, "What's Cookin', Doc?", *WCN*, 11/47. • Jones remark on A.C.T.I.O.N. from Joel C. Don, "In a World Where People and Animals Never Die."

The Masquerader

Jones quote at opening from Francesconi, "What's Happening." Jones on "golden age of comedy" from Benayoun, "The Roadrunner and Other Characters"; on "a human exclamation point" from Ford and Thompson, "Jones Interview." • Sennett's financial success from David Yallop, *The Day the Laughter Stopped*, New York: St. Martin's Press, 1976; Chaplin on personality from *My Autobiography*. Maltese anecdote from Adamson, Maltese Interview. Andre Bazin quoted from *What Is Cinema?*, Edited and Translated by Hugh Gray, Los Angeles: University of California Press, 1967. "Shabby Pierrot" from Payne, *The Great God Pan*. Walter Kerr quoted from *The Silent Clowns*, New York: Alfred A. Knopf, 1975. Derivation of The Tramp draws on Sobel and Francis, *Chaplin: Genesis of a Clown*. Chaplin on the clowns in the pantomimes from a syndicated newspaper interview of 1917, quoted in Robinson, *Chaplin*. • Corliss quoted from "Warnervana"; Jones on Keaton influencing Bugs and Daffy from Musilli, *The Boys from Termite Terrace*. Jones on animation as an extension of silent comedy from Jones, "The Naked Art," Expo '67; the same passage reappears in Jones, "Animation is a Gift Word," *AFI Report*, Vol. 5 No. 2, Summer, 1974. Otto Messmer on Chaplin and Felix from John Canemaker, *The Animated Raggedy Ann and Andy*, Indianapolis, Indiana: Bobbs-Merrill, 1977. Huemer on Mickey and Chaplin from Adamson, *Oral History of Dick Huemer*. Jones on Disney being the backbone for everybody else partially from "The Naked Art," and from Alex Ward, "Master Animator Chuck Jones: The Movement's the Thing."

The Briar Patch

Jones on "gentle pictures" from Needham, Jones Interview, 1979. Curtiz and Wellman stories from Silke, *Here's Looking at You, Kid*. Studio's financial situation in late 20s from Thomas Schatz, *The Genius of the System*, New York: Pantheon Books, 1988. The fact that the key reason for bringing Looney Tunes into existence was to promote Warners music is from Adamson, *Oral History of Friz Freleng*, backed up by Barrier and Gray, "Clampett Interview." Some of Clampett's Cagney and Bogart quote from Kilday, "Zounds! Not That Cwazy Wabbit!." • Early Warner Cartoon history from Adamson, *Tex Avery*; Maltin, *Of Mice and Magic*; and Schneider, *That All Folks!*, with supportive details and Freleng quotes from Beck, "Interview with Friz Freleng"; Adamson, *Oral History of Friz Freleng*; and Adamson, Freleng Interviews, 1989. Adults in lobby from Adamson, Maltese Interview. • Avery being the spark that ignited the flame at Warner Bros. is another source of contention, but is a point of view supported by Jones, "Confessions of a Cel Washer," *Take One*, 9/78, and Jones, *Chuck Amuck*, as well as Ford, "Tex Avery," and "The Hollywood Cartoon: A Soft-Cel Retrospective." Jones on "climate" from Needham, *Tex Avery*, and on "enthusiasm" from Solomon, *Enchanted Drawings*. Clampett "risky" quote and specific influences on the Warners Cartoon style from Andre, Clampett Interview. Date for Unit System from Unsigned, "Schlesinger Adopts Units." Freleng on finding a "path" from Beck, "Freleng Inteview." • Quotes from *Showmen's Trade Review*, 12/28/39, and from David Golding, "The Most Popular Shorts of 1939," *Boxoffice Barometer*, 2/24/40. I am indebted to Jerry Beck for the idea that Avery's travelog gags may have paved the way for Bugs Bunny's famous entrance and ensuing character development. That rabbits won't eat carrots in the wild from Sandy Sycafoose conversation with Michael Dee, Curator of Mammals at the Los Angeles Zoo, 10/12/89; "unlikely" was the adverb he used. Zomo from Tremain, *The Animals' Who's Who*, with details on Harris from *Benet's Reader's Encyclopedia*.

Wabbits, Wabbits, Wabbits!

"Bugs": Harold Wentworth and Stuart Berg Flexner, *The Pocket Dictionary of American Slang*, New York: Pocket Books, 1968, Popular Abridgment of *Dictionary of American Slang*, New York: Thomas Y. Crowell Co., 1967; *Random House Dictionary of the English Language*, Second Abridged Edition, New York: Random House, 1987; Carl Sifakis, *The Dictionary of Historic Nicknames*, New York: Facts on File Publications, 1984, and *The Encyclopedia of American Crime*, New York: Facts of File, Inc., 1982.; and Jay Robert Nash, *Almanac of World Crime*, Garden City, New York: Anchor Press/Doubleday, 1981 • Dizzy D: Alfred Steinberg, *The Man from Missouri: The Life and Times of Harry S Truman*, New York: G.P. Putnam's Sons, 1962; Merle Miller, *Plain Speaking: An Oral History of Harry S Truman*, New York: Berkeley Publishing Corporation, Distributed by G.P. Putnam's Sons, 1973. Lowell Elliott quote from Adamson, Lowell Elliott Interview, Studio City, California: April, 1981. • Norman Moray's hand in the development of The Rabbit from Barrier and Gray, "Clampett Interview," and Unsigned, "Bugs Bunny and His Father," *Milwaukee Journal*, Undated Clipping in Jack Warner's personal clipping file, now contained in the Jack L. Warner Collection at the University of Southern California Cinema-Television Library and Archives of Performing Arts, in Los Angeles. *Hare-um Scare-um* review from *Showmen's Trade Review*, 8/12/39. Jones on variations in stance from Bogdanovich, "Hollywood," *Esquire*, 3/72. • Earlier versions on this "evolution" have appeared in Adamson, *Avery*; Maltin, *Of Mice and Magic*; and Schneider, *That's All Folks!* McKimson's debunking from Nardone, "Robert McKimson Interviewed." • "What's Up, Duke?" from Andre, Clampett Interview; Carole Lombard business from David Butler, backed up by both versions of the film; Freleng's "cocky" comment partially from Unsigned, "Bugs Bunny, Carrot Crunching Comic."

THIS IS YOUR LIFE, BUGS BUNNY

Super Rabbit—1940-1944

Priore from "The Most Popular Shorts of 1942." People at Disney and Freleng on "unbelievable change" from Solomon, *Enchanted Drawings*. Story of Bugs' name from Brasch, *Cartoon Monickers*; Andre, Clampett Interview; and Tex Avery to author, 1975. McKimson on Bugs being "exhausted" from Nardone, "Robert McKimson Interviewed"; "different twists" from Butler, McKimson Interview, 1976. • Freleng on music from Maltin, *Of Mice and Magic*. Jones on Bugs' development partially from Jones, *Chuck Amuck*, and Ford and Thompson, "Chuck Jones Interview." Freleng on *Wacky Wabbit* from Unsigned, "Bugs Bunny, Carrot Crunching Comic." Clampett on Bugs knowing the script from Andre, Clampett Interview. • New design on Bugs from Barrier and Gray, "Clampett Interview," and Barrier, "Of Mice, Wabbits, Ducks and Men"; McKimson quoted from Nardone, "McKimson Interviewed," Jones on Bugs Bunny's new look from Broughton, Ed., *Producers on Producing*, and "Sun Up," CBS. Caption p. 63: Appropriate issues of *Boxoffice* and *Showmen's Trade Review* have been consulted to tabulate poll results, including *STR* 12/28/39, 12/26/40, 12/12/41, 12/26/42, 12/25/43; *Boxoffice* and *Boxoffice Barometer* 2/22/41, 2/21/42, 2/27/43. Date for "Bugs Bunny Specials" arriveed at by checking *MPH* release charts: series not mentioned in issue of 2/5/44 or before; first mention found in issue of 2/19/44. • Story of *Any Bonds Today?* from Unsigned, "Schlesinger Artmen Finish Bond Briefie"; Schickel quote from *The Disney Version*. Bugs' War record and servicemen's letters in caption from *Chicago Tribune*, 4/2/47; Warner Cartoon Publicity Brochure, c. 1946; and from Unsigned, "Bug Bunny, Carrot Crunching Comic." • Theater-owners' claims from "What the Picture Did For Me," *MPH*, 2/7/42. • Celery business from Warner Bros. Cartoon Publicity Brochure; broccoli gag from Los Angeles *Valley Times*, 5/28/47; carrot chewing being saved for last from, among others, Hubbell, "What's Up, Doc?", *WCN*, 5/59. • Memorabilia Photo Caption: Comic books from Adamson, Chase Craig and Mark Evanier Interviews, 1989; merchandise from Unsigned, "Schlesinger Corp. Forms For Toy Manufacture." • Real ending to *The Heckling Hare* from Unsigned, "Cartoon Man Walks Out on Leon Schlesinger," combined with personal testimony from Tex Avery related to Author in 1975 and to Greg Ford at about the same time. • Bugs' expressions: Chief sources are Schneider, *That's All Folks!* and conversations with Schneider, 1/28/90, and Friz Freleng, 1/27/90; Tashlin quoted from Johnston and Willeman, *Frank Tashlin*. "Nimrod" from Steve Oney and Joe Adamson, *Master Toonsmiths*, *Bugs Bunny Magazine*, May 1990; more specifically, Nimrod is from *Genesis* in the Old Testament—a mighty hunter whose name became metaphorically applied to *any* mighty hunter.

The Bugs Bunny Spirit—1945-1949

"We can feel certain of maintaining the top position in the cartoon field that the Warner Cartoons have attained this past year," said Warren Foster in "What Cookin', Doc?", *WCN*, 5/46. *Hare Conditioned* reaction from Thomas di Lorenzo in New Paltz, N.Y., from "What the Picture Did for Me," *MPH*, 12/15/45. *Herr Meets Hare* writeups reprinted in "Warner Bros. Cartoon Publicity Brochure"; New York letters from Maltese, "What's Cookin'," *WCN*, 12/44; Ten Best results from Becker, "Short Subjects Outlook." Maltese 40s quotes from "Animated Cartoons," *WCN*, 4/45. • Robert McKimson: Nardone, "Robert McKimson Interviewed"; Blanchard, What's Cookin', Doc?", *WCN*, 9/47; Clampett quotes, impressions of his drawing style, and one version of accident story from Korkis, Clampett Interview, 1976. Mark Kausler cited in Schneider, *That's All Folks!* on impact on McKimson's style on rest of studio. "Charlie Chase" and corroboration of accident story from Butler, McKimson Interview, 1976. • Schlesinger sale from Adamson, Alvarado and Givens Interview. Jones on Big Yes partially from *Chuck Amuck* and Francesconi, "What's Happening." Cohen quote from "Looney Tunes and Merrie Melodies," *The Velvet Light Trap*, No. 15, Fall, 1975.

The Rabbit in the Grey Flannel Fur—1950-1958

Bugs' drawing power from Sykes," "Short Subjects, Also, Better Than Ever," *Boxoffice Barometer*, 1/27/51. Jones on "severe" movement from Jones and Goldman, USC Address, 1966. • 3-D Caption: Unsigned, "All WB Eggs in 3-D Basket"; Pryor, "Warners Order Halt in Cartoons." Story is basically covered in Maltin, *Of Mice and Magic*, but this errs in assuming that *Lumber Jack-Rabbit* was photographed in 3-D *before* studio closing. • Jones' early experiences in live action from Needham, Jones Interview, 9/79. See Jones, *Chuck Amuck*, on his admiration for Avery and Freleng. "Only love should show" from Jones and Goldman, USC Address, and Hall, "The Fantasy Makers." Treg Brown quote from "What's Cookin', Doc?", *WCN*, 8/49; Jones-Maltese chemistry from Hubbell and Schilt, "What's Up, Doc?", *WCN*, 1/56, confirmed by Jones in interview. Freleng on Jones: *Boys from Termite Terrace*, 1975. Caption: Jones on *Hare-Way to the Stars* from Barrier and Spicer, "Interview with Chuck Jones." • Merchandise Caption: Sources include Unsigned, "WB Cartoons up to Manufacturers"; and Warner Bros. Studio Publicity Release, Burbank, Calif.: 8/8/49.

Wideo Wabbit: 1959-1964

McKimson quoted from Nardone, "Robert McKimson Interviewed." Warner Cartoon history during this period from Maltin, *Of Mice and Magic*, and Schneider, *That's All Folks!*, bolstered by interviews with Freleng and Maltese. Challenge to *Gunsmoke* from "Blanc, Mel(vin Jerome)", *Current Biography*, June, 1976.

The Unsinkable Bugs Bunny: 1965-1990

Opening quote from Kilday, "Zounds! Not That Cwazy Wabbit!." Barrier from *Funnyworld*, No. 11, 5/69. "Bugs Bunny Tech" from Rowland Barber, "Cheer, Cheer for Bugs Bunny Tech," *TV Guide*, 6/10/72. Avery and Freleng experiences from author's interviews. • Revues: "Four Bugs Bunny Units Are All Over the Map," *Variety*, 12/14/77; "Unit Review: Bugs Bunny Meets the Super-Heroes," *Variety*, 2/22/78; Lawrence Christon, "Bugs' Follies: What's Up, Doc?", *LAT*, 3/28/78; "Arena Show: Bugs Bunny in Space," *Variety*, 2/79; " 'Bugs Bunny Follies' Goes Latin in Caracas," *Variety*, 4/11/79. • *Variety* quote from A.D. Murphy, " 'Bugs Bunny' Retro Pic Is Full of Laughs, As Well As Serious Credit Omissions," *Daily Variety*, 11/20/75. *That's Entertainment* cited as precedent in Charles Schreger, "Chuck Jones Stitching Pic from Cartoon Shorts for CBS," *Daily Variety*, 8/30/78, and Schreger, "Warner Brothers' Cartoon Collage: That's Animation!", *LAT*, 2/17/79. • Bugs Today: Adamson, Bleier and Helppie-Shipley Interviews, 1990, as

—TIME FOR WITTO BABIES' NAP

well as informal conversations with Darrell Van Citters, Terry Lennon, and Greg Ford throughout 1989.

BUGS AND "FRIENDS"

Elmer: Fudd's continued popularity from *Appeal of Warner Bros. Cartoon Characters.* **Daffy:** Regarding Fields' *admiration* of Chaplin, see Wes Gehring, *W.C. Fields: A Bio-Bibliography*, New York: Greenwood Press, 1984. Jones on Daffy is a combination of many ruminations, including CNN, Jones Interview, and Kaplan, "Bugs Bunny at the Modern—Is That All, Folks?" • **Daffy and Elmer:** Opening discussion based on *Rabbit Seasoning* Story Conference Notes, 11/6/50. Thompson quoted from "Duck Amuck"; Bullis quoted from *Thematic Study.* •**Yosemite Sam:** Maltese quoted from *Cartoon Monickers*; Freleng on Sam partially from Brasch, *Cartoon Monickers*, and Group W, *The John Davidson Show*, which is also source for discussion of mask; Ford from "Warner Brothers"; Blanc quote from *CBS Morning News*, CBS, 3/20/84. •**Marvin:** Spelling of "Illudium Pew-36" from *Hare-Way to the Stars* bar sheet, Warner Bros. Archive, USC. • **Wile E. Coyote:** Bugs' line from Jones, *The Bugs Bunny/Roadrunner Movie.* •**Tasmanian Devil:** Creation partly from Brasch, *Cartoon Monickers*, as is "Taz Boy." Blanc story, quote, and transcription from Stamelman, "A Chat with Mel Blanc."

BUGS BUNNY'S GREATEST HITS

Jack-Wabbit and the Beanstalk: Chicago exhibitor referred to is H. Goldson of the Plaza Theater, quoted in "What the Picture Did For Me," *MPH*, 10/30/43. I am indebted to Steve Schneider for the concept of Warner Bros. Animation *being* the very sort of underdog vanquishing the oppressor they depicted in their cartoons. • **Baseball Bugs:** Freleng's conga for Selzer from Unsigned, "What's Cookin' at Cartoon Studio," *WCN*, 10/44. Shipped in June, '45, from Maltese, "What's Cookin', Doc?", *WCN*, 7/45. • **Hair-Raising Hare:** Jones quote from *Chuck Amuck.* • **Rhapsody Rabbit:** Agee's review appeared in *Nation* 9/14/46, reprinted in *Agee On Film, Vol. I.* Collaboration between Technicolor and layout men from Adamson, Alvarado and Givens Interview, 1989. Avery's story of MGM mixup from informal conversations from *Rhapsody Rabbit* had been seen again in the compilation feature *Bugs Bunny Superstar*, 1975. Lind's backgrounds dated by Foster, "What's Cookin', Doc?", *WCN*, 5/46, which is one source for Technicolor logjam, the other being Becker, "Short Subjects Outlook," which also attested to raw stock shortage. Jack Warner's praise from Burton, "What's Cookin', Doc?", *WCN*, 10/46. • **Rabbit of Seville.** Jones quote from *Chuck Amuck.* • **Bully for Bugs:** Jones' discussion essentially from Jones and Goldman, USC Address, 1966; Needham, Jones Interviews, 1979; Jones, "Animation: The Naked Art," and "Confessions of a Cel-Washer," *Take One*, 8/76. "Most satisfying structurally" comment from *Chuck Amuck*, and Schneider quote from *That's All Folks!.* • **What's Opera, Doc?:** Ken Moore's "spotlight" from Adamson, Noble Interview. Budget figures from *Warner Cartoon Summary*, Report Compiled by Warner Bros.-Seven Arts 10/31/69, for in-house reference. Lloyd Vaughan in caption from Needham, Vaughan Interview. • **Show Biz Bugs:** Corliss from "Warnervana." • **Knighty Knight Bugs:** "Complaints" from both Maltin, *Of Mice and Magic*, and Schneider, *That's All Folks!* Campbell from *The Hero with a Thousand Faces*, Princeton, New Jersey: Princeton University Press, 1949. • **Baton Bunny:** Details on production from Adamson, Jones Interviews, 1989.

SELECTIVE BIBLIOGRAPHY

Books:

Joe Adamson, *Tex Avery: King of Cartoons*, New York: Popular Library, 1975; Reissued New York: DaCapo Press, 1985.

__________, *The Walter Lantz Story*, New York: G.P. Putnam's Sons, 1985.

James Agee, *Agee on Film, Volume 1*, New York: Grosset and Dunlap, 1969.

Jerry Beck and Will Friedwald, *Looney Tunes and Merrie Melodies*, New York: Henry Holt and Company, 1989.

Benet's Reader's Encyclopedia, New York: Harper and Row, 1987.

Mel Blanc and Philip Bashe, *That's Not All Folks!*, New York: Warner Books, 1988.

Walter M. Brasch, *Cartoon Monickers: An Insight Into the Animation Industry*, Bowling Green, Ohio: Bowling Green University Popular Press, 1983.

Irv Broughton, Ed., *Producers on Producing*, Jefferson, North Carolina: McFarland & Company, Inc., 1986.

Charles Chaplin, *My Autobiography*, New York: Simon and Schuster, 1964.

Manny Farber, *Negative Space*, New York: Praeger Publishers, 1971.

Claire Johnston and Paul Willeman, Editors, *Frank Tashlin*, Edinburgh: The Journal of the Society for Education in Film and Television, 1973.

Chuck Jones, *Chuck Amuck: The Life and Times of an Animated Cartoonist*, New York: Farrar, Straus and Giroux, 1989.

Leonard Maltin, *Of Mice and Magic: A History of American Animated Cartoons*, New York: McGraw-Hill Book Company, 1980.

Ethan Mordden, *The Hollywood Studios*, New York: Alfred A. Knopf, 1988.

Robert Payne, *The Great God Pan*, New York: Hermitage House, 1952.

Danny Peary and Gerald Peary, Editors, *The American Animated Cartoon*, New York: E.P. Dutton, 1980.

David Robinson, *Chaplin: His Life and Art*, London: Collins, 1985; U.S. Edition, New York: McGraw-Hill Book Company, 1985.

Richard Schickel, *The Disney Version*, New York: Simon and Schuster, 1968.

Steve Schneider, *That's All Folks!: The Art of Warner Bros. Animation*, New York: Henry Holt and Company, 1988.

James Silke, *Here's Looking at You, Kid*, New York: Chanticleer Press, Inc., 1976.

Raoul Sobel and David Francis, *Chaplin: Genesis of a Clown*, London: Quartet Books, 1977.

Charles Solomon, *Enchanted Drawings: The History of Animation*, New York: Alfred A. Knopf, 1989.

Charles Leland Sonnichsen, *The Story of Roy Bean, Law West of the Pecos*, New York: The Macmillan Company, 1943.

Frank Thomas and Ollie Johnston, *Disney Animation: The Illusion of Life*, New York: Abbeville Press, 1981.

Ruthven Tremain, *The Animal's Who's Who*, London: Routledge and Kegan Paul, Ltd., 1982.

Articles:

Mike Barrier, "Interview," in Johnston and Willeman, Ed., *Frank Tashlin.*

__________, "Of Mice, Wabbits, Ducks and Men: The Hollywood Cartoon," *AFI Report*, Vol. 5 No. 2, Summer, 1974.

__________ and Milton Gray, "Bob Clampett: An Interview with a Master Cartoon Maker and Puppeteer," *Funnyworld*, No. 12, Summer, 1970.

__________ and Bill Spicer, "Interview with Chuck Jones," *Funnyworld*, No. 13, Spring, 1971.

__________ and __________, "Interview with Carl Stalling," *Funnyworld*, No. 13, Spring, 1971.

Jerry Beck, "An Interview with Friz Freleng," *Animato*, No. 18, Spring, 1989.

Charles Becker, "The Short Subjects Outlook for '45-'46," *Boxoffice Barometer*, November 17, 1945.

Robert Benayoun, "The Roadrunner and Other Characters," *Cinema Journal*, Vol. VIII No. 2, Spring, 1969; Translated and Reprinted from *Positif*, July-August, 1963.

Peter Bogdanovich, "Hollywood," *Esquire*, Vol. LXXVII No. 3, March, 1972.

Lawrence Christon, "Bugs' Follies: What's Up, Doc?", *The Los Angeles Times*, March 8, 1978.

Michell S. Cohen, "Looney Tunes and Merrie Melodies," *The Velvet Light Trap*, No. 15, Fall, 1975.

Richard Corliss, "Warnervana," *Film Comment*, Vol. 21 No. 6, November-December, 1985.

Joel C. Don, "In a World Where People and Animals Never Die," *Orange Coast Daily Pilot*, March 27, 1981.

Fame: The Annual Audit of the Creative Personalities of Screen and Radio, New York, Hollywood, London: Quigley Publishing Co., Issues of 1947-1961; Editor 1947-50 Terry Ramsaye, 1951-52 Red Kann, 1953-61 James D. Ivers.

Manny Farber, "Short and Happy," *The New Republic*, September 20, 1943; Reprinted in Farber, *Negative Space*, New York: Praeger Publishers, 1971.

Greg Ford, "The Hollywood Cartoon: A Soft-Cel Retrospective," *Take One*, Vol. 5 No. 1, 1976.

__________, "Tex Avery," *That's Not All Folks!*, London, BFI Distribution, 1984.

__________, "Warner Brothers," *Film Comment*, Vol. 11 No. 1, January-February, 1975.

__________ and Richard Thompson, "Chuck Jones Interview," *Film Comment*, Vol. 11 No. 1, January-February, 1975.

Mary Harrington Hall, "The Fantasy Makers: A Conversation with Ray Bradbury and Chuck Jones," *Psychology Today*, April, 1968.

Chuck Jones, "Animation, the Naked Art," Address given at the World Retrospective of Animation at Expo '67 in Montreal, Canada, 1967; Part I reprinted in *Funnyworld*, No. 9, May, 1968.

__________, "Confessions of a Cel-Washer," *Take One*, Vol. 5 No. 3, August, 1976.

__________, "132 Takes/Th-Th-That's All Folks," *Film Comment*, Vol. 25 No. 2, March-April, 1989.

Peter W. Kaplan, "Bugs Bunny at the Modern—Is That All, Folks?", *The New York Times*, September 11, 1985.

Gregg Kilday, "Zounds! Not That Cwazy Wabbit!", *The Los Angeles Times*, November 11, 1975.

D. Keith Mano, "Mano Whistles a Loony Tune" (sic), *Qui*, June, 1976.

Mark Nardone, "Robert McKimson Interviewed," in Peary, Ed., *The American Animated Cartoon.*

Tim Onosko, "Bob Clampett—Cartoonist," *The Velvet Light Trap*, No. 15, Fall, 1975.

Joseph Priore, "The Most Popular Shorts of 1942," *Boxoffice Barometer*, Vol. 10 No. 3, February 27, 1943.

Thomas M. Pryor, "Warners Order Halt in Cartoons," *The New York Times*, June 17, 1953.

David Rider, "That's All, Folks!" *Films and Filming*, March, 1963.

Franklin Rosemont, "Bugs Bunny," in *Cultural Correspondence*, No. 10-11, Fall, 1979; Reprinted from the Catalog of the 1976 World Surrealist Exhibition.

Leon Schlesinger, "Schlesinger Offers New Ideas for Coming Season," *The Hollywood Reporter*, September 4, 1940.

Tom Shales, "Bugs, Abe Score as TV Pitchmen," in *The Washington Post*, Reprinted in *The Los Angeles Times*, December 6, 1977.

Ron Smith, "Mel Blanc: 50 Years of Magical Voices," *Daily Variety*, April 29, 1983.

Charles Solomon, "What's Up, Doc? Bugs Gets His Star," *The Los Angeles Times*, December 21, 1985.

Peter Stamelman, "A Chat with Mel Blanc," in Peary, Ed., *The American Animated Cartoon.*

Velma West Sykes, "Short Subjects, Also, Better Than Ever," *Boxoffice Barometer*, January 27, 1951.

Richard Thompson, "Duck Amuck," *Film Comment*, Vol. 11 No. 1, January-February, 1975.

Unsigned, "All WB Eggs in 3-D Basket," *Daily Variety*, May 29, 1953.

__________, "Bugs Bunny, Carrot Crunching Comic," *The New York Times*, July 22, 1945.

__________, "Cartoon Man Walks Out on Leon Schlesinger," *The Hollywood Reporter*, July 2, 1941.

__________, "Fred Avery Heads MGM Cartoon Unit," *The Hollywood Reporter*, September 2, 1941.

__________, "Irrepressible Bugs Bunny 5 Years Old," *Chicago Daily News*, April 2, 1947.

__________, "Leading Short Subjects," *Showmen's Trade Review*, Vol. 39 No. 23, December 25, 1943.

__________, "Schlesinger Adopts Units for Cartoons," *The Hollywood Reporter*, May 15, 1936.

__________, "Schlesinger Artmen Finish Bond Briefie," *The Hollywood Reporter*, December 16, 1941.

__________, "Schlesinger Corp. Forms for Toy Manufacture," *The Hollywood Reporter*, September 21, 1937.

__________, "WB Cartoons Up to Manufacturers," *Variety*, July 5, 1949.

Alex Ward, "Chuck Jones, Animated Man," *The Washington Post*, October 27, 1974.

__________, "Master Animator Chuck Jones: The Movement's the Thing, *The New York Times*, October 7, 1979.

Warner Club News, In-house Newsletter containing Cartoon Division Column, variously titled "What's Cookin'," What's Cookin', Doc?", "What's Cookin' at Cartoon Studio," and "What's Up, Doc?"; variously authored by Jean Blanchard, Treg Brown, John W. Burton, Warren Foster, Elsa Hubbell, Michael Maltese, Tedd (sometimes Ted) Pierce, Barbara Richards, and Phyllis Schilt; also including one entry written by Michael Maltese and entitled "Animated Cartoons," in issue of April, 1945.

"What the Picture Did for Me," Regular Feature of *Motion Picture Herald*, reporting reactions to specific films from theater owners; Issues consulted from 1938 into the 1950s.

Bob Young, "A New 'Golden Era' of Animation?", *The Los Angeles Times*, November 28, 1981.

Charles M. Young, "Oryctolagus Cuniculus—a.k.a. Bugs Bunny," *The Village Voice*, December 29, 1975.

Interviews:

Joe Adamson, Heck Allen, Encino, California: April 1, 1971.

__________, Peter Alvarado and Robert Givens, Burbank, California: September 29, 1989.

__________, Tex Avery, Hollywood: June 19, 1969; November 13, 1969; March 25, 1971, and several informal conversations during 1974 and 1975.

__________, Edward Bleier, New York-to-Los Angeles Telephone: January 19, 1990.

__________, Chase Craig, Los Angeles: November 22, 1989.

__________, Mark Evanier, Los Angeles: November 18, 1989.

__________, Friz Freleng, Westwood, Los Angeles: August 31, September 5, 1989; January 27, 1990; in addition to informal conversations throughout the summer.

__________, Kathleen Helppie-Shipley, Los Angeles: January 24, 1990.

__________, Chuck Jones, Hollywood: March 29, 30; December 30, 1971; April 5, 1974; Newport Beach, California: August 17, 1989; Corona Del Mar, California: August 24, 1989.

__________, Walter Lantz, Hollywood: March to September, 1981.

__________, Michael Maltese, Hollywood: April 3, 1971, and several informal conversations during 1971, 1974 and 1975.

__________, Maurice Noble, La Crescenta, California: December 29, 1971.

__________, Leo Salkin, Studio City, California: June 9, 1981.

__________, Steve Schneider, Los Angeles: August 21, 1989; LA to New York Telephone: January 28, 1990.

__________, Gary Wolfe, Los Angeles: November 12, 1989.

Tom Andre, Bob Clampett, Hollywood: Summer, 1975.

Roger Bullis, Robert McKimson, Los Angeles: April 14, 1970. Included in Bullis, *A Thematic Study of the Post-War Warner Bros. Animated Films.*

David Butler, Robert McKimson, Hollywood: June, 1977.

Cable News Network, Chuck Jones, August 19, 1984.

Bob Francesconi, Chuck Jones, Erie, Pennsylvania: "What's Happening," WQLN Television, August 22, 1985.

Jim Korkis, Bob Clampett, Hollywood: October, 1977.

John Needham, Chuck Jones; Patrons in line for *Bugs Bunny/Roadrunner Movie*; Lloyd Vaughan, Hollywood: September, 1979. Interviews shot on 16mm film for *Omnibus*, BBC, episode on Chuck Jones.

Charles Solomon, Paul Julian; Phil Monroe; Virgil Ross, Los Angeles: 1985-1989. Interviews conducted for *Enchanted Drawings*, some passages quoted here not included in published version.

"Sun Up," Chuck Jones, San Diego: KFMB Television, CBS, August, 1985.

Special Sources:

Joe Adamson, *Oral History of Friz Freleng, Oral History of Dick Huemer*, UCLA-American Film Institute Joint Oral History Project, 1968-69.

The Appeal of Warner Bros. Cartoon Characters, brochure distributed by Licensing Corporation of America, containing results of C.A. Walker, Poll, June, 1989.

Treg Brown, Sound Effects File, Examined at the Editorial Department of The Burbank Studios, Burbank, California, October 27, 1989.

"Bugs Bunny's Star": Videotape of Dedication Ceremony, December 21, 1985; Property of Warner Bros. Animation.

Roger Alan Bullis, *A Thematic Study of the Post-War Warner Brothers Animated Films*, Madison, Wisconsin: Master of Arts Thesis in Communication Arts at the University of Wisconsin, 1971.

Bob Clampett, Address Given at Chapman College, 1974; Audio Tape in Clampett Collection.

Ralph Edwards Productions, *This Is Your Life, Mel Blanc*, Hollywood: Syndicated Television Special; Los Angeles Broadcast February 11, 1984.

Larry Jackson, Producer-Director, *Bugs Bunny Superstar*, Hare Raising Films, Released by United Artists, 1975.

Chuck Jones and Les Goldman, Address Given to Arthur Knight's Class in Cinema Studies, Los Angeles: University of Southern California, January, 1966; Audio Tape at Doheny Library, USC.

Group W Productions, *The John Davidson Show*, Los Angeles: Syndicated Television Program, April 14, 1981.

Lorne Michaels, Executive Producer, *Bugs Bunny/Looney Tunes 50th Anniversary Special*, NBC Broadcast, January 14, 1986.

John Musilli, Producer-Director, "The Boys From Termite Terrace," Episode of *Camera Three*, CBS Series, 1975.

John Needham, Producer-Director, *Tex Avery*, London: Moondance Films Production for BBC Television, 1988; United States Distribution under the title *King of Cartoons: Tex Avery* through Independent PBS Stations throughout 1989.

Warner Bros. Animation: Story and Direction Staff, Story Conference Notes, Hollywood and Burbank, California: *Blueprint Bunny (Homeless Hare)*, December 11, 1947; *Bunny Hugged*, May 26, 1949; *Operation Rabbit* (sic), November 3, 1949; *Robbit Seasoning*, November 6, 1950; *Forward, March Hare* (sic), March 23, 1951; *Dick! Rabbit, Duck!*, November 8, 1951; *Lumber Jack-Rabbit*, April 28, 1952; *Be-Witched Bunny* (sic), August 7, 1952; *Baby Buggy Bunny*, November 7, 1952; *Up in the Hare (Hare-Way to the Stars)*, Undated.

"Warner Bros. Cartoon Publicity Brochure," Burbank, California: Distributed by Warner Bros. Pictures, c. 1946.

Layout drawings from The Old Grey Hare, *1944.*

ACKNOWLEDGMENTS

All I wanted was to get my book written.

I was beginning to think that Bugs Bunny was the toughest taskmaster in the world. Everywhere I turned there was another anvil, another DETOUR sign, another stick of dynamite. Every time I saw the light at the end of the tunnel, I ran up against the stone wall it was painted on.

Not only that, he never once granted me a single interview.

But Friz Freleng and Chuck Jones spent hours with me, and they told me where Bugs came from. So did Pete Alvarado, Bob Givens, Mark Evanier, and Chase Craig. And, many years ago, so did Michael Maltese, Maurice Noble, and Tex Avery.

On past projects, I had relied on James Morrow, David Shepard, Mark Kausler, Leonard Maltin, Nanci Cook, Michael Barrier, and David Stone to point me in the right direction and help me locate resources, and they didn't fail me this time. They popped out of the woodwork, did whatever was needed, and had a lot of fun telling me what I was doing wrong, too.

But this time Howard Green, Gordon Kent, Sandy Sycafoose, Randy Skredvedt, Howard Prouty, David Butler, Roger Bullis, Jim Korkis, and Jerry Beck came out of nowhere and did the same thing, like they *had* to or something, and now I can't figure out how I ever got anything done without them.

People like Lorri Bond, Rick Gehr, Greg Ford, and Kathleen Helppie-Shipley at Warner Bros. Animation went out of their way to help me, like it was their job or something (actually, it was, but I think they stretched the definition of "job" a little if Bugs wanted them to).

Meanwhile, out in New York, my editor Lori Stein was doing the impossible to get all these words and pictures on these small pages--and had little patience with me while she was doing it. Our supervising editor, Don Hutter; our packager, John Sammis; our designer, Allan Mogel; Bugs' supervisor, Edward Bleier; and my agent, Timothy Seldes, all stepped in long enough to see that I had want I needed, and then left me alone.

Steve Schneider, Robert McKimson, Jr., Marlyn Niemann, Robert Clampett, Jr., Pam Martin, Steve Ferzoco, Harry Kleiman, Louis Marino, Steve Ison, and Mike and Jeanne Glad made available material I would have thought had long since vanished from the earth. Certain dealers and galleries were unbelievably helpful: Animation Plus! Gallery, (8610 West 3rd Street, Los Angeles, California 90048, 213-275-5513; 790 North Milwaukee Avenue, River West, Chicago, Illinois 60622, 312-243-8666); Cel-ebration! (P.O. Box 123, Little Silver, New Jersey 07739); Gallery Lainzberg (200 Guaranty Building, Cedar Rapids, Iowa 52401, 1-800-553-9995); The Shine Gallery (8012 1/2 Melrose Avenue, Los Angeles, California 90046, 213-653-7558).

Ruth Clampett, Linda Clough, Marian Jones, Charles Solomon, Roger Bullis, David Butler, Alain Silver, Erwin Dumbrille, Bill and Lennie Cascioli, Mack Eads, Jay Hyams, Mel Kaplan, Carmine Laietta, Jim Landis, Doug LeBlanc, Eric Marshall, Ann Miller, Barbara Miller, Madeleine O'Sullivan, David Pryor, Marty Richman, Edith Rudman, Kathy Sammis, Teddy Slater, Wendell Smith, Raynard Stapleton, Deena Stein, Michelle Stein, Chani Yammer, Lindsay Doran, John Francis, John O'Connor, Chris Walsh at Warner Bros., New York, Bill Exter, Ted Marburgh, Chuck Champin, Terry Lennon, and Darrell Van Citters at Warner Bros., Los Angeles, Mary Corliss at the Museum of Modern Art, Susan Sennet at MGM/UA; Dick May at Turner Entertainment, Julie Dolan at the Copy Spot, Michael Dee at the Los Angeles Zoo, Dennis Doros at Kino International, Robert Cushman and Sam Gill at the Margaret Herrick Library at the Academy of Motion Picture Arts and Sciences, Leith Adams at the Warner Bros. Archive and Ned Comstock at the Jack L. Warner Collection, both at the University of Southern California Cinema-Television Library and Archives of Performing Arts—all were able to work miracles on Bugs' behalf, just so long as nothing they did had anything to do with my original game plan.

Finally it became clear. Bugs had no intention of letting me get my book written. He wanted to get *his* book written.

And I guess he succeeded, because that's the one you're reading.

JOE ADAMSON

PHOTO CREDITS

We'd like to thank the following individuals and organizations for granting us permission to use illustrations from their collections:

Academy of Motion Picture Arts & Sciences: pp. 16 left, 63

Peter Alvarado, pp. 20 right; 181

Animation Plus! Gallery: pp. 11 right; 97 right; 111 top

Mike Barrier: pp. 62; 71 bottom left

Jerry Beck: p. 61 top

Robert Clampett Collection: pp. 49 bottom; 89 bottom left; 133 bottom

Steve Ferzoco: pp. 2; 6 bottom; 7 top; 11 bottom center; 23 bottom center; 37 bottom; 64 bottom; 70-71; 74; 117 top; 119 top left; 126 top; 127; 141 top center, 179, 184

June Foray, p. 78 top

Friz Freleng: p. 56

Gallery Lainzberg: p. 89 bottom right

Mike and Jeanne Glad: pp. 20 bottom left; 23 right; 52 top right; 60 top right, 180, 186

Steve Ison: pp. 17 bottom left; 80-81; 83 top; 100 right; 101; 110 top; 170 bottom; 157 top; 164-165; 170 bottom, 183

Jack L. Warner Collection, University of Southern California: p. 36 bottom

Chuck Jones: pp. 22 bottom left; 28 bottom; 30-31; 34 bottom right; 41 top; 68 bottom; 76 top; 91; 94-95; 98 upper left; 115 right; 119 center; 158 bottom left; 175 right.

Linda Jones Enterprises: p. 89 center

Harry Kleiman: pp. 66 top; 66 top; 69 bottom

Harold Lloyd Estate: p. 45

Leonard Maltin, p. 178

Robert McKimson, Jr. and Marlyn Niemann: pp. 34 bottom left; 73 top; 86 center left; 99 top left; 117 bottom right

Pam Martin: pp. 113 top; 119 bottom

Museum of Modern Art Film Stills Collection: p. 42 top left

Odradek Productions: pp. 8, 9

Shine Gallery: pp. 66 right; 85

Steven Schneider: pp. 4-5; 10 top left; 11 left; 14 right; 17 bottom right and center; 21; 22 bottom right; 23 bottom left, top left and center; 24-25; 26 top; 27; 33 right; 35; 38; 41 right; 43; 47; 48 bottom; 52 bottom and center; 53; 54 right; 58; 59 bottom; 60 top right, bottom right; 67 top; 68 top; 69 top; 70 top; 71 right; 72; 79; 86 top, bottom right; 87; 96; 99 top right, bottom left; 108; 109 right; 113 bottom; 114 left; 116 bottom; 118; 119, top row, 3 right; 120-121; 126 bottom; 128 bottom left; 130 bottom; 132 right; 133 top; 134 left; 135 top right; 139 top right; 140-145; 152-153; 153 top; 157 bottom left; 162-163; 168 bottom; 173 top; 176 (all rights reserved, including the right to reproduce in any form)

David Shepard: p. 43 top

Warner Bros. Archive at the University of Southern California: pp. 26-27; 76 bottom; 85 bottom right; 106 top left; 112 left; 114 right; 115 left top and bottom; 116 left; 117 bottom left; 167 top; 169 bottom; 174 center

Wisconsin State Historical Society: p. 42 bottom left

This book was typeset in Bookman by LCR Graphics, New York. Color separations were made by Mandarin Offset, Hong Kong. Additional separations and film preprations were provided by Chroma Scan, Monsey, New York. Jackets were printed and stamped by Color Art, St. Louis. The book was printed and bound by Arcata Graphics, Kingsport, Tennessee.